I0605081

PRAISE FOR *HALF-JEW—FULL LIFE*

"This is the astounding story of someone who belonged to a group that seldom get their histories told—*mischlings*—in this case with an Aryan mother and Jewish father. Amidst terror and mass death 'Pips' is always larger than life—choosing, out of love, to be Jewish rather than save himself from deportation, going underground and surviving Gestapo arrests and imprisonment, hiding pillar-to-post including in a brothel run by a giantess; protected as the 'pet Jew' of an SS officer, somehow walking away, leaping off a train, doing whatever it took to make it through the war. Georgette Bennett's jaw-dropping, page-turning book reads as comedy amidst horror, invincible life force against the odds of survival, and then, in America, an epic of genius chuztpah. And like all the most brilliant biographies it makes you wish you had known Pips in person. But by the end of the book you pretty much do."

—Sir Simon Schama, broadcaster, historian, documentarian, and author of many groundbreaking books and TV series, such as *A History of Britain, The Story of the Jews, and The Holocaust: 80 Years On*

"If Pip's journey in Dickens's *Great Expectations* was marked by ambition and transformation in the world of fiction, meet 'Pips'—the real-life 'Gary' Phillips (born Gerd Philipsohn)—whose expectations were shaped by history itself. *Half-Jew—Full Life* isn't a novel. It's a riveting plunge into the heart of the Holocaust and the hope that survived its darkest depths. What makes Pips's extraordinary life so unforgettable is Georgette Bennett's remarkable gift as a storyteller. With a detective's determination and a historian's understanding, Bennett crafts his story from years of Pips's own tape recordings, blending his voice, her memories, and deep historical context into a narrative as intimate as it is cinematic. In fulfilling her pledge to tell Pips's story, she has not only given her late cousin-in-law his due. She has given us a character for the ages."

—Henry Louis Gates, Jr., Alphonse Fletcher University Professor, Harvard University

"Georgette Bennett magically weaves the extraordinary tale of Pips—the blond and blue-eyed child of a Christian mother—who embraces Judaism at the worst of times. Against all odds, he grabs hold of life, survives and prospers, and always finds and builds love to pull him through. This story, so wonderfully told, could not be more evocative of how we all need to live and so uplifting for our times. *Half-Jew—Full Life* is a book that belongs on everyone's night table! But be warned, you won't be able to put it down!!"

—Anthony Marx, President of the New York Public Library

"My work, in the theatre and in film, is constantly focused on one thing—storytelling. As Shakespeare repeatedly demonstrates, the drama is magnetic when exposing criminality, or celebrating moral fortitude, but these aims are most successfully achieved in his tragedies, comedies, and histories, through the narrative. The true story we are told in *Half-Jew—Full Life* is riveting, as the reader experiences the nightmare of living through the Nazi determination to eliminate all Jews, but then, onwards through to life in New York during the second half of the twentieth century, and on into the twenty-first. Following the journey of Gerd Philipsohn, whom we come to know as Pips, through persecution to survival to happiness, we become deeply emotionally involved in his story. That is the achievement of the brilliant storyteller, Georgette Bennett."

—Sir Trevor R. Nunn, Tony Award–winning former artistic director of the Royal Shakespeare Company and the Royal National Theatre

"As an actor, I've had the privilege of playing many memorable roles. The greatest endorsement I can offer Georgette Bennett's book is that I'd like to play Pips, the subject of her deeply intimate recounting of a unique character. She has succeeded in bringing an exceptional man to life, while humanizing the Holocaust and recent history. Along the way, she educates us about modern European history—Germany and Berlin, in particular—Jewish cultural life, the plight of refugees, celebrity culture, and 'the American Dream.' All this is done in a fast-paced, poignant narrative that reads like a novel. Pips's adventures are funny, harrowing, and improbable. But they're real—and that makes his story all the more compelling. *Half-Jew—Full Life* takes you through the arc of an exceptional life, from birth to death, and stays with you long after the last heartrending sentence."

—F. Murray Abraham, Academy Award, Golden Globe, and Grammy Award winner

"In her searing, deeply personal memoir, Georgette Bennett provides a guided tour of history's darkest landscape during its cruelest hour. Steeped in history, the narrative is at the same time chillingly, ominously contemporary. Confronting the incendiary issue of our era, racial and religious identity, *Half-Jew—Full Life* offers an eyewitness account of unthinkable, unspeakable horror that is also an eloquent testament to the resilience of the human spirit."

—Richard Walter, author of *Deadpan*

"The story of Gary 'Pips' Phillips slices through the history of Germany like a bleeding sword, a sharpened knife, a cleaver to the heart—I'm weeping and laughing and crying as the story of this little boy emerges from the vivid writing of his friend, Georgette Bennett. She paints the picture of his traumatic life as a child born of a Christian mother and Jewish father—whose faith he follows. This brought him close to death one thousand times and then life flung him into the world like a broken shining shield. Georgette Bennett has written the portrait—and she is a wonderful writer, bringing pages to the life of the story of her friendship, shared by her husband, Learned Polanski with their friend 'Pips' and his kindness to them both. I could not put down the book. Bennett's story of her friendship with Pip and his kindness to her through her life paint a picture of a hero, a gentleman, a survivor, and a truly determined soul whose whole life was survival; a flag against the demons of history, the horrors of dictatorship. His life breaks the heart. I was so moved by the story—the one we know and the one that rips through our hearts. We need his story today, to arm us, to inform us, to give us the courage to go on, to be brave, to be fearless. God bless you 'Pips,' and thank you."

**—Judy Collins, Grammy–winning
singer-songwriter & author**

Half-Jew —Full Life

Half-Jew —Full Life

The Unlikely Journey of a Voluntary Jew from Nazi Persecution to the American Dream

Georgette F. Bennett

Heresy Press books may be purchased in bulk at special discounts for sales promotion, corporate gifts, fund-raising, or educational purposes. Special editions can also be created to specifications. For details, contact the Special Sales Department, Skyhorse Publishing, 307 West 36th Street, 11th Floor, New York, NY 10018 or info@skyhorsepublishing.com.

Visit our website at skyhorsepublishing.com.

HERESY PRESS
P.O. Box 425201
Cambridge, MA 02142
heresy-press.com

Heresy Press is an imprint of Skyhorse Publishing.

10 9 8 7 6 5 4 3 2 1

Library of Congress Cataloging-in-Publication Data is available on file.

Jacket design by David Ter-Avanesyan
Photo credits: © Georgette Bennett (unless otherwise indicated)

Hardcover ISBN: 978-1-949846-74-4
Ebook ISBN: 978-1-949846-75-1

Printed in the United States of America

In memory of Gary "Pips" Phillips and his wife, Olga Phillips, along with the six million Jews who perished in the Holocaust, and dedicated to my beloved husband, Leonard Polonsky, who died before this book about his dear friend, Pips, was finished.

CONTENTS

AUTHOR'S NOTE

Gerd Philipsohn, Gerald Phillips, Gary, Pips. The evolution of his name from German Holocaust survivor to American citizen tracks the arc of his life. He was only my third cousin-in-law but my closest extended family. He thought of himself variously as my father and uncle. He and his wife, Olga, were at the pier to meet me and my parents when we arrived in New York in 1952 as stateless refugees. The day before he died in 2015, I, then a sixty-nine-year-old woman, leaned over his bed as he reminisced about the five-and-a-half-year-old girl, who had been me. With his death, there's no one left who shared that history, so it's up to me to do that.

He and Olga Horvath, my cousin, met in a Displaced Persons camp after the War. They came to America a couple of years before I arrived with my parents and they lived the American dream. Pips started out as a waiter, graduated to bicycle messenger, and—although he never owned a camera in his life—ended up co-owning the largest photo agency in the world. That brought him into contact with Hollywood luminaries of the day—and also landed him in a *Playboy* photo layout in which he's posing, fully dressed, flanked by a cluster of nude women. Vintage Pips!

Olga and Pips were a golden couple. OlgaandPips. I never said one of their names without the other. He was handsome and she was beautiful. They were popular and always in demand by a beloved circle of interesting friends. They were in demand by me, too. I was elated anytime my mother told me we were going to see OlgandPips.

They had no children—a choice about which they felt a bit guilty. On my fifty-ninth birthday, Pips wrote me a note saying: "That's why I always loved you as my virtual (though not always virtuous) daughter and continue loving you."

My own father died when I was six years old, and I remember being a rather sad child. So, Pips was very important to me. With funny hats, a macabre ability to wiggle his ears, and the weird facial contortions he produced, he was huge fun. I desperately wanted to have more playtime with him. I once dreamed of Scotch-taping Olga to the wall so that I could have Pips to myself. He was the person who grabbed me by the legs and swung me around in dizzying circles. He was the first person with whom I tried to play tennis. Neither of us knew what we were doing. We looked like a pair of spastics trying—and failing—to keep the ball in play.

Then there were the drives in his Thunderbird to Jones Beach or into the country. During our drives, I would ask him to stop in the middle of the highway so that I could pick flowers. Never one to indulge children, he wouldn't do it. Or, as he would often recall, I would demand a "jus d'orange." That was early on, before I learned to speak English.

But it wasn't all fun and games with him. Oh, no! Every time he came to visit, Pips would sit with me in my room and drill me on world capitals. Only a few weeks before his death in 2015, he gave me a pop quiz on the capital of Mongolia. He was stunned when I came back with "Ulan Bator."

As I grew older, he retained bragging rights over anything I achieved. And he was always the stand-in for the father I had lost.

He was there for Soph Father's Weekend at Vassar. He walked me down the aisle and gave me away when my late husband, Marc, and I were married. For years after, he would ask me: "Do you remember what you said to me right before we started down the aisle?"

"Yes," I replied. "I need to pee."

He and Olga were the first ones to hold my son, Joshua-Marc, at his birth. Joshua's father had died seven weeks before and never met his son. But Pips became a virtual grandfather.

When my current husband, Leonard, came into my life, Olga and Pips immediately fell in love with him. Because Leonard was fluent in four languages and had lived in Germany, Pips had someone with whom to speak German and share impressions of the old country.

Pips spent the Holocaust hiding in Berlin in the belly of the Nazi beast. More than anything, he wanted to live—and that informed many of the choices he made during those years. His goal was to live to a hundred. But his medical problems piled up, and in the last years of his life, he was never free of pain. Yet, no matter how ill or uncomfortable he was, he insisted: "It beats the alternative."

His notorious sense of humor and his outrageous inappropriateness stayed with him until the end. He shamelessly flirted with his nurses in the Palliative Care Unit at Mount Sinai Hospital in New York City. And, only a few hours before he died, he confided to one of his last visitors: "I have a deal with the guy upstairs. I don't bother Him and He doesn't bother me."

If God was ready to take him, Pips was having none of it. On the contrary, he instructed the doctors and me to "keep me going as long as you can." Of course, that didn't include any measures that would involve more suffering. When the question of intubation came up, both Pips and I said, "No way!" Intubation would have kept him breathing, but it would have prevented him from talking.

For Pips, who always talked way too much, life without that outlet was no life at all.

Pips didn't believe in God or any other comforting fantasies. He knew that death is the end. When it came time to bury Pips, the grave would not be an unfamiliar place to him. After Olga died, he had his own name added to their shared headstone so that only the date would need to be added when he joined her. While he was still able to drive—and he drove much longer than he should have—he took enormous pleasure in going to the White Plains Rural Cemetery to visit his own grave. That, too, was vintage Pips.

Pips was a rascal. In one of the many missives I received from him with instructions for his death, he told me to take care of Olga. "I ain't no angel (at least not yet)," he said. But he was concerned about Olga's lack of financial know-how. So, he instructed me, "Please take care of my affairs (I mean the financial ones) when the time comes."

With Pips's death, all that remained of this couple is the extraordinary story that Pips left behind. It was a story that he told to anyone who would listen. I've lost count of how many times I heard that story. Now, as a seventy-nine-year-old woman, I want to give Pips his due and share his story.

The only child of a mixed marriage, Gerd Philipsohn decided to be a Jew and become a bar mitzvah in the very week that the Nuremberg Laws were enacted in Germany. With a Lutheran mother, he didn't have to identify as Jewish at a time when it could be fatal to do so. He was repelled by the extremism of the Nazis and didn't want to be part of them—even though he identified completely as a proud German. As such, the pageantry, Teutonic marches, Goethe, Schiller, and Wagner were hardwired into his DNA. But "Hitler made me a Jew," he quipped.

He also had a more mundane reason to opt for the Jewish rite of passage into adulthood: he wanted a bicycle. Ironically, that bicycle was stolen two weeks later. But the label he had imposed on himself stuck and led him to become a fugitive in his own city, Berlin.

In 1933, as the Nationalist Socialist Party rose to power, Berlin's Jewish community of 160,000 was the largest in Germany. That number dropped by half as the persecution of Jews unfolded. By the end of 1943, 30,000 Jews had been deported from Berlin and almost all of them were killed.

Of the remainder, 6,500 decided to go into hiding under the noses of the Nazis. Gerd/Pips was one of them. During his years underground, he was captured by the Gestapo four times, spent two years as a prisoner, and escaped three times. After one of his captures, he was slated to be put on a transport to Auschwitz. But his paperwork couldn't be found. That's because the secretary (and mistress) of a prison Kommandant had taken a liking to him and disappeared his file by dropping it behind a file cabinet. The Germans, being very methodical, couldn't deport a Jew without the proper paperwork. That was one of several times that his life had been saved by a Nazi—in this case, at the very last moment. The secretary's SS boss was fully aware of what she had done. He let it go because Pips had become his pet Jew.

This is just one of many close calls and harrowing stories contained in dozens of audio tapes on which Pips recorded his life story in therapy sessions with a psychiatrist. As his closest relative, Pips left me the rights to his story. This book is based on transcripts of those tapes, my personal knowledge of him, and contextual research.

There are many stories about how Jews died in the Holocaust. Far fewer about the ambiguities with which survivors lived and the wrenching choices they had to make. Pips was ten years old when Hitler came to power, and life under the Nazis was all he knew. His life in hiding was marked by close calls, betrayals, and painful compromises that allowed him to survive. Indeed, his journey was a series of paradoxes. With his Aryan mother, he could have been spared persecution, but he chose instead to identify as Jewish. His adventures are at once comical and terrifying. He hated the Nazis but pretended to befriend them in order to live. He felt German to his core but loathed what Germany had become. The Nazis persecuted him but they also saved his life on more than one occasion.

The price of his survival was guilt—not just general survivors' guilt, but guilt over things he did that never stopped haunting him.

For his entire life, he struggled with his identity. Early on, he longed to be part of the majority, which in his childhood circle was Jewish. Later in life, he pondered, "You were German, you were Jewish, and right when you turned Jewish, someone tried to separate out German from Jew. Now you add American to the pot, but how can you be Jewish and German and American meshed into one being with one identity? And in some people's eyes, you're none of these."

According to Israel's Law of Return, Pips was not a Jew. Indeed, the more Orthodox did not accept Pips as a Jew. But his self-identification as such ran deep and permeated his life. He spent his life trying shed his "goyishe" side. "I want to be a full Jew, not a half Jew," he said. He wished his parents had given him at least a bit of a feel for the life of a Jew—some foundation in Hebrew, Jewish history, the practice of Jewish rituals. "I need an identity," he told his therapist. "Since my own personal identity doesn't amount to much, I need identity by belonging to a tribe." That tribe was not Germany. Whenever someone observed that he was German, he retorted: "No, I'm not German; I'm *from* Germany."

He was passionate about Israel and worried endlessly about its survival. When he was finally able to visit Israel in his old age, he returned several times. During those visits, he also made stops in Berlin, where he met some young Germans who became his most cherished late-life friends. The irony of having made his peace with Germany and Germans was a source of wonder for him.

A childhood and young adulthood marked by loss scarred him for life. His first memory of loss was seeing the family's piano removed from their apartment in order to raise money. The piano meant almost nothing to him, but it was an ominous sign of things to come. That first loss grew into an avalanche, until he lost everything but his own life.

Pips saw the absurdity in life—and never hesitated to point it out. He was determined to live every minute he had. He was matter-of-fact about his problems and saw everything clearly. He was straightforward—perhaps too much so—and never kidded himself or anyone else—unless it was to make a joke. He had an endless supply of those and he was a formidable storyteller.

In his will, Pips left me his apartment and its contents. The most precious item in this inheritance is the Jew Star he refused to wear but was eventually forced to wear during the Holocaust. He tried trading the "Jude" star for chocolates after liberation. Fortunately, he didn't succeed. That "Jude" star sits, framed, in the center of a ledge of family photos in my study. Having devoted more than three decades of my life to conflict resolution and advancing interreligious relations, that "Jude" star is my lodestar—a daily reminder of why I do what I do.

As witnesses to the Holocaust die and Holocaust deniers ascend, such stories need to be told. Eighty years after the fact, the public seems to have an insatiable appetite for such narratives. Bestselling author Dara Horn helps explain why: people love dead Jews. Pips is one such dead Jew—but with a unique life-affirming story to tell.

PART ONE

NOWHERE TO RUN, NOWHERE TO HIDE

CHAPTER 1

THE MAKING OF A VOLUNTARY JEW: A CHILDHOOD IN BERLIN

Before World War II, Berlin's Bayerisches Viertel—the Bavarian Quarter—was a leafy enclave with streets named after Bavarian cities and towns. Known as the "Jewish Switzerland," it was an upper-middle-class neighborhood and a hub of intellectual life in Berlin. Hannah Arendt called it home and Albert Einstein lived at Haberlandstraße 5 from 1917 to 1932. No doubt, Arendt's and Einstein's peregrinations took them to the Bayerischer Platz, a green area, landscaped in 1908, with fountains and promenades. Ringed by cafés, exclusive shops, banks, and professional offices, it was one of the most popular gathering places in Berlin. Grand residential buildings, adorned with stucco and marble, were set back from the street with wide pavements and pleasant gardens. Many boasted balconies and gabled roofs. By spring 1945, three quarters of the Bavarian Quarter would be rubble.

The Bavarian Quarter is nestled in the borough of Schöneberg, an agrarian village from the 1300s to the end of the nineteenth century. Then, with Berlin's population surging, developers bought extensive swaths of land from local farmers. The most prominent of these developers was Georg Haberland, the son of a Jewish textile manufacturer. The street on which Albert Einstein lived is named after him. But the Nazis, with their loathing of wealthy Jews, later renamed the street. By the end of February 1943, the entire borough would be declared *Judenrein*, free of Jews.

In 1933, the year that Adolf Hitler took power, more than sixteen thousand Jews lived in the Bavarian Quarter—10 percent of Berlin's Jewish population. Among these were a married couple, Ernst Philipsohn, a Jewish interior architect, and Marie Wollbrecht, a Lutheran housewife. Neither were religious. Marie went to church only at Christmastime and Ernst was a "High Holy Day Jew." But the couple's entire social life revolved around Jewish friends. Ernst and Marie may even have crossed paths with Einstein, Arendt, and other Jewish notables as they went about their quotidian lives.

Ernst, like so many German Jews, lived well and prospered. He did a good business revamping villas and building spacious apartments. He drew the plans, got them approved, and hired carpenters to bring his projects to fruition. A member of the Jewish War Veterans, Ernst suffered a wound in combat that ailed him for the rest of his life. But he was proud of his service in World War I. In one photo, a grave mustachioed Ernst, with dark hair and a widow's peak, sits bedecked in his uniform, a Schirmmütze field visor cap poised on his lap. He frequently retold stories of his battles against Russians, and like many German Jews, he felt very, very German.

Ernst and Marie lived in a third-floor apartment on Berlinerstrasse, a broad, tree-lined avenue, with ornate baroque buildings. Theirs was near the main street, where street cars came and went, clanging as they passed every few minutes. Notwithstanding the start of production by Mercedes-Benz in 1928, there was little automobile traffic because few Berliners owned cars.

Marie came from a lower-class background. A no-nonsense person, she was street smart but was neither well educated nor cultured. She was talkative and well-liked, however; friends found her to be very entertaining. She had a sister who died of TB. Her niece, Marichen, obese, nearly blind, and with no education, had nowhere to go. Ernst kindly took her in and employed her as the family's housekeeper. Because he made a good living, he also helped his wife's two nephews, Ernst and Curt, one of whom, with his low IQ, could find work only as a day laborer.

In contrast, Ernst hailed from a solid upper middle-class family. His father had a lumber business in Berlin. Pre-cut lumber arrived by train on a track that led directly to his cavernous warehouse. When the patriarch died, the business was taken over by Ernst's older brother, Martin. Martin had been married to a Jewish woman and had a son, Kurt, with her. But he was now married to Gertrud, a gentile. They harmoniously blended their family of a Jewish father, Christian mother, Jewish son, and Christian daughter, Irmgard. Ernst's younger brother, Adolf, was an opera singer and had moved to Paris with his Jewish wife. They had no children.

Such is the world into which Ernst and Marie's only child, Gerd Louis Philipsohn, was born on July 17, 1922.

They were older parents, having conceived only after fifteen years of marriage. Marie was the boss of the family. As such, Ernst, a malleable person, was a perfect match for her. He adored Gerd and was the softer parent. Marie loved her son, too, but adoration? No.

Circumcision was controversial in Germany during the interwar period. Gerd was circumcised anyway, but without the ritual *brit milah*.

One of Gerd's earliest memories is being left alone, at age four, while his parents went to a movie. "In Germany, I never heard of babysitters. People who were rich had servants. But anybody else?" Gerd was edgy about being left on his own, so he was allowed to sleep in his parents' big double bed. But he woke up, and finding himself alone, he panicked. When his mother and father finally walked through the door, he had a total meltdown, with piercing screams dissolving into wails. "What's all the fuss about? Why are you crying," asked his mother coolly. "I told you we'd be back and it's only eleven o'clock." His father, on the other hand, deeply felt his boy's terror and tried to soothe him, intoning, "My poor darling; my poor darling." It's the first time that Gerd was angry with his mother. But it was the beginning of a lifelong anger.

When Gerd was five, he had a painful accident, in which he, again, sensed the great contrast between his parents. To urinate, he had to hold up the seat because his penis only reached to the edge of the toilet. On this particular day, the seat slipped from his hand and slammed down on his penis. Hearing Gerd's loud yelp, Ernst rushed in, distraught. In searing pain, Gerd clambered into his father's arms and bled on his clothes. "My mother, as usual, took things in stride. She knew I wasn't going to die from this, so she didn't waste any energy on being upset."

Using the bathroom was not one of Gerd's strong suits. "Even though I was duly potty-trained, I was prone to occasional accidents caused by my unwillingness to interrupt whatever I was doing to go to the bathroom. I tried to hold it in and finally it would explode. On a trip to the Rhineland, we were on a hilltop and I was squirming and twitching. My mother said, 'What's with you?' I was just too lazy to go to the bathroom so I made in my pants. Other occasions, where I was playing marbles on the street with my neighborhood friends, I was so intent on the play, and so unwilling to interrupt it, that I kept trying to hold it in. Finally, I had to go home, which was just around the corner from where we lived. When I got home, I rang the apartment bell and just a second before my mother opened the door, I couldn't hold it and I let loose. The poor woman opened the door to see an enormous puddle, so I was not all milk and honey. And I think my mother resented me ever since."

There was a maid to help clean. When his parents went out, she sometimes took five-year-old Gerd into her bed and let him play with her breasts. "I was absolutely delighted. I wanted to also get down to her behind. I didn't know anything about what's up front. But she wouldn't let me. It certainly wasn't harmful. In fact, it's one of my earliest and fondest memories. It was so warm and comfortable between her tits."

At that age, Gerd was in kindergarten, where he met his first love, Ruth Michaelis. Berliners were supplied with big wooden boxes that stored sand to strew on snow and ice-covered streets. Spying one of those crates, Gerd and Ruth decided to climb in and do something very daring: sneak a kiss. "At the age of five what else do you want? I was in seventh heaven. That was my first amour."

At age six, Gerd started *Volksschule*—public school—carrying with him a large satchel. It was 1928, and for the first four years of school, students had the same teacher for all subjects. Gerd's teacher was Fräulein Eckert, a Valkyrian blonde—big bosomed and strong, with hair piled in a braid on top of her head. She was strict but not overly so. Among other classes, the Teutonic Fräulein Eckert taught religion. The Jewish children were excused but Gerd's mother encouraged him to attend. He complied, only to hear Eckert instruct that Jews are Christ-killers who have murdered their savior. Shocked, he refused to attend religion class again. Eckert awakened the first stirrings of Gerd's Jewish consciousness.

Gerd knew many children and was often invited to their birthday parties. At one, he recalled, "They had cake, and all the kids ate it. But I wouldn't touch it. Somehow, I'd gotten it into my head that it was bad manners to eat a piece of cake at a birthday party." The next day, the birthday child's mother called Marie, concerned that

Gerd refused to eat. Gerd's mother admonished him: "*Wenn man dir gibt, dann nimm; wenn man dir nimmt, dann schrei.*" (When one gives to you, take; when one takes from you, yell.) "One of those typical Berliner pearls of wisdom. My mother was full of them. So, I learned from that moment on not to be shy about accepting something that's offered to me."

After graduating from public school in 1932, Gerd attended the Treitschke Gymnasium (the German name for high school), located on Prinzregentstrasse, one of the magisterial avenues of Berlin. That grandeur was not reflected in the school's interior. The yawning classrooms, illuminated by only two hanging lamps, were furnished with long wooden tables and hard-backed chairs. The sparse gym had a few wooden horses, a suite of dangling ropes for straining through pull-ups, and ceiling lights encased in iron cages. The gloomy lab room, with long tables and glass cabinets, bore silent witness to the chemical experiments and animal dissections that had occupied generations of budding scientists.

The school bore the name of Heinrich von Treitschke, a prominent German historian and political publicist of the 1800s. Treitschke coined the phrase, "The Jews are our misfortune," which was later adopted as a slogan by the Nazi propaganda newspaper, *Der Stürmer.* Gerd keenly felt that "misfortune" when he looked on as a gang of his classmates tied a Jewish boy to a tree, where they kicked and beat him. Gerd was not Jewish, and nothing happened to him. But antisemitism was starting to turn him into a Jew.

Gerd shirked homework from his earliest school days. But he never shirked an adventure. When he was six or seven years old, joined by three friends, he took his long European-style wooden sled to a nearby park to take advantage of the good snow. The sled had a pull rope attached. All four jumped aboard in preparation to sled down the hill, with Gerd at the helm. But Gerd had no idea how to steer. He vainly tugged the rope to the left and right but had yet to learn that steering is done by digging one's heels into the snow. As the quartet barreled down the hill, Gerd sensed disaster looming: they catapulted at top speed into a wrought-iron fence. A protruding rail smacked him right between the eyes and broke his nose. For a few weeks, Gerd had the face of a monkey, and his mother could not look at him without laughing. "I learned early in life to survive all kinds of mishaps."

There would be many more.

Gerd, ten years old in January 1933 when Germany's president, Paul von Hindenburg, installed Adolf Hitler as chancellor, was captivated by the Nazis massing through the streets of Berlin with their imperial colors and fiery torches.

In March, Jewish doctors were suspended from the city's social welfare services.

In April, Jews were removed from government service; denied admission to the bar; and largely ejected from public schools.

In July, naturalized Jews were deemed "undesirables," and their German citizenship was revoked.

In October, Jews were banned from editorial jobs in the press and radio.

Gerd and his friends didn't yet feel the brunt of these decrees. Yes, they'd seen Brownshirts, daggers dangling from their belts, marching with torches down Münchener Strasse. They'd heard them loudly caroling the Horst-Wessel song with its chorus: "*Wenn's Judenblut vom Messer fließt, dann geht's nochmal so gut.*" (When Jewish blood flows from the knife, then it works twice as well.) But Gerd didn't see this as having anything to do with his family. That only came later.

"My father was not a lawyer; my father was not a teacher or a college professor. And I think the feelings of youth, whatever you call them, your hormones are so strong that even these events could not override my optimism, my fun, my ability to learn."

Gerd developed a lifelong love of German marching music. And yet, much later in his life, when these long-ago songs invaded his consciousness, they caused severe heart palpitations and drove him into psychotherapy.

April 20 is Hitler's birthday, a national holiday on which children were off from school. Gerd's mother took him on a three-hour boat ride down the river Havel—a sort of pilgrimage that Berliners made to celebrate their Führer. The boat sailed past Potsdam, arriving at Werder, where orchards stood laden with apple and cherry trees in full bloom. Mother and son hiked up a hill to arrive at one of several garden restaurants at the summit. There they sipped last year's apple cider—another tradition—and gazed at the sea of blossoms. In the evening, they embarked on the return voyage, to the sound of harmonicas and singing wafting through the ship. "It was altogether a pretty nice thing, but it did nothing to endear Hitler to me."

Nor did his classmates manage to spark this enthusiasm. One boy, who, at the prodding of his parents, loudly proclaimed himself to be a German nationalist, recited a poem. The rough translation goes like this: *God, who let iron grow, didn't want any slaves or serfs, so he gave the man a sword or spear—the iron—to defend himself and fight for his liberty.* On one occasion, unprovoked, the boy looked Gerd in the face, stood in front of him, and declared: "The God who let iron grow didn't want any Jews."

Gerd was dumbfounded. "It was so ridiculous: if God didn't want Jews, why did he make Jews?"

Gerd, like so many Germans, was steeped in Teutonic paganism with its Germanic gods: Valhalla, Wotan, Tor, Loki. Richard Wagner's opera cycle, *Der Ring der Nibelungen* is akin to a national saga! The rituals of the Nazis—the big bonfires, some of which were used to burn books; the martial music; the massive structures—they were all steeped in paganism. Ironically, it wasn't in his German schools but in a Jewish institution that Gerd was indoctrinated with Teutonic imagery. “I grew up in that atmosphere, and I didn’t at first reject it. I felt German, part and parcel of this, until the age of twelve. It’s not from one day to another that I decided to turn my back on these things. It was a gradual process.”

He later theorized that one of the many elements that went into the Nazi ideology was a rejection of Christianity and its Jewish roots. "What was emphasized, even in the very early days of Hitler, was our Germanic background, our Germanic gods. The Germans, in my opinion, had never properly digested Christianity.”

When Gerd was twelve, he got a small turtle. The apartment on Berlinerstrasse had a balcony where Gerd kept his pet in a box filled with munchable leaves. One day, while Ernst was at work, his mother had a visitor, Mr. Schleier. Gerd had seen him around before. A friend of the family? His mother sent Gerd to buy some groceries. Instead of going right out, he went to the balcony to check on his turtle and decided to sneak up on his mother and surprise her, shouting “I’m here!” He crept through the living room toward the kitchen. And there stood an unresisting Marie with Schleier’s hand up her blouse, furtively warning him “Not now.” Gerd was devastated. He didn’t show himself. He said nothing. He just retreated from the room, went downstairs, and bought the groceries.

But there was another episode that shook Gerd to his core: the time his mother kissed him and put her tongue in his mouth. “It was only a second, but I was very shocked by it. My mother, what is this? She never did it again, and I never mentioned it. But I haven’t forgotten it.”

There was no hint that Ernst suspected his wife’s perfidy, but his business suffered precipitously from 1933 on. After Hitler took power, many Aryans wouldn’t work with a Jew, leaving Ernst with very few gentile customers. He still had some Jewish customers. But, in the 1930s, Jews were insecure and there wasn’t much interest in renovating property. So long as Hitler and the Nazis were in power, they reasoned, this was not the time to invest. They made do with what they had, and Ernst could no longer afford to pay for his son's school.

It made no difference, because the April 1933 Law Against Overcrowding of German Schools had been enacted. "Philipsohn" was deemed a Jewish name and all Jews were commanded to leave Aryan schools. After only two and a half years of attendance, Gerd was evicted from the Treitschke Gymnasium.

The accretion of Gerd's Jewish identity continued to build through experiences like these.

Having been exiled from high school, Gerd attended the Jewish Children's School, established in 1933 for Jews who had been expelled from public schools. Founded by Vera Lachmann, the school was housed in the chauffeur's residence on the grounds of an estate at 29-33 Jagowstrasse, which was owned by Lachmann's cousin and her husband, Siegmund Bodenheimer. The owners had fled Germany for a resort in Switzerland but kept the house in the expectation that they would return some day.

"Our principal loved Germany with a passion," Gerd reminisced. "She said that they could kill us, but they cannot take our Germanness away from us. She also shared a passion for German romanticism. Germans are very romantic, in verse, song, in anything. All this influence, of course, made me love Germany, German culture, particularly literature and music. I don't remember that we ever talked about Jewishness in any shape or form. The school principal told us, 'We are Germans, no matter what the Nazis or Hitler say.'"

The Jewish school offered an English course, which Gerd avoided by jumping from a swing and faking a broken leg. "Little did I know that someday it would be my daily language."

He later faked appendicitis and endured an operation to get out of taking his exams. His doctor warned him to eat lightly. Instead,

Pips convinced his father to take him to the swanky Kempinski Hotel restaurant, where he stuffed himself to the gills. That left him violently sick after the surgery. To ease his nausea, he was given tea, which he hated. Spotting a carafe of water across the room, he drank the whole thing, which made him even more sick. When he was released from the hospital, the first thing he did was go to the movies. School could wait!

The entire student body was comprised of approximately fifty kids grouped into classes of six or seven. There were no classrooms. Some students sat on the couch and some on the floor. Everything was informal and the teaching methods were somewhat unorthodox. The music teacher was a Jew who could no longer practice his profession as the conductor of a German orchestra. But there was a grand piano in the school, and he announced, "Today we're going to hear *The Magic Flute*." He then proceeded, for two hours, to give his charges the highlights of Mozart's opera by singing and playing all the parts himself. The following week, it could be Verdi's *The Masked Ball* that got a similar treatment. "It opened our minds. We developed a taste for this kind of music. And even I, who would never do homework, was stimulated enough to develop a lifelong interest in music."

The German literature class was taught by a Professor Herrmann, who, like the music teacher, had been fired from her faculty position at a university. One Sunday, she read *Macbeth* to the students. Gerd Hoffnung, nicknamed "Loki" after the Norse god of mischief and trickery, was in her class. Loki kept gazing out the window during Professor Hermann's lecture. Suddenly, he turned to her in alarm. "What is it?" she asked in dread. "There are men out there with ten heads and animals with heads on both ends," Loke breathlessly reported. Eventually, Hermann realized that Loki was up to his usual tricks and admonished him to stop his nonsense. But, no! Loki insisted that he was seeing these bizarre creatures outside. He whipped out sketch paper and a pencil and within two minutes, he brought the strange figures to life on his pad. Loki, one of many oddball characters in the school, would become a famous humorist and well-known cartoonist for *Punch* magazine in England.

Sports were a key activity at the Lachmann school. Up until 1935, there was still a Jewish sports field with a running track, where various Zionist youth organizations competed. Gerd was especially drawn to 5000-meter long-distance running. He was a good runner and practiced by running laps around the garden of his school.

As one of the older children, Gerd was also captain of the boys' *Völkerball* team, in which players try to hit players on the opposing team with a heavy medicine ball while avoiding being slammed themselves. Ilse Rosenthal, a somewhat masculine girl with large breasts, led the other team. "I loved to throw that heavy ball directly at her chest. I got a big kick out of it when the ball gave a bang against the tits, but it wasn't a sexual thing; it was amusing." Gerd and Ilse became friends, often jumping on their bicycles and riding into the nearby Grunewald, up and down hills and through the forest and lakes. "We loved that."

Soon a new neighbor arrived: Heinrich Himmler, principal architect of the Holocaust, moved into Hagenstraße 22, the house immediately to the left of the Jewish school. Like the Bodenheimers, many wealthy Jewish families were leaving Germany, and the Nazis helped themselves to the vacated homes.

"The SS guards with their steel helmets patrolled the perimeter of the garden. Sometimes our ball would fly over the fence, and they would kick it back. I don't think they knew what was going on next door, that this was a Jewish school."

A testimony by a Bodenheimer descendant tells a similar story: "It was quite strange to have SS Nazi guards return the ball, ruffle our hair, and kindly tell us Jewish children to not kick the ball so high."

Vera Lachmann had another bizarre connection to the Nazi high command. Her parents had earlier adopted Magda Friedlander, who grew up with her as a sister. But in a stunning twist, Magda would become the wife of Josef Goebbels, the chief propagandist of the Nazi party. Prior to her marriage, Magda had a brief relationship with Haim Arlosoroff, an ardent Zionist, who eventually emigrated to Palestine and headed up the Jewish Agency there. He gave Magda a *Mogen David,* which she wore for a time. Arlosoroff was assassinated in Tel Aviv the same year that Hitler became Chancellor.

The Nazis closed Lachmann's school in 1938, shortly after Kristallnacht. Lachmann left for the United States with the help of friends and, a few years later, established Camp Catawba in the Blue Ridge mountains of North Carolina. Siegmund Bodenheimer became an American citizen in New York City in 1943.

Gerd and his parents stayed put. In 1934, he joined a right-wing Jewish youth organization, Bund Deutsch-Jüdischer Jugend—Association of German-Jewish Youth—which was founded a year earlier. A youth movement had been spreading through Germany since the beginning of the twentieth century. As it became increasingly nationalistic, Jews were excluded. In response, assimilated middle class Jews created their own youth movement, which combined German patriotism with Jewish identity. Children and teenagers came together for retreats, social events, and hiking. But given the pressure on Jews to leave Germany, the members were now taught agricultural skills that would prepare them for emigration to other places, such as Australia, South America, Kenya, and the US. Notably, because of the British Mandate Authority's restrictive policies, Palestine was not one of the target countries for emigration. Also, notably, the Bund was not Zionist.

Three years after the Bund's founding, the Gestapo prohibited it from using the word "German" in its name, and the group of five thousand members and sixteen regional associations were rebranded,

"Ring, League of Jewish Youth." The Ring was banned altogether in 1937.

In Gerd's Bund, everyone was given a pet name. Gerd, a skinny little guy with a high "pip-sy" voice, was dubbed "Pips." The name stuck for the rest of his life, and that's the name that will be used going forward in this story.

The Bund was very nationalistic. The members almost never talked about Jewish matters. Rather, the Bund emphasized and strengthened Gerd/Pips's German consciousness and played into his reckless impulses. Naturally, girls were beneath contempt.

Cossack songs were popular with the Bund, and they went to hear the Don Cossack choir whenever it came to Berlin. "I don't know where the hell that came from. We knew nothing about Russia, we didn't speak Russian, we had no sympathy for the Communists. We had some kind of a sentimental thing."

The Bund's eighteen-year-old leader had a sadistic streak. "He wanted to make real boys out of us, real men. In winter, our legs were naked. But we didn't just march or hike; we went on forced marches till it hurt. We went on all-night marches and stole chickens from farmers, not because we had no money to buy a chicken—in those days our parents still had some money—but that was the sporty thing to do. It's amazing we survived this thing."

Pips sensed a homoerotic aspect to the Bund and its values—the vision of the blond hero who draws his sword and fights and dies. "Everything always ends in catastrophe and tragedy, which is a strong draw for the Germans." Pips recalled Sigi Sternfeld, a good-looking boy in the group. The leader always put his arms around his shoulder and insisted that Sigi sleep next to him in the tent.

During one of his adventures, Pips broke his leg for real. "On one of my wild trips, we slept in a barn, but the farmer didn't know anything about it. We sneaked in after dark." While the cows milled around downstairs, the boys slept in the hay loft upstairs. But Pips fell through a trap door. "It wasn't a serious break. I know how to fall. They took me to a hospital, which was run by nuns, and they were very sweet women. They put on a cast and took good care of me."

When Pips was twelve years old, he took swimming lessons with his class at a lake in West Berlin. The lifeguard used a zip line with a harness to lower each child to the surface of the water so they could practice their swimming strokes without sinking. When Pips's turn came, he began to work on the crawl, but the lifeguard was distracted and the contraption slowly sank, leaving Pips struggling under water. "I learned to swim in a hurry!"

Pips was subject to further mishaps at Krummhübel, a pastoral village nestled amid rolling hills at the foot of the Silesian mountains on the German-Czech border. Known as Sudetenland, it would, in 1944, be the site of a meeting of Nazi officials in which they agreed to intensify antisemitic propaganda in Europe and in which one participant called for the elimination of Eastern European Jews. But when Pips was a small child in the 1920s, it was an idyllic place where he was sent for sojourns at Althaus, a kind of children's camp. "I liked it; the only thing I didn't like was that after lunch they made us nap. What a waste of time, when one could be playing hopscotch! Why, in the middle of the day, do I have to close my eyes? Ridiculous!"

Krummhübel imbued Pips with a love of nature—especially mountains. As he entered his teens, he had difficulty finding someone his age to go to the village with him. He made do with a nerdy boy from his school. The two boys took a train to Krummhübel. It was winter, the snow was deep, and they checked into a cheap pension. But the boy's family was religiously observant and he kept kosher. There was no kosher restaurant in Krummhübel and there were already signs on street corners: "Jews not allowed." They went to restaurants, where the boy pretended to be a vegetarian on a strict diet. He ate only carrots while Pips feasted on wurst or ham sandwiches. "It didn't exactly make me happy to be with a guy who has that handicap."

On New Year's Eve 1935, at about eight o'clock, Pips convinced his companion to go to the top of the mountain. They lugged a sled to the summit of a five-thousand-foot ridge. They were so close to the border that "with one foot, I could stand in Czechoslovakia; with the other in Germany. It was beautiful, there was a full moon. A full moon in the mountains with snow, there aren't many things better than that!"

The two boys wandered around the ridge for an hour. Nearing midnight, they decided to sled down. Pips mounted the front and his friend, the back. In no time, they hit a steep slope and the sled gathered speed. Pips didn't know how to brake. By then, they were in the forest and the moonlight was obscured. In the semi-darkness, Pips felt a push and heard a cry. The other boy had jumped off the sled, and by jumping off, inadvertently propelled Pips further down the slope. Now, it was easier to stop because there was only one person on the sled. But Pips kept going, picking up speed. Finally, he threw himself off the sled. "This was the kind of mini adventure that I always loved in nature. I was often very careless and really in danger—the word for that is stupid—but I love nature and I'm not afraid of it. I tend to be afraid of people much more than nature."

Pips returned to Krummhübel with his friend, Karl Weirauch (who later Americanized his name to Charlie Wyle), with whom he had previously done some climbing. Pips sported a walking stick with a bent handle. At one point, he lost his balance at the edge of a two-hundred-foot cliff. There was a tree growing out of the rock face and, just as Pips was about to careen over the precipice, he managed to hook his stick onto a branch of that tree. "Here I was, suspended over the abyss, and the one thing I yelled was 'halt'—stop!"

Pips, now thirteen years old, attended a Jewish school and was a member of a Jewish Bund. All his friends and his parents' friends were Jewish. The *pintele yid*—Jewish spark—in him had been kindled by the rising antisemitism that engulfed his world. He felt closer to his Jewish father than his Aryan mother, with whom he became increasingly uncomfortable. So, he made a fateful decision. Pips chose to become a bar mitzvah in September 1935—the very week the Nuremberg Laws were enacted.

CHAPTER 2

THE RISE OF THE NAZIS AND THE FALL OF THE PHILIPSOHN FAMILY

Pips's father never pushed him to become a bar mitzvah. Quite the contrary. Like many German Jews, the Philipsohns had a Christmas tree, which Ernst set up. Along with the tree, there was a roast goose dinner, with the radio tuned to Christmas songs. There was nothing religious in this. It was simply a matter of enjoying the exchange of gifts and the festive decorations. No thought was ever given to Chanukah.

On the High Holy Days, Ernst attended synagogue services on his own. Pips had no interest in going. The few times Ernst took his son with him, Pips was bored and had no idea what the service was about.

That was the extent of Pips's religious upbringing. So, there was no religious motivation for his decision to undergo the Jewish initiation into manhood and responsibility. He wanted it for only two reasons: to fit in with his Bund friends and, because it's customary for the bar mitzvah boy to get special gifts—and Pips wanted a new bicycle.

But Pips was too lazy to learn to speak and read Hebrew. So, his father phonetically wrote out the ritual prayers and Pips's Torah portion. "He should have said, if you're so lazy you can't even be bothered to learn the words, you should not have a bar mitzvah. But father assisted me, conspired with me, because he was so crazy about his son. He would have walked through fire for me."

Pips faked his way through the bar mitzvah ceremony. Among the family and friends who came to celebrate was Mr. Schleier, his mother's lover. "I kicked up a hell of a fuss. I looked at my mother and said, 'Get rid of him, I don't want him at my party.' And my mother played innocent. 'What's the matter with you? It's Mr. Schleier.' 'Get rid of him.'" Pips ran into his small room and locked himself in. He refused to come out until he was assured that Schleier has left. His father had no clue what Pips's tantrum was about. But for the sake of the party, he asked Schleier to leave.

Pips got his new bicycle. Three weeks later, he rode it to see the Circus Krone, an iconic German circus that Hitler had left untouched because, unlike many circuses, it was not owned by Jews. Pips had no tickets, so he was unable to get into the tent. But he wanted to look around and smell the sawdust, just to soak up the atmosphere. He leaned his brand-new bicycle against a post while he wandered around. When he returned ten minutes later, the bike was gone. "I became a Jew for nothing."

From then on, he had only old, dirty bicycles that no one would want to steal. But the label "Jew" stuck.

With the promulgation of the Nuremberg Laws, the German population was classified by racial categories. The "Special Cases with First Degree Mischlings" decree issued in September 1935 spelled it out: *A mixed-race child that is the issue of a marriage with a Jew that is born after 17 September 1935 will be classified as a Jew.*

Those already born before 17 September 1935 will still be classified as Mischlings.

With his Aryan mother and Jewish father, and his 1922 birth year, Pips was eligible to be a *Mischling* first degree. As such, Pips only partly belonged to the German race and nation; but he was approved to have Reich citizenship—leaving him in a position of relative safety. However, the moment he became a bar mitzvah, he was deemed to be a registered Jew and lost his protected status as a *Mischling* first degree. He was now a *Geltungsjude,* meaning he was no longer a citizen of the Reich and was subject to almost all the restrictive laws pertaining to Jews.

"My official status was a Jew; my emotional status was a Jew—even though I didn't know a damned thing about Judaism, Jewish history, or anything. My world was within Germany. I was still a German. I couldn't help it. I have never been totally sure of my own identity. That has followed me throughout my life. As a six-year-old I didn't give these matters any thought. But I became a bar mitzvah at thirteen and there I drew the line."

It was a line that his mother frantically tried to erase. She set about trying to Aryanize Pips by swearing to the authorities that his father was not a Jew. She averred that an Aryan cousin of hers was Pips's biological father. But her claim would be put in doubt when blood tests and her statement were sent for verification to the Kaiser Wilhelm Institute, a research facility in Berlin. Marie understood the value of her Aryan-ness and desperately tried to use it to save her son from the fate of German Jews.

"The fact that I am alive had a lot to do with the fact that my mother was not Jewish."

The Nuremberg Laws were issued in four decrees that gradually tightened a noose around every aspect of Jewish life in Germany:

The Reich Citizenship Law of September 15, 1935, mandated that: *A citizen of the Reich may be only one who is of German or kindred blood, and who, through his behavior, shows that he is both desirous and personally fit to serve loyally the German people and the Reich.*

The Law for the Protection of German Blood and Honor further states: . . . *the purity of German blood is the necessary prerequisite for the existence of the German nation and, inspired by an inflexible will to maintain the existence of the German nation for all future times,*" it criminalized marriage between Jews and non-Jews. It further forbade the hiring by Jews of German maids under the age of forty-five and prohibited Jews from displaying the national colors. The First Supplementary Decree for the Execution of the Law for the Protection of German Blood and Honor, issued on November 14, went on to depict the genealogy that defined who is a Jew, and it specifically excluded Jews from citizenship. It was the first time in history that Jews were persecuted not for their religious beliefs, but for their "race."

Using violence and economic pressure, the goal of the Nazis was to terrorize all Jews into voluntarily leaving Germany. But, when they did leave, Jews had to pay a tax equal to 90 percent of their wealth. Anyone caught transferring assets overseas was deemed an "economic saboteur" and subject to a long prison sentence.

Jewish stores closed due to lack of customers. Non-Jews stopped socializing with Jews. Jewish businesses were transferred to Aryan ownership at a fraction of their market value. Jews could no longer work in brokerages or stock exchanges. German theaters were closed to them. Jews, now excluded from all the professions, took menial jobs—if they could find any work at all.

Ernst Philipsohn was among them.

Trying to find another source of income, they moved from Berlinerstrasse to a larger apartment in an elevator building, just ten blocks away, at 15 Münchener Strasse. It was a better neighborhood than the one they left behind. Down the street, at number 35, was the domed synagogue that Ernst attended on the occasional Shabbat. Also on their street was the Münchener Strasse Gymnasium.

Marie and Ernst hoped to make a living by renting out rooms in their spacious seven-room flat. At first, all their tenants were Jews. They started by letting two large rooms to a frail woman in her seventies and her gentile caregiver. The caregiver had the title Baroness, because she had formerly been married to a Polish Baron. The second rental was to an aged couple named Ballin whose family formerly owned one of the biggest shipbuilding companies in Hamburg and Bremen. Having been stripped of everything, they were now poor. A third room was rented out, and Pips's parents ended up with just one room for themselves. That room served as both living room and bedroom. By this time, their marriage was crumbling. Ernst's bed was on one side while Marie's was on the other. Pips was in the maid's room, behind the kitchen.

But they had high quality, solid furniture, thanks to Ernst's former business. To raise some cash, they sold their piano. Pips had never practiced and didn't even want a piano. But when the piano went out the door, it looked to him like a black coffin.

"The piano meant next to nothing, it wasn't important, it was a piece of furniture. But having it taken away was a sign of things to come, the first loss. From then on, like an avalanche, it grew and grew, until just about everything was gone."

Gradually, Marie and Ernst's social life shrank as Jewish families fled Berlin. One of the remaining families, the Rosenthals, were in the clothing business. Their daughter, Ilse, was one of Pips's early crushes. All of them emigrated to Cape Town. Later, they tried to pull some strings in South Africa to get Pips out of Germany, to no avail. Another family, the Pragers, owned an antique bookstore in which the proprietor produced manuscripts. When Pips was a young boy, Ernst took him to visit that store, and he was fascinated by the old books. The Pragers escaped to Rome. The second Ilse Rosenthal in Pips's life—his *Völkerball* opponent—was a classmate from the Jewish school. She and her family absconded to the Netherlands, where they were hidden by a Dutch baker, whom Ilse married after the war. They ended up in California.

Pips was now fourteen years old and caught up in the thrill of the 1936 Berlin Olympics. He had no tickets to the stadium but listened to the games on the radio and saw them on newsreels. He was elated with the gold medals won by Jesse Owens in the long jump, the 100-and 200-meter dashes, and the 4 x 100-meter relay. Owens, an African-American, was a living refutation of Hitler's racial theories. But the only event Pips saw in person was the end of the marathon, which was open to everyone. Pips stood at the end of the route, an autobahn on the outskirts of Berlin. He vividly recalled his excitement as he saw the first runner, a Japanese man, break through the tape. And, even into his old age, he remembered the names of the three Finns who won the 10,000-meter run: Ilmari Salminen, Arvo Askola, and Volmari Iso-Hollo.

For now, Pips was still in the Lachmann school, where Vera arranged a vacation for him near Geneva. Among her acquaintances was a Mr. Levy who owned a villa there. She told him that she had a pupil whose parents were struggling and implored him to offer the boy a good summer holiday. Levy invited Pips to visit for a month. A thousand kilometers from Berlin, the village to which Pips traveled felt like the end of the world. He crossed a border and went to a strange country—the longest trip he had ever taken.

Pips arrived in July and was picked up by a surly Swiss German caretaker. "The Swiss German tend to be surly anyway, not the most sociable bunch." Pips was dropped off at the mansion, where he met the rest of the staff. His host was nowhere to be seen and, in the four weeks that he spent there, Pips never laid eyes on him. Pips was instructed to eat with the staff in the kitchen and told that he would be expected to do some work, mostly picking berries in the vast garden. Pips was happy with that, so long as it didn't interfere too much with his amusement.

Pips was shown to a well-appointed room, and the next morning was instructed on the proper method for picking raspberries. And so, he began. But the berries were irresistible. For each one he put in the pot, he put another in his mouth. He did this for the whole morning. Then it was time for lunch, followed by more berry-picking. He complied for a couple of days and then began to protest. He made it clear that he was, after all, a guest of Mr. Levy and was supposed to be enjoying his holiday here. While he didn't mind spending a few hours a day picking berries, he didn't want to spend the whole day doing that. This did nothing to improve the caretaker's sour mood. It was quite clear that he saw Pips as a nuisance and resented having the boy imposed on him.

To make things worse, Pips committed an embarrassing *faux pas*. His room didn't have a private bathroom but there were several other bathrooms in the house. He was directed to a spacious one he was meant to use. There was a toilet, of course. But, to his shock, there was another basin next to it, shaped like a figure-eight. He'd never seen one of these and puzzled over its purpose. Flummoxed, he concluded that the toilet was for defecating while the other object was for urinating. "I thought that was rather gilding the lily, but when in Rome do as the Romans do. So, I peed into the basin, flushed it, and two hours later the caretaker came to me with fire in his eyes and said, 'You peed in the bidet.' I had no idea what he meant by 'bidet,' and when it became clear what he meant, I denied it. I still didn't know what it was for, but I didn't go near the damned thing again."

Looming behind Geneva is one of the Prealps of France, Mont Salève, which is also called the Balcony of Geneva. One day, Pips took off to hike up Mont Salève, where he had a beer and savored the view of the Mont Blanc massif to the southeast. He felt very adventurous stepping into France—how foreign can you get? It was on that outing that he first lay eyes on eighteen-year-old Lucienne

Levy, his host's niece. "She was absolutely gorgeous and it took me no time at all to fall in love with her."

Lucienne was very well educated—fluent in English, French, and German—so communicating was no problem. Pips spent all the time he could with her. They hung out in the back of her uncle's estate on a terrace festooned with ivy-covered columns. "For me this was heaven, to sit next to her. I could hardly contain myself."

Lucienne, marooned in a small village, had no other company than this fifteen-year-old German boy in knickerbockers. Pips was ashamed of his baggy, knee-length pants and told people that his long pants were at the cleaners or being fixed. But Lucienne didn't seem to mind. She sunned herself as Pips read to her in German—and later took him to her boudoir, which was conveniently outfitted with a couch. They soon ended up entangled there, "to the extent I was capable, which was kissing." It didn't enter his mind to go beyond that. "There were times when I was lying on top of her, it never occurred to me to touch her breasts, to undress her, to open her blouse, or any of that. I was deliriously happy kissing."

Lucienne taught Pips French kissing. The other thing she taught him was to inhale when smoking. "Whether that was much of a favor is another story." The French kisses didn't do any lasting damage, but inhaling cigarettes started him on the path to nicotine addiction and emphysema.

"I cannot imagine that she loved me. I was fifteen. To an eighteen-year-old girl, I was a kid. An eighteen-year-old girl wants to screw with a twenty-two-year-old. To this day I say to myself, if I only had known how to do it, I would have had a terrific time. I was a late bloomer as far as sex is concerned, but I was very much in love."

The month ended and Pips left his idyll. With an aching heart, he bade farewell to Lucienne. The caretaker was relieved to be rid of him. Pips was scheduled to cross Lake Geneva on a steamer. After a three-hour ride, he disembarked in Montreux, at the far end of the lake. From there, he took the train up the Rhone Valley to get on the Cog Railway, which chugged through a narrow valley to Zermatt. He disembarked in the late afternoon, knowing he would never see Lucienne again. As he stood on the platform, a train came in the opposite direction, with a sign saying *Geneve*. He said to himself, "I could take this train and, within two hours, I could see her again. What the hell do I want to go to Zermatt for? I want her." Just as the train was about to leave the station, he hopped aboard.

When he reappeared in Geneva, the caretaker looked at him as if to say, *What the hell—what do you want? We got rid of you, and you were leaving.* Pips concocted a story about suddenly falling ill and not knowing where to go. "It was a thin lie, quite transparent, but I was out of my head." When Pips arrived back at the estate, Lucienne was taken aback. He spent another few days there, but the bloom was off. "I was no longer an honored guest; I was an intruder being suffered, not very happily. So, that's when I finally did leave. The leaving was easy because, by now, cold water was poured over my head."

Six months later, at Christmastime, Pips received a card from London with a banal message, written in English: 'I am sending you this Christmas card with loving wishes fond and true, wherever you are, whatever you do, may fortune ever smile on you.' It was signed "Lucienne." She had not forgotten him, but it was the last goodbye.

When Pips returned to Berlin, he finally acquired his first long pants.

In October, Pips's parents registered him at Gross Breesen, a 567-acre working farm established in Silesia, eastern Germany, run by the Central Association of German Jews. The land was previously owned by Willi Rohr, a wealthy Jew. The Association hired Curt Werner Bondy, a former full professor in Göttingen with a PhD in Social Psychology, to establish an agricultural school for Jewish teens. The curriculum he developed included vocational training, science, and the humanities, with the goal of nurturing cultured farmers to prepare for emigration in the face of rising Nazi persecution. About a hundred students were in residence at any given time, with boys and girls on separate floors, sleeping in bunk beds, twelve to a room. By the time the Gestapo closed down the school in 1941 to turn it into a forced labor camp, 240 teens had gone through its program. Many emigrated and sustained lifelong connections to one another.

"Gross Breesen was allowed because it was a way to get rid of Jews. Until a year later, the Germans were still satisfied with kicking the Jews out of Germany rather than killing them.

"I still remember my father bringing me to the railroad station and being very sad. He didn't know whether we would ever see each other again. He didn't know what was going to happen to him; he didn't know what was going to happen to me. I could see that he was trying to control the tears. I was uncomfortable, as I often was, to see my father suffer like that. He was not a complainer, not a whiner, not at all. But he was very sensitive. I also felt sad, but nowhere near the kind of sadness that he felt." Ernst gave his son a parting gift—a carton of cigarettes.

In a way, Pips looked forward to Gross Breesen. He was still fifteen years old and this was, after all, a new escapade.

But Bondy, who ran the camp, was a strict disciplinarian and maintained a rigorous daily routine. Trainees rose at 5:00 a.m. to do farm tasks. After they finished their chores, they pivoted to academic studies. Twice a day, they underwent military roll calls. Dinner followed, with mandatory attendance at an evening concert.

"We were all city kids, and we were put to work right off the bat." As a new arrival, Pips was assigned to muck out the pond from which the animals drank. It had been completely drained to clean out layers of mud. Standing in the sludge, the trainees shoveled the mud into carts and wheeled it off to be dumped. "For somebody who had never done any physical work it was hard. For days, I had blisters on my hands."

Pips's parents wrote to him almost every day. His mother's letters were full of love and practical concern. In one of her letters, she wrote:

> *"My dear boy, I am sending you the sweater you asked for, the old washcloth, a wool scarf, and three bananas, since you like them. I hope that you have received the work boots by now. Papa went promptly to a wholesaler to buy them. As you know, he himself urgently needs a pair of shoes, but he will have to do without them for now . . . . I am also enclosing the wool socks. You had torn them to shreds when you put them on, so I was barely able to sew them up. For the time being, wear them in high-top boots. I will send you a few more in the next package."*

Her attentiveness surprised Pips "because years later, we ended up pretty much hating each other."

Pips recalled a herd of thirty cows and other livestock at Gross Breesen. There were no milking machines, so those assigned to do the first milking literally had their hands full. "If you're not used to this, it's terribly difficult. If you're lucky, some milk will come out. If you're not lucky it won't come out and you try again. Then, the cow realizes this is a greenhorn who doesn't know what he's doing and takes his tail out of the shit on the floor and hits you on the head with it."

The cows didn't make it easy. They rocked back and forth, causing hands to lose their grip on udders and teats. "Three hours later, half dead, the people could eat breakfast. It was very hard work that scared the hell out of me. I was always lazy to start with, but the work was very demanding. I decided after three months that agriculture wasn't my cup of tea." To make matters worse, Pips was freezing in the eastern European cold.

Pips reached out to his parents, and they let him return to Berlin.

There, he met Gerd Blach, a boy his age, who, like Pips, was at loose ends. Studying was now prohibited to Jews, and Jewish schools were closing, so continuing their education wasn't an option. All worthwhile occupations were off limits. But the boys desperately needed money, so they hired themselves out to Jewish families as house cleaners, specializing in carpets and windows. German windows swing out so they can be washed from the outside. Carpet cleaning involved beating the carpets with wicker switches on a large wooden frame to get at the deeply ingrained dust that vacuum cleaners missed.

"Of course, they didn't give us the carpets that were not so dirty. They gave us the filthy ones and the dust that came flying out was horrendous. We put handkerchiefs around our mouths, so we didn't breathe in the crap. In no time, the handkerchiefs would be black; our foreheads would be black; and we kept beating these carpets like crazy. Then you turned them around and beat them from the other side." Pips was very thorough, but slow.

However, he was a very fast cyclist, more at home on a bike than on his feet. Fittingly, his next job was making deliveries for an electrical appliance store. He mounted his bicycle in the morning, reported for duty, and was given a couple of items—perhaps a vacuum cleaner, a hair dryer—in a big sack, which he mounted on the rack of his bike. He rode around and made his deliveries in good time. "I thought they don't expect me to come back for an hour and it's only forty minutes. I might as well goof off for twenty minutes and sit on a park bench—which was not exactly straight, but one of my lesser sins."

Pips went everywhere on a bike. One day, he was making his rounds and came to Fasanenstrasse, the site of a monumental synagogue by the same name. The Fasanenstrasse Synagogue, completed in 1912, was built in the Romanesque Revival style, with three domes, and Byzantine features. The vast sanctuary held more than 1,700 worshippers, and the epic structure made no attempt to cower in the shadows. Its main portal boldly proclaimed itself a Jewish house of worship. At its opening, the synagogue was led by Rabbi Leo Baeck, who attained international renown as a liberal theologian and advocate for Christian-Jewish dialogue. But, in 1931, antisemitic gangs attacked the temple—the largest in Berlin—and the Nazis shuttered it for good in 1936.

On this day in 1938, there was a large crowd milling on Fasanenstrasse. Pips spotted smoke and flames. He dismounted from his bike and ambled into the crowd to see what was going on. As he inched closer, he saw that the synagogue was engulfed in flames. History later recorded that Joseph Goebbels personally ordered the destruction of that great tabernacle.

"I was terribly upset. Something like that had never happened before, even under the Nazis, and it meant the beginning of the destruction of the Jewish community." Unbeknownst to Pips, a mile away, the synagogue where he became a bar mitzvah was also in ashes.

Suddenly, a man broke out of the crowd and ran toward Kurfürstendamm. Dozens of people chased after him shouting, "A Jew, a Jew! Kill the Jew!

Pips jumped back on his bicycle and followed the crowd. There is a subway under the Kurfürstendamm, with vents at street level. The crowd grabbed hold of the hapless Jew, lifted him over the grill, and flung him onto the tracks. A minute later a train rushed by and ground him to smithereens. Pips heard the man's screams and the shouts of the crowd: "Ha ha! We got him!"

"To say this shook me up, is putting it mildly. This was the first time I saw violence with my own eyes. Real violence, not just people being kicked out of their jobs, but real violence, real murder. That left an impression on me that I will never forget. It gave me a foretaste; it's going to get worse."

It was the night of November 9, 1938. Pips didn't yet know it, but he had just borne witness to Kristallnacht.

"The Germans at that time were anxious to get rid of the Jews. The idea of exterminating them had not yet ripened, so it was a question of pushing them out of the country, which was not that easy. The majority were so German and so rooted in Germany that it was difficult to pry them loose. So, I think the SS, the Gestapo, and the government had the idea that they had to do something more drastic to put a fire under their asses to get them to move."

The Nazis found the perfect pretext.

On November 7, 1938, a distraught seventeen-year-old Polish Jew, Herschel Grynszpan, living illegally in Paris, shot Ernst vom Rath, a German embassy official stationed there. It was a symbolic act of revenge to protest the expulsion of Jews of Polish citizenship living in Germany, including his parents. His family, initially denied entry into Poland, was stranded in the squalor of a refugee camp in the border region between the two countries.

Kristallnacht, a well-orchestrated pogrom, was billed as a spontaneous outburst of public sentiment in response to vom Rath's assassination. But, in truth, Jews had long been targeted before the events of that night. "Prior to that, Jewish store owners had been required to mark their windows first with their name, and later with the Star of David, so that they were easily recognizable. During the night, all these Jewish-owned stores were smashed and the rioters helped themselves to whatever there was."

Thirty thousand Jewish men were arrested after Kristallnacht and sent to Dachau, Sachsenhausen, Buchenwald, and other concentration camps. It was the first time that Jews were rounded up en masse based on their ethnicity. The regime deemed the Kristallnacht devastation to be the fault of its victims and imposed a one billion Reichsmark "Atonement Tax" on the Jewish community. Lest German insurance companies bear the cost of paying for the property that Jewish clients had paid them to cover, the Reich confiscated all payments made to Jews for the damage to their homes and businesses.

Kristallnacht achieved exactly what it was intended to do: spur Jews to leave Germany.

Finding a destination was daunting, but despite the obstacles, 113,000 Jews managed to leave Germany and Austria in 1938 and 1939. By the end of 1939, there were only 202,000 Jews left in Germany out of a population of 523,000 only six years earlier.

The Philipsohn family went from consulate to consulate, searching for a host country. In July 1938, President Franklin Roosevelt convened the Evian Conference to address the problem of Jewish refugees. Only one country, the Dominican Republic, was willing to open its doors. It agreed to accept up to 100,000 Jews to work as farmers. The Philipsohns hoped to be among them. "It was then under the thumb of Trujillo, who was smart enough to figure out that if you get a bunch of Jews in here, it could help the economy." Rafael Trujillo also saw it as an opportunity to increase the white population of his backward country.

In preparation to leave, Pips took a few weeks of Spanish lessons. He didn't learn much but recalled a couple of sentences: *Juan Pérez es un joven español de 18 años que trabaja en la empresa López Hermanos.* He also took a course in window dressing, which happened to be available to would-be emigrants. He learned how to drape material around a dummy and arrange shop windows. The classes ran for a few weeks, but he didn't achieve anything worthwhile. "My artistic sense was not grandiose."

Between 1938 and 1945, Trujillo issued only 5,000 visas and accepted only 645 Jews. The Philipsohns were not among the lucky few.

Shanghai was another option. Thousands of Jews fled there after Kristallnacht. As an open city, with an International Settlement largely controlled by the United States, France, and Japan, it was one of the few places that didn't require an entry visa or extensive documents. "We heard some terrible things about Shanghai, which were mostly true, but we didn't know that staying in Germany would be a lot worse. So, we weren't anxious to go to Shanghai. You know how it is: when something is for free, you respect it less than when you pay money for it. Shanghai would open its doors—that already demoted it in our minds. There must be something terribly wrong in Shanghai if they let us in."

Eventually, twenty thousand Jews took refuge there, traveling by boat from Italy or by Trans-Siberian Railroad through the Soviet Union. Many were destitute, isolated, living in cramped quarters, and exposed to tropical diseases. Later, after the Japanese conquered Shanghai, Jews would be relegated to a one-square-mile ghetto in the Hongkou District. It seemed that, because Japan had no appetite for killing Jews, they created this ghetto to placate their Axis ally, Germany. But one of their diplomats, Chiune Sugihara, heroically issued life-saving transit visas to 2,140 Jewish refugees in Lithuania.

The door to Shanghai slammed shut in August 1939. But the Philipsohns persisted in their attempts to find an escape route. Siam (Thailand) looked promising. Ernst and Marie approached their Jewish friends and relatives for money to pay for passage on the ship they booked—and for Pips to buy a cheap tropical suit, which immediately lost its shape.

About a week before the sailing date, the Siamese government added a new requirement: refugees must each carry at least twenty pounds sterling. Because Jews were forbidden to hold foreign currency, the Philipsohns could not produce the sterling needed to board the ship and were turned away.

"The Jews who left Germany after '35 or '36 were penniless, unless they had already stashed away money in Switzerland. Not that all Jews had money to stash away, in the first place. My parents certainly didn't. So, we pretty much gave up."

With nowhere to go, Pips kept his job at the electrical appliance shop when summer came. In the early part of the season, he was invited to pay a weekend visit to a girl in his group of friends, whose parents lived in Angermünde, forty miles northeast of Berlin.

CHAPTER 3

WAR BEGINS AND CHILDHOOD ENDS

Angermünde was a small town, where Pips's Jewish hosts had managed to hold on to their modest house. Pips arrived in pleasant weather and, on Sunday morning, he and his friend went for a walk. It wasn't long before they found themselves in open fields. They settled on a grassy slope to eat a sandwich. While she was lying in the sun, Pips began to open her blouse. When she didn't resist, he removed her bra. He kissed her breasts, and being innocent and virginal, she turned very red in the face. But she returned Pips's kisses and demurely accepted his advances. Neither of them knew where to go from there, so she got dressed and that was that. "I don't know if she was ready, but I certainly wasn't ready to go below the belt. She liked me and I liked her, but we were friends, and we never became lovers or did anything like that again. This was a one-shot deal, so to speak."

But Pips had another vivid memory of that weekend trip. He and the girl trekked across a bridge that led over railroad tracks. As they got to the middle of the bridge, they spied a train approaching. The first wagons were passenger cars, filled with German officers. Then came flatbed cars bearing cannons and tanks, and freight cars laden with war materiel. While officers relaxed in their comfortable quarters, regular soldiers shared space with the ordnance.

"That train must have had at least a hundred cars and was going east. We said to each other, 'It looks an awful lot like war and war doesn't bode well for us Jews.'" It was Pips's first inkling that hostilities were about to erupt.

By fall, Pips lost his job at the electrical appliance store. But he soon got another job: catching tiny crustaceans, misnamed water fleas, for Mr. Furchert, who lived about twenty-five minutes by bus from Münchener Strasse. Furchert had made arrangements with the owners of several ponds to fish their water for these near-microscopic creatures. Each morning, he and Pips set out in his BMW, "But they weren't like BMWs today. It was a crummy little car—like these French sardine cans. They look exactly like sardine cans and sound like a sewing machine, with a horsepower of three and a half."

The duo carried nets with them and stretched them across the entire span of the ponds, dragging the nets just under the waterline. When they came to the end of the pond, they pulled up their nets, removed grainy, reddish clumps of water fleas, and laid them on wooden frames. Four hours later, they had two hundred frames. Furchert took 120 frames to his car. Pips put the remaining frames in a wooden crate on his bicycle.

Pips went from pet shop to pet shop. Each had a bucket of water near the entrance in preparation for the fleas, which would feed fish and help keep their water clean. Pips took out one frame at a time, and poured water through it, so that all the fleas would float in the bucket below.

Then, winter came—the winter of 1939, when Central Europe suffered one of the coldest winters of the twentieth century—and war had just broken out in the early fall.

"Every second evening I would get on my bicycle and ride to my boss's apartment over icy, snowy roads. I was used to it. Then I would park my bicycle someplace and we would get into his car and drive for an hour or two out to the country, where he had paid for the authority to fish." The ice was so thick that Furchert drove his car right onto the ponds, where there was no shelter from the frigid wind.

Furchert and Pips arrived at eleven o'clock at night. The first order of business was to hack four holes in the ice to get to the water—and the fleas—lurking below. This was no easy feat with ice that was six inches thick.

There were two holes for each of them. Every half hour or so, when the net felt heavy enough, they brought up their haul. This routine went on every other night. It took six or seven hours to catch their quota. By the time they were done, it was six in the morning.

It became easier later on because there were only two accessible ponds remaining. The temperature kept falling. "I was wearing just about everything I had, including newspaper under my pullover. My mother gave me a very thick scarf, which I wrapped around my face. It didn't do much good because, within five minutes, I had ice on my breath. It was miserable. But you can stand a lot when you're seventeen years old."

Berlin was in the throes of the coldest winter in 110 years.

"When I say cold in Berlin, it's different from cold in New York. Berlin gets colder. Berlin is on the same parallel as Calgary, Canada. Most people don't realize that. New York is on the same parallel as Naples. And when the wind comes from the east, Berlin gets the weather from Siberia."

Notwithstanding the weather, Pips prepared for wartime deprivation in his own way. As soon as the war broke out, he got on his bicycle and went from store to store to pick up all the chocolate bars he could find. He managed to garner fifteen of them, feeling confident that he had a sufficient supply to see him through the war. "I had a sweet tooth and couldn't stare that chocolate in the face. Within two weeks, it was all gone."

Food ration cards started being issued on August 27, 1939. One could not purchase goods without them. The six-by-eight-inch sheets, divided into tear-off coupons, doled out items like butter, meat, coffee, and honey in quantities ranging from 62.5 grams to 750 grams. For Jews, the ration cards were stamped with a big red "J"—and their allotments were lower than those for Aryans.

"At first the rations were pretty livable—generous—and some things weren't rationed, like potatoes. The potatoes we would get were frozen, even though the peasants had stacked them up, as they do every year, with straw. And frozen potatoes didn't taste very good. They're mushy and they were sickly sweetish. But if you're hungry, you eat them."

Soon Jewish ration cards excluded meat of any kind, along with white bread, butter, eggs, milk, and, of course, chocolate, cigarettes, and luxury items. "The only things you could get on a Jewish ration card were small amounts of margarine and you could buy vegetables. You became a vegetarian." In Pips's case, it wasn't bad, at first. His Aryan mother had a regular ration card so she could buy meat and ask the butcher to throw in a bone to make soup.

Given the limits of a Jewish ration card, Pips was privy to a great perk: After their long nights of catching water fleas, he and Furchert drove to the house of the farmer who owned the ponds where they fished. There, they feasted on a breakfast of ham, eggs, and home-baked bread with thick butter. "Really good stuff that you couldn't get in Berlin unless you were a Nazi big shot." Then they drove back to the boss's house, where Furchert's wife gave them a cup of coffee with a cookie.

At that point, Pips was only midway through his shift. He now had to get back on his bicycle with a crate of frames and deliver them to pet stores in the icy weather. "So, I went from store to store and finished at four or five in the afternoon. I had pretty much a twenty-four-hour gig." He then went home and had the next night free.

"When I heard on the radio what the German soldiers are suffering on the Eastern front in Poland, I said they should try to do what I'm doing. They didn't have to stand on ice for four hours when they had guard duty for maybe two hours."

Spring came and Pips resumed his job water flea catching. But he decided to go into business for himself and tried to wean away some of his boss's customers. He was earning a fraction of what Furchert was making for the same amount of work. So, he reasoned, why not just work for himself and get more money for the torture he endured every other night? Of course, his boss didn't earn much money either—one Reichsmark per frame, 70 Reichsmarks for 70 frames.

"For the rest of my life I've been unable to figure out how I could possibly have been so depraved and so idiotic. This man had treated me decently and had never made any remarks about me being a Jew. He had always treated me as a human being and as a helper, whom he needed. It was, from a moral standpoint, outrageous. But from a practical standpoint, it was even more outrageous. There was no way in the world I could have pulled that off. First, I had no car and Jews, of course, couldn't get cars. Secondly, it should have occurred to me that the people I started talking to would tell him about it. They had worked with this man for many years. Of course, he found out about it in no time, and he called me on the carpet. He was still relatively civil. He didn't beat me up—even though to beat a Jew was no big deal. He just told me how disgusted he was with me, and then he said, 'What you did was typically Jewish.' He normally would never have said anything like that, and it really hurt. But I deserved it and then some."

Despite Pips's betrayal, Furchert needed him and kept him on. But he became a shade less friendly from that time on. "It stayed with me, and I've been feeling guilty ever since."

Starting in 1939, the year in which Pips got his job catching water fleas, Jewish property was systematically appropriated, and Jews were methodically deprived of their ability to work. “The only thing Jews were still allowed to do was die.”

Nineteen thirty-nine was a hard year, but it was also the year that Pips had his first real girlfriend, Alice, a passionate sixteen-year-old, who was eager to go to bed with him. “I just wasn’t ready for it. I would fondle her breasts, and she was very anxious to go further. I said we should save ourselves for marriage. What a schmuck! I was very naïve, very immature, and I was just afraid of going all the way. I spoke like a Catholic priest, and I believed, for the moment, my own crap that one shouldn’t do this before marriage.” Although Alice persisted in talking about marriage to her “little Pips with blue eyes and blond hair,” she never succeeded in taking his virginity.

The following year it was the turn of Ilse Cohen, a student nurse in the Jewish hospital. “I always had a thing for nurses. Maybe it started with her.” Ilse lived at the other end of Berlin and had to travel a long distance to get to Pips. “I wasn’t in love with her, but she was in love with me. We both enjoyed each other’s bodies, we enjoyed lying together, spending a night together in bed. We didn’t go all the way, but we were steady for about a year.”

One day, he sent Ilse a note with an erotic message. He deliberately wrote it on a postcard so other people would see it before it reached her. Infuriated, she called Pips from a telephone booth. (Jews could no longer have phones.) He was out, so she spoke to his parents instead. Her message to Pips: *She is deeply upset, and he should go to hell!* Pips wrote her back, sarcastically:

> *You called tonight. Unfortunately, I was not home. My father loyally and dutifully relayed me your blessings and kind compliments . . . When you say I should have myself buried, you . . . make the flattering assumption that I am dead. I can, however,*

> *report—which will surely bring you unspeakable joy—that I find myself as alive as a spring chicken and in full possession of my intellectual and physical abilities—and if requested, I am happy to grant you the opportunity to convince yourself of the unfaltering strength of this vitality.*
>
> *I truly must thank you for turning your face—which is a picture of innocence—toward me in an act of selfless willingness for sacrifice . . . even though . . . you are so utterly convinced of the profound depravity of my character.*
>
> *Since you seem to worry about your already wrecked reputation taking another hit, I have dutifully obeyed your wishes. I shall now ensure that the eruptions of our passionate affection will be confined solely to the safety of closed blinds. . . .*
>
> *Having come to realization . . . that our union—confined to written correspondence, and moreover also one-sided, as all great loves are—will hardly make the desired progress, I politely ask you to be so kind to inform me via writing . . . when I might have the pleasure of seeing or calling you. . . . We could then arrange a little rendezvous so we can again gaze deeply into each other's eyes.*
>
> *With high hopes of soon being able to wrap my arms around your virginal form again, I remain . . . still fond of you.*

"I remember that, even in those days, I had a cruel streak. I didn't mean to be cruel. It was my idea of a practical joke. I don't do slapstick. I do it verbally instead, and sometimes it's cruel and almost always tactless."

Marie respected her son's privacy and stayed away from his room. Because it was opposite the back door of the apartment, he could discreetly spirit in his girlfriends, Alice, Ilse, and a bevy of others who spent many nights there. "I was not deprived but I didn't go all the way." But then it happened.

Pips's best friend was Gerd Blach, with whom he earlier started a window and carpet cleaning business. The Blach apartment was five minutes away by bicycle and the boys were regulars in each other's homes. They, and a small circle of friends, whiled away weekday evenings chatting, and they went to the countryside on weekends. The girls in this clique were their age or a bit younger. One evening, they were joined by a young woman in her early twenties. "She was an awfully nice person but not particularly pretty. She wasn't ugly either, but nothing to write home about." The group broke up at about midnight. Pushing their bicycles, she and Pips ambled to his apartment. He invited her to come up and finally had his first complete sexual intercourse.

"She introduced me, which wasn't easy because I spilled my beans before I even got in. Of course, it was embarrassing, but she was very understanding and very soft and very sweet and loving. Later that night, I was able to perform and consummate it for her. But we didn't become an item." Yet, a few weeks later, Pips was on his bicycle and had a sudden urge to see her.

"I wanted to have sex with her. She received me, but she was embarrassed. I said, 'What's the matter, why are you so hesitant?' She said she had her period. I didn't know much about periods, and I was horny as hell at that point, so I said, 'Period or no period, just go.' I was a little shocked when I pulled out and saw the blood, but still a good time was had by all, particularly by me."

It was now 1940. Pips was eighteen years old, sexually active, and he hung out with his friends until late into the night. Ernst worried about his son's safe return home. "My father was a very soft-hearted man who loved me beyond description." In Berlin, the doors of apartment buildings were locked at eight o'clock at night. Residents had a key. But visitors either had to call ahead or whistle "hello" to alert residents of their arrival. Residents threw their key down or came down to admit the visitor. The entrance lights turned on with the press of a button, but they remained on for only a few minutes. It was an awkward arrangement!

"So, many a time, when I came home, my father was walking up and down. It must have been for hours. When I finally arrived, it was, for him, accompanied by a mixture of pent-up frustration, anger, and relief that I was safe and sound. This was my father's way; I was everything to him."

Despite all the restrictions, Pips still indulged his amusements. Jewish performing artists were excluded from all public performances before Aryan audiences. But, in 1933, the Gestapo approved the formation of the Jüdischer Kulturbund, the Jewish Cultural League. Its performances were limited to Jewish audiences.

Pips attended a Kulturbund performance of the Hungarian operetta, *Countess Maritza*, which was permitted only because the composer was a Jew. "It was a very charming performance despite all the difficulties they had getting stage material and costumes." Pips had always been interested in theater and even considered becoming an actor—something his parents encouraged because of his talent in reciting poetry. "They thought this was a sign that I would make a great actor. I learned in time that it wasn't."

The middle-aged male lead's performance in the operetta impressed the aspiring actor and Pips reached out to him. "We made a deal that he would give me acting lessons, which in 1940 was quite optimistic. I went to him on weekends when I didn't have to work, and he gave me some lessons. But I was uneasy with him because it became very obvious that he was a homosexual. Even though he didn't make a pass at me, I wasn't comfortable. Also, I had a feeling I wasn't really getting anywhere."

Neither was his parents' marriage of thirty-five years, which finally broke up after years of them drifting apart. The differences in their temperaments were irreconcilable. But mostly, the relentless government campaign to isolate Jews from the rest of society made

Ernst a drag on his wife. He was no longer earning a living and the family now lived on the money Marie made by renting out the rooms in their apartment.

Once they were divorced, their Jewish boarders became a liability, and Marie urged them to find housing elsewhere. From that point on, Marie took in only Aryan boarders. But her son was still living with her.

Ernst moved to a tiny, dreary room, with only a bed and a chair. He had smoked cigars all his life, but as a Jew, tobacco was *verboten*, so he could no longer access even this small pleasure. He managed to get hold of a few cigarettes from time to time, but he didn't like them or inhale the smoke.

Ernst was flagged by the Jüdisches Arbeitsamt—the Central Office for Jews of the Berlin Employment Office. "The SS had set up an employment agency, except this was compulsory and it was staffed by Jews. They wouldn't waste their own personnel on this. The rule was that every Jew had to be assigned work and there were only a few types of jobs to be had. One was garbage collection, and the other one was on the railroad tracks. Both jobs were very hard on the Jews in Germany because—in contrast to Eastern Europe—those Jews were generally not used to physical labor. German Jews were professionals, businessmen, teachers, any number of things, but they were not garbage disposal people. They were not railroad workers. And, of course, the SS wouldn't give them a break. You had to be there, and you had to work. If you stopped work, there were SS men there with whips."

Ernst was spared either of these jobs. Instead, he was conscripted to forced labor in a factory, where Jewish sweat was needed for the war effort. But his work was interrupted when, suffering from a painful hernia, he was admitted to the Jewish hospital for surgery. "I visited him once or twice but not as often I should have."

There was no animosity in Ernst's and Marie's divorce—just great sadness—so Marie visited her ex-husband from time to time to bring him food. Of course, the rupture was much harder on him than on her, and Marie encouraged Pips to visit his father.

"I was such an egotistical mess. All I cared about was my sex life, my love life, and, of course, the pressure of the situation. I visited him only a few times. And every time I visited, he practically kissed my feet, so grateful that I came. My father had brought me up so lovingly and given me everything that I needed as a child. I had nothing to give him, no food or anything. But just my presence was such a great honor for him, such a great *mitzvah*. Sometimes he had a cigarette or two in his pocket that he saved for me and gave me as a treat—and, also, perhaps to bribe me to come back soon.

"I felt very, very guilty, as I should have, and yet I didn't change my ways. I felt guilty for neglecting him, for not seeing him at least once a week, for leaving this poor sixty-year-old man, this miserable man, to go schlepping early every morning to the factory. He had been an architect. Now he was a factory laborer, trying to live on the meager Jewish ration cards, which were cut down more and more, and being totally alone. I, his own son, his flesh and blood, for whom he had paced the streets at night to make sure I was all right, I couldn't find the time to see him more often than maybe every few weeks. It was so painful for me because I felt intensely uncomfortable that he had to demean himself by begging me to come back. As it turned out later, my parents' divorce caused my father's death."

Fearing backlash from Aryans if their families were broken up, the Nazi regime didn't deport Jews married to Aryan spouses. But Ernst no longer had that protection.

In fall 1940, the Jewish labor office discovered Pips's illicit work as a water flea catcher. Furchert had to let him go and they never saw each other again. Pips was now among the jobless Jews who were conscripted for hard labor in segregated work battalions.

But, even in his degraded circumstances, Ernst came to his son's rescue. As an interior architect, Ernst had done a lot of work with carpenters. He importuned an old friend, to whom he had given a lot of work, to write a letter attesting to Pips's carpentry skills. So instead of being assigned to garbage disposal or track bed repair, Pips was sent to Holzbau GmbH, a woodworks company that built prefabricated barracks for the German army. Located on the opposite side of Berlin from his home, Pips had to take a one-hour streetcar ride each way. This, on top of working eleven hours a day, five days a week, with a half hour for lunch; Saturdays, six hours; Sundays off.

"I show up and they have a large factory building with lots of machines. Some of them are quite dangerous because of very sharp rotator blades. If you pushed the wood in there, your fingers might go with it, which happened several times."

All the workers were Jews; all the foremen were Gentiles. A foreman gave Pips a plank of wood and a plane. "I'd never held a plane, and I just couldn't hold it straight. I chopped that wood into matchsticks. A blind man could see that I didn't know what I was doing. The foreman came and took one look and said 'You're not a carpenter. Come to the office.' I went to the office and was roundly shamed. 'You son of a bitch, you lousy Jew, trying to put one over on us, I'm going to call the Gestapo now. They'll take care of you.' That could have meant arrest and a labor camp. I pleaded, practically on bended knee, and he gave me a chance to work the machines on the night shift."

After a few weeks, Pips was reassigned to work outdoors, along with thirty Jews ranging from young to old. Stacking the finished barracks parts as they came in from the sawmill, into twenty- and thirty-foot piles, was not unduly hard work—especially in good weather. But in fall and winter, each worker ducked into the lunchroom every couple of hours to warm up by the stove.

During 1940, a young girl appeared among Pips's informal group of friends, joining their talk fests and going on hikes with them. She was Ilse Rosenthal—the third girl in Pips's life with that identical name. This one, a blond, blue-eyed, Germanic type, "with a touch of Jewish softness about her," was sixteen at the time, and she would become the great love of his life.

"To me she was the most beautiful thing—the loveliness of her face, the smile, the sweetness. She was not a glamorous woman, like Ava Gardner, but she had this natural sweetness."

Doom was engulfing Germany's Jews. Yet, Pips and his friends—including Ilse—were still in the mood to celebrate Silvester, New Year's Eve. But, where? The occupants of the apartment where they had celebrated the prior year had been kicked out and their home was now a slum. But the Baroness, former nursemaid to the rickety old Jewish woman who rented rooms from Pips's mother, now had a small apartment of her own. As an Aryan, no one bothered her, so her home would be safe. Pips had stayed in touch with her, and she agreed to let his band hold their Silvester party in her flat. They had a record player. They danced. And Pips got jealous. To his mind, Ilse was a little too friendly with Kuli, one of his comrades.

"I know that this was utter insanity on my part. But I was such an immature fool that I let this jealousy get hold of me. I gave her a very hard time towards the end of the party and the next day. Then things calmed down and we got back to normal."

Pips made a note of January 5, 1941—the day that Ilse declared her love for him. "Probably the happiest day of my life."

The lovers lived only twenty blocks apart and saw each other at least twice a week. On those evenings when they didn't meet, Ilse wrote Pips a letter. Sometimes, the letters were full of raw emotion. Other times, they were infantilizing and moralistic.

My beloved, it was so wonderful in your arms, I feel that I belong to you. Everything I write now is nonsense, I'm so mixed up, but I have to think of you. Darling, darling, I would like to say all

> *the time I love you, I love you, I love you! Will we ever be together and peaceful and happy, will we ever achieve that?*

Later she wrote:

> *Darling, did you sleep enough? I didn't. This morning, I could hardly wake up. I'm now sewing some stuff and am very bored. You know, I think how wonderful it would be when I awaken this night to have you close next to me. Ach, my boy, I have tremendous longing. Please, when you come on Tuesday, bring me Dr. Doolittle and Mark Twain. Today, I am reading* Peer Gynt. *I am very excited about it. You know, this Peer is unbelievably similar to you. But this is not what I meant to write to you and I'll probably bore you with this. My darling, I embrace you and say to you how I love you, I wish I could express it. I think of you always, my beloved boy . . .*

And yet, Ilse wanted Pips to see her as she was.

> *I am not the girl in your dreams. I am real and alive and I ask for nothing more than that you don't take me for the girl in your dreams, but that you love me as I really am. Everything else will only disappoint you.*

"Here's a girl who loves me very, very much. But when she writes, it's not just moon and June and honeymoon. It's very tough love, in a way. She wants me to be a *mensch*. She wants me to improve myself."

> *You know Pipusch, you let everything go and procrastinate. But this is not going to get you anywhere, because from nothing comes nothing. You have to do something, but first of all you have to know what it is you want it to be.*

Your Aryanization, you say that your mother forced you to that. Nobody can force you to do anything. You have to choose between me and the future. One thing brings you all advantages and possibilities for life. With me you have none of this, only love.

In other matters, you're not particularly concerned about your parents. Just as you can turn your back in an ugly way from your father, so you can do it with your mother, if the need arises. If you would insist on your right strongly enough, you could tell your mother, listen, I do not want this.

If you do it anyway, we are finished with each other . . . But of course, that would mean that you have to stand on your own feet and not always have somebody who feeds you and makes your life possible. You would have to work very hard to live at all. You would have the advantage of knowing that you are capable of standing on your own feet and would gain confidence in your own strength.

Only to be, to exist, is not living. You know, to be active one has to take one's fate in one's own hands and one has to risk something.

Now you lose nothing, but I do not think you are very happy about this. Because if you are, you would be worthless as a human being and you would really deserve contempt. You can say I will Aryanize, I will live, I want to succeed. Then you would have to take the consequences for that, to sacrifice anything that holds you back in the least, that binds you. Above all, it is important that you choose a way. Let us not kid ourselves, the chance that we can be together in the future is less than smooth . . .

Ilse was clear-eyed. Pips needed to make a choice between survival as an Aryan and an uncertain future with her. If Marie succeeded in Aryanizing Pips, Ilse and he would have no future.

"I've always been egotistical, but my love for Ilse became greater and greater. I can truthfully say that if it had come to that, I would gladly have died for her. In those days you didn't bandy that around easily, especially the next year when the deportations started.

"In 1941, we were still pretty safe in Berlin, if you didn't step over the line; if you didn't do something that was against the rules; and if nobody just had it in for you, denounced you as having done this or that, whether it's true or not."

Around Christmastime that year, Ilse and Pips had a fight. "I didn't always treat her with kindness." Coincidentally, that was also the time when he heard about a man in Innsbruck who could smuggle refugees over the 5,900-foot Arlberg into Switzerland. Pips decided to find him.

Presumably, he wanted to find an escape route. But he also wanted an adventure. What Jew would do this in the tightening grip of the Nuremberg Laws? But Pips was on friendly terms with his supervisor at Holzbau. "I gave him some kind of bullshit story and he said, 'I want you to be away for a week, just disappear and nobody will know the difference,' which was quite decent of him. I figured that if I make it to Switzerland, the disappearance will have no end, and if I don't make it, I'll be back in a week.

"So, I went partly out of spite to punish Ilse and partly out of a sense of adventure. Ilse was, by far, the most important thing in my life. Why would I run away from her? It makes no sense, and I can't understand it."

Austria, now annexed by Germany and designated "Ostmark," no longer existed as an independent country. Pips boarded a train to Vienna and whenever he saw patrols approaching, he ducked into the toilet until they passed.

"Dumb luck! I didn't really believe I would make it to Switzerland. That was too much of a dream. And in a way, perhaps I didn't want to do it, because I didn't want to leave Ilse."

In Vienna, Pips checked into a tiny pension off the beaten track. Police made their rounds of every hotel in the late afternoon or early evening to collect passports. Pips made sure to check in after they left. The next day, he went to another hotel and did the same thing. During his two days in Vienna, like any tourist in peacetime, he visited Schönbrunn Palace, Emperor Joseph I's imperial hunting lodge, and attended the Burgtheater, the most important German-speaking theater in the world. And he got away with it.

Pips then boarded another train, but it didn't go directly to Innsbruck. He needed to connect through Kitzbuhel, then already a world-renowned ski resort, east of his destination. There, he found a little inn but there was no vacancy. He was about to leave when the receptionist intercepted him. "If you don't mind it, we have a small room with two beds. One bed is occupied but you can have the other bed." She showed Pips the room and he nearly fainted. Slung over the chair was a uniform jacket with the insignia of a high Nazi party official. "So, he would be my roommate. I would sleep with him."

That didn't deter him. "I found out there was a shindig that night in one of the big hotels. It was in a ballroom with lots of tables and table telephones. In Germany, that was the *dernier cri*. So, if you were a single guy and saw a pretty girl sitting by herself, and if there was a number on the table, you could phone and ask her to have a drink with you. There was also a dance band, and I had hardly sat down when they announced a conduct-the-band contest. I volunteered as one of the contestants. Here I am, a Jew surrounded by Nazis, and I tell the band what I want them to play. And what did I want them to play? 'Begin the Beguine.' I directed it and I won the contest. My prize was a bottle of champagne. Sure enough, a pretty young woman came to my table, and I shared the bottle of champagne with her. Then I went to the inn to hit the sack. The Nazi was already snoring. Sheer insanity! The next morning, I got up and took the train to Innsbruck."

Pips arrived in Innsbruck and went off in search of the smuggler-guide. When he arrived at the address he was given, he was told that the guide had left weeks before and was not expected to return. Pips suspected that he had been arrested.

"Now what? No way could I make my way without a guide over the Arlberg to Switzerland in the middle of winter. I wasn't equipped for that. Even if a guide did take me over; even if I'd satisfied him with what little money I had; these areas were patrolled by the ski patrol on the German side and on the Swiss side. If the Swiss border patrols caught me, they would have taken me right back over the German border. But in a way, I thought it was just as well. At least I had fulfilled half of my desire, which was adventure. The desire to escape, I didn't. I took the train back to Vienna and from Vienna I took a train to Munich."

It was late evening and bitter cold when Pips caught the express train from Munich to Berlin. The only seat he could find was in a compartment with six seats, five of which were occupied by SS majors and colonels. Undaunted, Pips took a seat. "That was the smartest thing I could have done, but I was scared shitless. They didn't ask me how come I'm in civilian clothes. I think they were too drunk and the last thing on their minds was 'Is this fellow a Jew?' And, in a way, I was protected from the military police because, when they came by, opened the compartment door, and saw these SS officers, they would just close it and move on. If I'd gotten caught by the military police without papers, they would have turned me over to the Gestapo and I would have been sent to a concentration camp. I got back to Berlin but the odds that I would have made it were a thousand to one. Shows you how *meshugge* I was."

Soon after he returned from his junket, Pips got Ilse pregnant. It was early 1942 and abortion was strictly illegal in Germany, as was contraception. "We tried to go by the Catholic rhythm method, which as far as I'm concerned, is for the birds." What to do? They couldn't have a baby.

Ilse confessed to her mother. "Her mother had sort of a jaundiced eye about me anyway, the son of a bitch who gets her seventeen-year-old girl pregnant." But her mother found a sympathetic doctor and paid him several hundred marks. "A fantastic sum, because, at that time, the mark still had some value." Pips accompanied Ilse and her mother. "I was sitting, shivering. Then Ilse came out. She could hardly walk. She was pale. We couldn't take a taxi, so we took a streetcar." At least, they could still take a streetcar. Within a short time, Jews would be banned from all public transport.

"You can imagine, to travel right after an abortion! I felt, with justification, that I was a real shit. How could I have inflicted on this poor girl this pain, this agony, this worry?"

A few months later, Ilse became pregnant again. They agreed: no more abortions. She would have the baby, come what may. But her uterus had been damaged from the earlier termination and, mercifully, she miscarried after a couple of months. Ilse was admitted to the Jewish hospital, on the corner of Exerzierstrasse and Schulstrasse. It was still functioning, albeit on a much-reduced scale. She was confined to bed for a week or two. Pips and her mother visited each day. "And again, I felt like a shit."

Life became progressively worse. Food was tight. Jews were deprived of their homes and belongings. Radios and telephones were forbidden. An 8:00 p.m. curfew was imposed, and the use of public transportation was denied—unless the riders had papers proving they had to get to work. The Jew star was introduced. "They even tried to imitate Hebrew letters to make us more laughable."

Cigarettes, on which Pips was now hooked, were among the deprivations. He dipped into the black market, making minor deals with an acquaintance whose source obtained cigarettes by the carton from Yugoslavia. "They were pretty shitty cigarettes." Pips took a couple of cartons on consignment, selling one and a half of them to pay his contact. That left him a half carton for himself.

"In spite of all the misery and trouble and the danger that was coming closer and closer, I was still happy, because of my love for Ilse. When I was with Ilse, I was happy. When I received a note from Ilse, I was happy. So, in a way, I'm nostalgic for that time. A Jew nostalgic for that time? Am I nuts?"

Emigration was banned in October 1941 and Jews were required to wear "*Jude*" stars on their clothes. "Most people believed that if they were good citizens and they did everything they were told to do, they would be spared. Of course, they hadn't been citizens anymore for a long time. Nobody understood yet that the plan was to kill all Jews, regardless."

Pips, ever the rebel, flouted the rules and refused to wear the Jew star, didn't respect the 8:00 p.m. curfew, and would not give up movies and other amusements—leaving Ilse frantic with worry.

> *I beg you, by everything that is important to you, wear the star now always.*

She underlined *immer*, the German word for "always."

There is one instance when Pips complied. He and Ilse were on the subway before subways were off limits to Jews. Ilse wore a green coat, which she had made out of curtains—echoing Scarlett O'Hara in *Gone With the Wind.* She insisted that they both pin on their Jew stars. They dared not sit down, but the other riders didn't pay them any particular attention. "It wasn't a traumatic thing. But for me, it was very unusual and very uncomfortable. Because once you wear the star, somebody might remember you as a Jew. It's better to never wear it at all."

Ilse's mother forbade Pips from entering her home without his Jew star. To appease her, he sewed it on his raincoat but left it visible only when he entered her apartment.

Ilse also implored Pips to be home by 8:00 p.m., lest he get arrested.

But Ilse could no longer bear living apart. Two of her friends had just gotten engaged and marriage was at the top of her mind.

> *They all can do it. We know we love each other so much, much more than all the others together. It can't go on any further like this. I wish so much that we can relax. The rings don't have to be gold—probably we wouldn't be able to get them anyway—and steel would be good enough. There are some very nice steel rings. I know, darling, that you will laugh and say I'm childish and these things are not important. But it seems wrong to be engaged without a ring. For me that's part of it, just as it's understood that one lives together when one is married. My darling, good little Pipeschein, I love you so much, so without end.*
>
> *We don't need a stamp from City Hall, we are for all practical purposes people who belong together, we are one.*

"We wanted more than a few hours with an occasional night of togetherness. We wanted a life where you could have a future. You may not know what the future will be, but you have a future together. But we couldn't live together. We had no apartment, we had nothing. So, we tried to think of ourselves as an old married couple with the comfort of knowing each other, being sure of one another. We were aching for normalcy. We even discussed when we should have children, how many children. We craved a room or a little apartment and being married."

> *Pipeschein, I cannot bear it anymore. We must marry. We must marry. Why don't you please speak with your mother?*

In July 1938, Hitler had decreed that men could not marry before the age of twenty-one without special permission. But permission could not be granted to a man younger than eighteen. Pips and Ilse were underage and needed their parents' consent.

Ilse approached her mother, asking her to try to put aside her complaints about Pips's lack of formality—he never wore a tie, rarely wore a jacket, and had been spied with his fly inadvertently left open. But Ilse's mother, a widow, wouldn't agree to their marriage because she disdained Pips, finding him egotistical, irresponsible, and an alarmist. Nor would Pips's mother agree because she feared that marriage to a Jew would derail the Aryanization she was trying to obtain for her son.

These were the last optimistic moments in which the young couple could harbor thoughts of marriage. Ilse bemoaned the impossibility of their love under the Nazi regime.

> *"If only we were together, but where could we live and what could we live on. Maybe the best thing is to make* schluss *to finish it all off."*

Ilse was disheartened by the cards life had dealt them. "She was in so much pain and agony that we couldn't be together. She was talking about suicide. This is the only time she ever mentioned it and I don't think she meant it."

Pips's possible Aryanization was still very much on her mind.

> *Everything whirls around me, I love you so much that I cannot describe it, this feeling is so strong I think I have to explode. Pipush, come or go, but do something. I know that I am one of those who have held you back, up to now. But now you must do something, but only if you really want it. Don't let me influence you. But don't let me wait too long for an answer. My darling, my body, my everything. You, only you, I don't want to be without you, I need you, help me this way or that way.*

The implementation of a 1939 "Law Concerning Jewish Tenants" laid the legal foundation for dispossessing Jewish property and segregating Jews in Berlin in *Judenhäuser* (Jewish houses). Ilse, her mother, and her brother were now forced to move to one of these. It wasn't quite a ghetto, because they were allowed to come and go. But they were squeezed together. In larger apartments, there were now two families in one room. Concentration in these Jewish houses would later facilitate the mass deportation of Berlin's Jews. Ilse writes:

> *This morning, I was with mother, and we have to move to this other place. Then we'll have even less privacy than I had before. I'm so longing for peace, which you have, at least at night in your little room. If you have it for yourself alone, I know it's not fair, but I wish it for myself too.*

In the midst of 1942's unfolding catastrophes, Pips caught a break. Holzbau assigned him to serve as co-pilot to a truck driver who delivered prefabricated barracks parts to army camps. Pips didn't know how to drive. Nor, under Nazi law, was he allowed to drive. His task was to talk to the driver to keep him awake and help with random problems. After driving a hundred miles or so and arriving at their destinations, there was no work for Pips to do. Other workers, mostly fellow Jews, were there to unload the truck. So, he just stood there and smoked a cigarette.

"It was a pretty easy life. The driver happened to be a nice fellow—not that he was altogether crazy about Jews, but we got along." En route, the driver often stopped at a *Kneipe,* a pub, where he and Pips had a meal. The driver had his ration card, but Pips's was of no use because of the "J" stamped on it. "Most of the food they served, I couldn't get on my card. So, he was very nice. If you ordered horsemeat instead of beef, you got a double portion.

On occasion, he would order horsemeat so he could share it with me. It tasted like chicken, it wasn't bad. It was very pleasant to ride around in the truck; it was nothing but a joy ride."

And then came the spring of '42. That's when deportations started and the flavor changed dramatically. Hopelessness and terror set in.

> *When I write you this letter don't think that I'm running after you. It is totally against my pride, but Pipush, when your love is as great as you say it is, then we have to try to make it clear to my mother that we love each other and must be together. Her whole attitude toward us is ugly and completely without any understanding and she tries to block us at every opportunity. And all the family, they strengthen her in her attitude. My darling, the best thing is that we are clear, that you see clearly and can decide for yourself, and then we will see that your will can be put up against them. I will do everything necessary, but we have to stay together.*

"She didn't mean just the two of us but also with her mother and family. That wasn't possible. The Germans were very strict in their policies. If I'm not a deportation case, I'm not a deportation case. I had my job—a fairly pleasant job—and I lived with my mother."

> *Beloved sweet little Pipush. I'm thinking of what will become of us since we are, after all, in the hands of the N-A-Z-I-S. Darling, we have so much tension and pressure from the outside, it should be possible that we, at least, reach inner peace between ourselves.*

But that was not to be.

In June, elderly Jews were transported to Theresienstadt in Czechoslovakia, a camp reserved for certain categories of Jews: in addition to old people, those wounded in past military service, or those who had achieved great renown as scholars, artists, or scientists were among them. Nazi propaganda described the camp as a "spa town" where elderly German Jews could "retire" in safety. In a seeming contradiction, at the same time, the public was informed that its occupants would be productively employed in forced labor. Although this was a "show" camp, trotted out to hide the true conditions in the Nazi concentration camps, nearly all the old people imprisoned there died. Those who didn't were transferred to Auschwitz, Majdanek, and Treblinka to be killed.

As a wounded former front-line soldier, Pips's father was sent to Theresienstadt to face starvation, hard labor, and disease.

"My mother wasn't losing any sleep over the Jews in general—the Jews in Poland, the Jews in Russia, the Jews in Budapest, the Jews of Bucharest, the Jews in Sofia, the Jews in France—but she was worried about me and she was worried about my father. She knew that my father had to be written off. She felt very guilty because, if they hadn't divorced, he wouldn't have been deported. But by the time they got divorced, there was no deportation yet in sight, so I cannot blame her directly. But she was not sympathetic."

Ernst died in Theresienstadt, along with 35,440 other Jews.

Ernst's brother, Adolf, was deported to Sobibor from Paris.

The family of Ernst's brother, Martin, declined step by step. "I still remember being at Martin's lumberyard once or twice. They had a car, which was rare. The couple of times I rode in that car, it was a big deal. Not that we went anywhere, just riding around the streets. All this disappeared. Jews weren't allowed to drive, and the lumberyard was taken away." In the first wave of deportations, Martin and his son Kurt killed themselves. "Kurt was justified in committing suicide because, as a full Jew, there was nothing that could save him from deportation. My uncle was a full Jew too, but he was in a mixed marriage and would not have been deported. But he didn't seem to have known that."

Pips wasn't a deportation case either, because he was a Jew living in the same household with an Aryan mother. But, like Uncle Martin, he was unaware that he was exempt.

"You didn't know whether tomorrow, without announcement, they decided to deport you, to deport the Geltungsjuden, who lived with their Aryan parent. There's no way of telling, so I can't say that I left the wonderful, warm bed of security to save Ilse. My security was a very iffy proposition, too."

The inner circle of Pips's friends—particularly he and the Blach boys—concluded "that once they get their hands on us physically, we're finished, they will kill us. So, we decided that when the time comes, meaning when we get the 'invitation,' we would go underground."

Ilse's mother was appalled by Pips's plan. "She called me a nut because I told her you're going to death. 'We will work hard, starving. We will have a very tough time, but kill us all? Ridiculous!' So, people like Ilse's mother wouldn't think of going underground. She was too law-abiding, middle class, and middle aged. To be an outlaw was not in her book. And there were so many of those."

Mrs. Rosenthal accused Pips of wanting to go underground only in order to hold on to Ilse. Yet, he wasn't responsible enough to take care of her daughter.

"There were various components to her mother's feelings. First, I'm sure she was jealous. Out of nowhere comes this young nobody—I was an eighteen-year-old boy when I met Ilse. All of a sudden, her daughter is smitten. I'm all she can think of. That bugged the hell out of her. Secondly, she felt that I was unworthy of her Ilse, which I probably was. And we were too young to be in such an intense relationship. A little later came the main reason why she began to hate me: I was taking Ilse away from her.

"The only thing I knew was that I didn't want to live without Ilse. I was too insensitive, too egotistical, too self-involved, and too dumb to understand what it meant when she had to say good-bye to her mother and her brother for the last time. I didn't even make a serious effort to understand."

Mrs. Rosenthal and Ilse's fourteen-year-old brother were deported to Riga, Latvia, where they were killed with at least twenty-five thousand other Jews massacred in the Rumbula Forest.

Pips's father, his uncles, cousins, and many of his friends had been deported.

Pips saw clearly where this was heading, and he was determined to survive with Ilse, at all cost.

CHAPTER 4

GOING UNDERGROUND WITH ILSE AND SEARCHING FOR AN ESCAPE

When Hitler came to power in 1933, the first step in the war on Jews was to deprive them of participating in public life. The second step was to steal their assets and take away their citizenship and their rights. The third step was to open an immigration office and get the Jews out of Germany.

"The Germans were again lousy with Jews. They realized that, with their conquests, they had not only *not* gotten rid of Jews, but inherited *more* Jews—particularly in Poland, where there were three million of them. Obviously, the emigration thing didn't work anymore, so now the Jews had to be concentrated, physically removed, separated from the whole world around them, in ghettos."

It wasn't until the Wannsee Conference in January 1942 that the decision was made to solve the "Judenfrage"—*the Jewish issue*—by exterminating all Jews. "In all haste, extermination camps had to be erected, not just concentration camps, but camps with the specific purpose of exterminating people. As soon as they could be erected, they could proceed to the final solution: No more Jews in ghettos; Jews up in the sky in smoke and ashes."

New Year's Eve 1942 was quite different from the previous year's festive costume party at the apartment of the Baroness. This time, Pips was gathered only with Ilse, her mother, and her brother in the semi-ghetto apartment to which the Rosenthal family had been relocated. They were able to scrounge a bottle somewhere and he stayed overnight. "I was with Ilse, which was the main thing."

But he and Ilse fell into terrible arguments with her mother. Mrs. Rosenthal confronted Pips after he warned her that the Germans were going to kill the Jews. "She said, like most German Jews would have said, 'You've read too many Wild West stories. This is the middle of the twentieth century. This is Germany, one of the most civilized countries in the world. Even though the Nazis are evil, to kill all of us? To murder all of us? This is insane! Yes, you will have to work hard. The Germans don't have it easy either. Millions of Germans are fighting at the front, being shot at. Why leave the Jews in comfort?" She dismissed Pips's concern for Ilse as selfishness. "You want Ilse to live the life of an outlaw."

But Pips knew what awaited Ilse as a full Jew, and Ilse had made up her mind.

"Ilse became the very breath of life to me, and I became the very breath to her. That's why we were willing to break all bonds with family, friends, legal life—sacrifice everything, not to lose each other. I was willing to leave my mother's apartment and the relative security of that. Ilse was willing to let her mother and brother go to stay with me."

But now Pips would have to protect Ilse. He would have to scavenge for food in the black market. He would have to find places to sleep.

"To buy groceries on the black market cost a lot of money. The prices had already gone very high until finally a pound of butter cost

250 marks. I had to make money. How do I make money? I worked at my job, but the salary I got was turned over to the Gestapo. I never saw a penny and it was a meaningless amount. So, now in '42, what could I do?"

He came up with an idea: canning fruit in glass jars. With his "J"-stamped ration card, Pips couldn't buy fruit. But his Aryan mother could. "I got hold of a dozen or so jars. I got hold of some peaches, strawberries, apples—mainly apples—and my mother showed me how to cook this stuff with the sugar she had. Of course, it was crazy because I couldn't produce enough—at most, a one-month supply. And there were years to go if we succeeded in staying underground. What was the point of this and where was I going to store it all?"

By now, all of Marie's subtenants had either been deported or gone into hiding. They were replaced with Aryans—one of whom was an apothecary, a rather quiet man, who had his own pharmacy. His wife, a lively blonde in her thirties, was a Nazi Party member wearing the Party emblem. Pips confided in her that he would be moving out of the apartment. "She wasn't terrible; not one of those foaming-at-the-mouth Germans. But she was a regulation Nazi who believed in Hitler and Germany and the importance of winning the war. Even so, she gave me a hand with the glass jars of fruit I made."

In Pips's circle, everyone was looking for a place to hide—no mean feat in the face of the ubiquitous German system of registrations. Early in the Third Reich, Hitler issued *Kennkarten*, identity cards that contained fingerprints, photo, age, place of birth, physical description. Germans were forbidden to leave the house without the six-page cardboard booklet. Jews' *Kennkarten* were prominently emblazoned with a "J."

Those of military age were also issued a *Wehrpass*, a comprehensive fifty-four-page, gray book kept until age sixty, documenting the holder's entire military history.

"You had to have a *Kennkarte* and a *Wehrpass* if you were of military age. You couldn't be overnight anywhere without being registered with a police precinct. You couldn't go to a hotel. You couldn't go even if there was room and you had the money. You couldn't ask anyone to take you in. You were illegal. So, finding a place to stay turned out to be most difficult. But that wasn't the only thing: you had to eat. To eat, you had to have ration cards. The cards had to be registered with the local butcher. You couldn't register with the butcher unless you also showed your ID card with your address. The butcher snipped off the coupon from the ration card and now he had a thousand customers and a thousand of these registration pieces and, on that basis, he got his allotment of meat. The same with the baker." But what if you had to leave your area for other reasons? For that, a *Reisepass* was needed to travel both within and outside Germany.

"Now I needed to get travelers' cards, which were very hard to get legally and were expensive to get illegally. I started to buy a few ration cards and managed at the end of '42 to get a fake non-Jewish *Kennkarte* for Ilse. I knew that for X amount of money, I could rustle one up."

Ilse was now in possession of a *Kennkarte*, with her photo but someone else's fingerprints. Pips had a valid *Kennkarte* but needed a *Wehrpass*. One of the Blach brothers had secured one from a German friend of his. But he was unable to get one for Pips.

"Now I was looking for what was really the most important thing: a place to stay." There was a drugstore a block from Pips's apartment. He had become a steady customer there, and a friend to both the owner and the manager. "The owner was not a very appetizing character, who turned out to be homosexual. But his manager was a very decent man. I told him what I was planning to do and asked him if Ilse and I could count on him for domicile. He said he needed to think it over, but I knew he wouldn't tell on us. He came back a few days later and said, 'I thought about it, yes, but only for a few days and only if you have no other place to go.'"

Having made what preparations he could, Pips waited to pull the trigger on his escape plan until Ilse's family received the summons to report for transit. That notice arrived right after the first of the year in 1943. The Rosenthals now had to report for deportation.

"They didn't come to pick you up. Jews weren't dragged out of their homes. It shows you how confident the authorities were in people's willingness to go along, to follow orders. Jews got postcards in the mail: Next Tuesday, at seven in the morning, you must report to such and such a place. Bring with you extra food and clothes for three days, but no more than you can carry, and you will be evacuated. The word 'evacuated' didn't sound so terrible since a lot of Aryans were evacuated, too, because of the air raids. They went, because they were told they will be shipped to places where they have to work hard. After all, the Germans have to suffer, you know, the armies have to fight on the fronts—by now the war against Russia had started—and the Germans were bombed, and you Jews are sitting here like in a spa. Most Jews accepted that. They couldn't believe what was really happening."

For the Rosenthals, zero hour had come. Ilse said good-bye to her mother and brother, knowing she would never see them again. It was a wrenching parting.

For Pips, whose relationship with his mother was fraught, it was easier. "She knew we were going underground, but she didn't know where we would go. We didn't know where we would go either. But I couldn't dare to go back home." A day or two after he vanished, the SS visited his mother to investigate Pips's absence from work. His mother informed them that he had disappeared. And it was true.

There was another problem: The air raids of Berlin by the British, which began on August 25, 1940, and continued sporadically until fall 1941, resumed in earnest in November 1943. But the lead-up to the big blitz was a bombing of Berlin by De Havilland Mosquitos on January 30 and another on Hitler's birthday, April 20.

"The air raids increased and altered life in Berlin. It finally came to the point where the British were so reliable, they would come at midnight almost every night. People scheduled themselves around the air raids. 'I'll see you half an hour after the all-clear.' Of course, nobody got much sleep, and it made hiding from the Gestapo much more difficult."

Each building had an air raid warden. It could have been an old man, a young boy, a woman, or a man unfit for military service. In addition to training residents in civil defense and guiding them to shelters, the wardens took it as part of their civic duty to snoop on their charges. "They missed nothing. Whenever they discovered someone out of the ordinary, they would go to the police and find out if they knew anything about this person." Navigating around air raid wardens narrowed even further the options for finding shelter.

It's in the face of these nearly insurmountable obstacles that Pips and Ilse went into hiding in Berlin in January 1943, right under the noses of their oppressors.

"I didn't have to go underground with Ilse. I did it for her and for me because I didn't want to lose her. I could have stayed at my job in the Holzbau. I would not have left home. I would not have been a fugitive. But since I didn't observe most of the rules, I could have been caught at any time."

Their two preoccupations were finding a place to sleep and finding something to eat.

The drugstore manager whom Pips had befriended took them in for three days in his small apartment. But he was fearful of being caught hiding Jews. The unwed mother of a friend of Pips's took them in for another couple of nights. She had no beds for them, so they slept on the floor. But even the floor was bliss because they were together at last. "We took a bath together. It was marvelous to be naked with Ilse in the warm water. It felt so good, you didn't want to get out."

Pips remembered a little village, with a couple of inns, where his mother had years before taken him for a summer holiday. He reasoned that it would be easier to get potatoes and bread there without a ration card because the peasants still had some stores.

"In my desperation we went on a train, which was really risky. We managed to get there and went to an inn. We told the owner some kind of bullshit story, about my exceeding my furlough in the army by a few days, to celebrate our honeymoon. She was romantic, so she swallowed that and didn't report us to the police. The room had a double bed with an enormous down blanket, like a mountain on top of you. It was so warm under this fluffy duvet, and Ilse and I snuggled up, even though the angel of death was hovering over us." They left after two or three days, afraid to push their luck any further.

They found shelter for another couple of nights with Ilse Friedlander, a middle-aged woman whom Pips knew through his friends, the Blachs. She was living illegally with an Aryan Communist in his apartment. They took in a Jew from time to time, but only for a limited time. Any longer, and the air raid warden would be likely to notice.

Given that Ilse and Pips were now illegal, they could not risk using their ration cards. Nor could they survive on what food the ration cards provided. "This was not exactly a cornucopia of goodies. It was strictly measured: so many grams of bread, of this and that. From the time I left home in January of '43, my nourishment wasn't up to snuff—practically no protein or vitamins or all the other foods that you need for potassium or minerals. Well, maybe a little from potato peels and vegetables. No fat, though once in a while, you got a little bit of margarine. We had hunger, a chronic hunger that lasted far, far past liberation. Hunger was a state of mind, a permanent condition. It's a constant pain in your stomach. It's constantly this dreaming about a piece of bread. And even when my mother managed to send me some food, I was just as hungry after eating it as before."

Pips scrounged what he could in the booming black market. "But I was never good at it, and I never liked doing it. Despite what they say about Jews, I was never a good businessman."

Once in a while, Ilse and Pips had access to a radio. They heard about Hitler's humiliating defeat in the Battle of Stalingrad, in which 220,000 German soldiers were encircled by the Soviets. Only 91,000 survived, and those surrendered in February 1943. "This lifted our spirits, although we realized that this defeat was not yet the beginning of the end. But it was, maybe, the end of the beginning."

And so it went for three and half months. "Always desperate. Where can we go? What can we do?"

Having run out of options, someone directed the frantic couple to a woman in a working-class neighborhood in the eastern part of Berlin. The woman took them in for a few nights, but not out of humanity; they had to pay. She tried to extort them on the basis that she was risking her life for a paltry sum. Pips would have to come up with real money if he wanted to stay longer. "I did have some money, three thousand marks, which wasn't much, but I couldn't trust this woman and we left."

They managed to get through the winter, and it was now the middle of April 1943. Ilse and Pips got on a subway and changed trains at the huge Alexanderplatz station, a major hub in Berlin. After Hitler's defeat, it would become the center of the Soviet-controlled sector of East Berlin. At the time, it was the headquarters for the Berlin Polizei, a wing of which was occupied by the Gestapo. As the fugitive couple stood on the platform waiting for their train, the unthinkable happened. Two men accosted them, flashing IDs.

In his confusion, Pips didn't know what he was looking at, but Ilse showed her fake *Kennkarte*. "We were not part of a general passport control, and I don't know how they managed to catch up with us in the subway station. But it was obvious they had been steered to us." Pips was sure the hateful woman who tried to blackmail them was the one who betrayed them.

"They walked us out of the station and into police headquarters. I was in shock and barely able to walk. It was as if I had been hit in the head by heavy artillery; as if my nervous system's circuit breakers had exploded. I couldn't even look at Ilse to gauge her reaction, to see how she felt, and to say something in support. If I did look at her, I wasn't seeing her. If she said anything, I didn't hear it. I didn't even try for a last embrace. Maybe I could have; maybe they would have let me kiss her once more. Then she was led away and all I could say was, '*Wir halten zusammen*,' we stick together. I knew I would never see her again. This was the girl who was the great love of my life and I of hers, and I collapsed mentally. It was the worst day and the greatest shock of my life."

Pips had been certain that if he and Ilse would ever fall into the clutches of the Gestapo, their lives would be shattered. Now it had happened. Ilse was gone and Pips was led to a kind of a cage. A tired and disinterested Gestapo officer posed some routine questions—name, address—which Pips answered mechanically. Pips later wrote, "I will never recover from this night, this evening, this situation. I will never recover, if I live to be a hundred."

CHAPTER 5

SURVIVING ALONE AND ON THE RUN

Pips was led down a barely illuminated corridor and shoved into a totally dark room. He had no idea where it was, but he could feel bodies underfoot. He laid down on the floor and fell instantly asleep. "Many people might say, how could you sleep? I could. I was so knocked out, I just conked out." The next morning, his jailors opened the door and Pips realized that he was in a small cell with a dozen people in it. But it wasn't a prison cell—just a regular room.

Pips was led down to the cellar. He wasn't yet capable of orienting himself. But he later divined that there were three large cells underground, and each cell held hundreds of prisoners. On the sides of the cells were four or five tiers of wooden shelves stacked to the ceiling for sleeping. There was no room for anyone to stretch out and prisoners sat cramped next to each other. The rest sat on the floor. Pips was one of the floor people. There was one toilet, which was overflowing.

As Pips's senses slowly returned, he noticed an awful smell that permeated everything. "I said to myself, these people must be farting and have body odor. A couple of days later, I realized this was garlic. I did not meet another Jew in that cell. They were Poles, White Russians, Czechs, Italians, prisoners from all over Europe. Many of these people eat garlic. Germans don't eat garlic. In fact, Germans have contempt for garlic eaters, the *Knoblauchfresser*. I had never encountered garlic in my life. I can't stand garlic, not the smell and certainly not the taste."

Once a day, the guards opened the door and shoved a large bucket containing a thin soup into the entrance. They handed out a dozen bowls but no spoons. "The prisoners lined up and their bowls were filled with some crap with a few potato peels floating in there. They had to eat that right away because the bowls had to be turned over to the next dozen. Since they had no spoons, they just drank that stuff down. At the beginning, it was very hot, so they burned their tongues. By the time they got to the tail end of the line, it was ice cold. This being my first prison, I was stupid and didn't know how to handle myself, so I usually ended up with the ice-cold stuff, and not much of it! That's what we got to eat once a day and nothing else."

But Pips was still too upset, nauseous, and numb to feel hunger. He felt as near death as possible, short of being shot or stabbed. He remained in that dank cell for ten days. "Every morning, they opened the door and read out a list of Polish names, Russian names. These people were taken out and you never knew what happened to them. At least once a day, we heard salvos in the courtyard above us. We figured that some of these guys were being shot. Even in the most gruesome horror films, you would not see anything like this, and this was real. I don't think I thought much of Ilse at that time, I was too crushed, too dazed, and I guess I had a strong survival instinct. My nervous system told me what I could and couldn't afford to think about."

After ten days, Pips's name was called. While he was relieved to get out of his hellhole, he was afraid that he was about to be shot. Instead, he was taken in handcuffs to another Gestapo office a few blocks away. Unlike the police headquarters he had just left, this office dealt mostly with Jews.

He arrived in a waiting room and much to his surprise, his mother was sitting there. "I have no idea how she found out that I would be there at that time and place. But she was there, and she brought me some underwear. I was allowed five minutes with her. Then they threw her out."

Pips was taken into an office. A man in civilian clothes sat behind the desk with a secretary seated beside him. "He was obviously a low-grade functionary, but at that moment I didn't analyze it. He was the Gestapo, the deadly enemy, the rattlesnake that would devour me or kill me. I stood there, and he bellowed a few questions at me. Then he said, 'You aren't wearing a Jew star.' He ordered the secretary to get one for me, along with a needle and thread. He threw it on the floor and said, 'Sew that onto your jacket.' I sat down on the floor and started sewing, which was not exactly my cup of tea. While I was doing this, I was vaguely aware that he was kicking me, but I didn't feel the pain. Later, I couldn't sit."

Pips finally managed to sew the Jew star on his jacket and could no longer avoid wearing it. Then the interrogation began in earnest. The officer got straight to the point: "What's the real name of the girl we arrested?"

Thoroughly shaken, Pips blurted out "Ilse Rosenthal."

"They asked me nothing else about her, only her name. I was totally unprepared for that. Ever since that moment, I've asked myself, 'Why did I say that? How could I have done this? Did I betray her?' I automatically assumed that the minute they get hold of us we are finished. That was ingrained. Ten days had passed since our arrest. If they wanted to know something about her that they didn't already know, they wouldn't have kept her for ten days."

Pips later learned that, during that ten-day period, Ilse had been transferred to Grosse Hamburger Strasse, a smaller Gestapo prison for Jews being shipped to Auschwitz. "With all reason, I tell myself that I did not betray her. There was no chance in the world that if she hadn't gotten out by then, that she would have gotten out later had I not revealed her name. I was not afraid of being beaten and kicked. I had simply taken for granted that she was gone, finished. So, when they asked me her name, it couldn't have made any difference. I still feel that I should not have done it, and I still feel guilty about it. Otherwise, they asked me only about myself."

When Pips had first arrived in the dungeon, he realized that his fellow prisoners were infested with lice. Soon after his interrogation, there was an outbreak of typhus and his cell was locked down in quarantine. The guards didn't dare open the door and for the first day or two the inmates received no food at all. Even though several prisoners died, no one was taken out. "Then they realized they're going to have a couple of hundred bodies on their hands. So, they unlocked the door, but this time it was prisoners who opened it. The SS wouldn't expose itself to this kind of problem. They brought soup again and asked if anybody was dead. They dragged the bodies out by their feet." The quarantine went on for about ten days. Still in a fog and frantically trying to pick off lice, Pips had no idea of the day of the week and whether it was day or night. At the end of the quarantine, an SS officer stood at the door with a list of names and called Pips along with fifty others. By now, he had been in the Polizeipräsidium dungeon for a full month.

The cohort was taken to a courtyard, where there stood an open truck and a trailer with a canvas over it. "I realized we were being taken somewhere and I had to get out of my fog to deal with what was happening. As it turned out, we were going to be taken to a labor camp."

It was a beautiful sunny day in early May. The prisoners were deloused in very hot showers and their clothes were fumigated. "Now we were supposedly free of lice and clean as a whistle." Because they were being released from the Polizeipräsidium, the prisoners were given back their belongings. Pips was handed the three thousand marks that were taken from him when he was arrested, along with a small batch of *Reisekarten*, traveler's ration cards.

"Germans are bureaucrats *par excellence*. They returned our belongings because their papers had to be in order. Of course, as soon as we arrived in the labor camp, we would have been relieved of this burden."

Pips was loaded onto the truck with the other prisoners. "The treatment in labor camps was at least as bad as in the worst concentration camps because they had only limited time to deal with you and they wanted to make sure they could maximize your humiliation. I knew that while I was in their hands, my life wasn't worth a plugged nickel. I had to try to escape, so I made sure that I got into the trailer rather than the truck."

The truck started moving. Pips couldn't see anything because of the canvas cover. But after a while, he could tell that they had left the local streets and were rolling at about thirty-five miles per hour down a major thoroughfare. He had no idea where the truck would end up but he knew it wouldn't be anywhere good. At the very end of the trailer, the canvas was attached by snaps and Pips noticed that one of the snaps was open. An SS man with a drawn revolver sat there "just in case somebody gets funny ideas." Pips stood next to a middle-aged Jew. "I had that little package of underwear that my mother had given me, and I pushed it into his hand, telling him I didn't need it. I wormed my way to the back of the trailer and stood there for a minute or two. I took a deep breath and tore open the place where the button was missing and jumped out head-first. I did a somersault on the street and didn't hurt myself at all!"

A woman on the street shrieked, thinking that Pips had been run over by the truck. "She didn't know what was in the truck and she didn't see me hop out. I got myself up and ran in the opposite direction." Pips heard shots behind him, but the truck was still moving. Once the driver heard the shots, he stopped the truck. But, by then, the truck was already a quarter of a mile away and Pips was long gone.

"I found out after the war that this gentleman from the Gestapo, who was my judge and jury, had recommended the lightest labor camp sentence, which was fifty-six days. My main crime was that I didn't wear the star, hadn't gone to work, and had been caught with a Jewess underground. So, the sentence was pretty mild. But you didn't know what your sentence was. You didn't know whether you were in there for eight weeks or forever. They made you work breaking rocks for twelve to fifteen hours a day and you got watery soup, but I probably would have survived it. I was young, reasonably healthy, and maybe it was foolish for me to have jumped off the truck because I made my situation much worse. Now I was an escapee. But I likely saved my life by jumping. If I had gotten typhus in the camp, I would have died, no question about it."

Had Pips served his sentence and survived, he would have been legal again. Instead, Pips chose to run. But where could he go?

The only place that came to mind was the home of Ilse Friedlander, a half-Jew, who lived with Heckers, a full German Communist. He and Ilse had spent a couple of nights with them before their arrest and Pips hoped they would take him in again. And they did—but only after getting rid of his clothes and washing him in a hot bath with delousing soap. Despite these precautions, typhus finally caught up with Pips, and within a week, their apartment was infested with lice.

Pips's fever shot to 105 degrees. Delirious and unconscious most of the time, he alternated between burning up and freezing. Having been put in one of his benefactor's beds, the soaked linen had to be changed every couple of hours. Of course, there was no medication with which to treat his illness. Friedlander and Heckers, convinced that Pips was going to die, deliberated on how to dispose of the body of this Jew on the run, whom they were harboring. They decided on putting him in a sack and loading him on a pushcart. Then, in a quiet moment, in the middle of the night, they would dump Pips's corpse in the river.

But Pips fooled them and slowly recovered. He emerged from his illness with a ravenous hunger. "Food wasn't exactly plentiful. However, I had been given all my belongings back before I went on the transport, so I had a couple of sheets of traveler's ration cards, which I gave to my hosts so they could buy some food for themselves, as well as for me. They were going to share what they had with me, so I certainly couldn't hold back with my ration cards."

Friedlander and Heckers knew of a Jew whom they had sheltered for a time while he was underground. He was reputed to have contacts in the Grosse Hamburger Strasse prison. "By now, general deportations were over but newly arrested Jews were sent there. Whenever they had a hundred people together for a transport—which was at first every week, and later on every two weeks, then three weeks—they shipped them off to Auschwitz. I knew with reasonable assurance that Ilse was at Grosse Hamburger Strasse. She might have already gone on a transport, but this guy—I only met him once—claimed he might be able to get her out from there if he had enough money."

Pips turned over the three thousand marks that had been returned to him when he was released and pleaded, "Do what you can. That's every penny I have."

"Ilse meant more to me than anything. If I could get her out of their clutches, I wouldn't hold back a single mark for myself." Of course, the money was gone, and Pips never saw the man again. He never learned whether the man had tried and failed or whether he was just a con man. "I knew from the beginning that this was a one in a thousand shot. The possibility that a few thousand marks would buy her freedom was just too far-fetched, but I had to try it."

In fact, Ilse had been deported to Auschwitz, where she perished a year and a half later.

After three weeks, Friedlander and Hecker felt it was no longer safe for Pips to stay with them. With no place to go, Pips toyed with the idea of dressing as a nun, because nuns weren't bothered in the streets. "First of all, where was I to get a nun's outfit? I would have to shave to make sure that I didn't have a beard. I would have to shave my legs and wear stockings. I had to get the right pair of shoes and I still would have to find a place to stay. So, I discarded the idea."

Pips reasoned you can live without food for days, but you can't go without sleep. "What came to my mind was the only relative I had besides my mother: Carl Muller, one of three first cousins from my mother's sister. Two of them were Nazis: Ernst and Marichen." Marichen had been the Philipsohn's housekeeper. Ernst, now of military age, was mentally defective. Carl Muller, the third of her children, was the only one who seemed normal. He was a clerk in the post office and was married to an ordinary woman. They lived a conventional life in a working-class neighborhood in Berlin. "On the second day of Christmas, we would go to them for another round of Christmas celebrations. We had a nice relationship with them, but it had fizzled out long before. I became so involved with my own problems that I didn't even pay much attention to my own father, let alone a cousin. I hadn't seen or talked to these people for years. But now, in my desperation, I figured maybe I can get some help there."

Pips rang the bell and Carl's wife, Lucy, opened the door. When she saw Pips, her eyes grew wide with terror. "She knew right away that I was poison. I was on the lam and touching me could kill them." When he asked her for help, he could see that she was shaking. She closed the door and didn't invite Pips in. Ten minutes passed before Lucy opened the door again. She pressed a large paper bag filled with food into his arms and said, 'I'm sorry, but that's all

I can do for you." Pips suspected that Carl was in the house but he didn't show himself.

"I wasn't terribly shocked by this. I had never shown any interest in them; they had never shown any interest in me. So, I didn't expect anything. Things became tough for my father, so he couldn't help them anymore, and we didn't go there for a second Christmas. But Carl was still my first cousin, and he still owed me something because my father had helped him. I would have hoped that they would say 'Come in. Plop yourself down on the floor and we'll give you a pillow and tomorrow we'll figure out what can be done.' That would have been the minimum that they should have done, but their fear of the police, of the Gestapo, was so great, that they wouldn't touch me with a ten-foot pole."

Contrasting his experience with Hecker with his first cousin, Pips was learning that Communists were among the few people who were willing to help Jews because they, too, were outlaws in Hitler's Germany—even when they were full Aryans.

With nothing but a bag of food, Pips racked his brains about where to go next. He remembered an acquaintance from his youth, Helga Matushek. He knew her through Hans Blach, who had been her tutor while she was in school. Helga was now in her early twenties and living with her parents in a fine neighborhood not far from the home that Pips had abandoned to go into hiding. Her family had extensive contacts in the diplomatic corps, giving them entry to the upper echelons of German society, despite not being Nazis. Pips's relationship with Helga was casual, at best. "She was by all measures the most beautiful young woman I've ever seen in my life. Ilse was beautiful, but this woman was an absolutely gorgeous blond beauty. Yet, she was not one of those preening girls—'Look how beautiful I am.' She was a really good person."

When Pips showed up at her door, Helga radiated compassion. She couldn't take him in because her parents wouldn't stand for it.

But she told him to come back in two days and hoped that, by then, she could arrange something for him. When Pips returned, she introduced him to a smallish man of early middle age, who had a passing resemblance to Goebbels. He wore the round emblem of the Nazi party on his lapel. The minute Pips saw it, he balked. But Helga assured him that the man would help him.

Her friend didn't express any great sympathy for Pips and was very matter-of-fact in telling him that he had a miniature dacha, where Pips could hide. The dacha was a one-room hut similar to those that many Berliners used in the summer, where they could garden and grow vegetables. This hut was in a remote part of the city, and his host took him there by streetcar. He instructed Pips to be discreet, water his plants, and keep the house clean. Food was not included. But he said he would stop by in a few days to see how his fugitive guest was doing. "I couldn't believe it. What luck! And a Nazi yet! Only later did it dawn on me what his motive was. It was not that he loved Jews or felt sorry for me. He was head over heels in love with Helga and he would do anything to get to her. So, he couldn't say no to her when she asked him to do this."

Pips spent several weeks in the Nazi's cottage. Then came the day when his host told him that people were beginning to ask who was in his house. It was time to leave, but he had another hiding place for Pips. He directed Pips to a woman who rented out a room in a lower middle-class section of East Berlin. The Nazi had lived there for a little while when he was in school. He told Pips, "We'll have to concoct some kind of cock-and-bull story and I will introduce you to her. She's not terribly bright and I hope she'll take you in." No Nazi had ever helped him that much.

"The story was that my name was Peter Martens, an engineer who was working on a hush-hush military project at Spandau, quite a distance away. And because this was secret work, they had barracks for the engineers and others who worked on that project. It wasn't the atom bomb—it was something I couldn't talk about. I had to sleep in the barracks with many other guys and I hated that. I loved privacy, so I wanted to get away—at least a few days a week—and sleep somewhere else. My friend, so-and-so, the Nazi, was kind enough to suggest her place and of course his recommendation meant that I was kosher. But I couldn't be registered with the police because I wasn't supposed to do this. She swallowed the story, hook, line, and sinker."

Pips was given a perfectly adequate little room at a rent that was next to nothing. He needed to go into black market bartering to get food, but he stayed comfortably ensconced there. "She was in her forties and very nice. She liked me from the first day. After all, I was a nice-looking fellow: blond, blue-eyed, Aryan type, twenty-one years old, and I didn't bother her." The landlady even went so far as to knock on Pips's door in the morning and say, "Herr Martens, I just made breakfast. Would you like to share it with me?" At first, Pips had trouble reacting to the name Martens. "But then I said, listen you've got to get that straight, and I had breakfast with her—and getting breakfast really helped a lot." His host worked in a munitions factory and was gone all day. She didn't know whether Pips was in or out. He went out only to meet someone for black market exchanges and then got off the street as fast as he could.

Air raids were in full swing. "The British came every night and once or twice there was an air raid just in our neighborhood. By that time the British had a good bomber force so we weren't talking about just a handful of bombers, but hundreds of bombers, always led by a scout. The scout would release Christmas Trees, glowing green colored flares that dropped from the plane on parachutes and fanned out, looking just like a Christmas tree. That was the area where they would drop their bombs. A couple of times it was very close to us. The anti-aircraft batteries were shooting up a storm and the searchlights were going crazy. I watched these air raids and for me every air raid was good: let the Germans get it—another small step toward their demise!"

One evening the landlady came home from work and told Pips that she had managed to score some flour, butter, eggs, and sugar. She also got hold of some real coffee, at a time when even Germans were drinking ersatz coffee. She used her bounty to bake a cake and invited Pips to share it in her living room. "I ate and drank, and we talked, mostly about the war because that was the only thing we had in common. And she said, yes, we are suffering some reverses. These air raids are smashing the cities and, of course, Stalingrad was terrible. Even Goebbels couldn't hide that from the public. She said, these things were bad signs that worried her greatly, but thank goodness we have our Führer. He will know what to do, and there's no question that he will win the war and avenge all that. She kept going on and on and I kept nodding sympathetically and she said, 'You know, we must win the war. If we don't win the war, the Jews will get us. And you are such an innocent young man, you don't know this, but the Jews are not like normal human beings. They are devils. They will rape the women and slit our throats.' She had an inventory of gruesome stuff—the Jews, oh my God! 'So we must win the war. We must destroy all the Jews because they will wreak revenge on us in the most horrible way.' This was the funniest bit I've ever seen. She's telling this to a Jew, an illegal Jew, a Jew on the lam. I would have loved to be able to get up and say, 'Well, you're looking at one,' and she would have fainted dead away. On the other hand, it gave me shivers down my spine. There are people who actually believe that the Jews are literally devils who want to get their claws into us. I didn't know what the fuck to say, so I said, 'Oh, gee, I didn't realize that' and ate another piece of cake and drank another cup of coffee. The grotesque quality of it all! And this woman said, 'Mr. Martens, have another piece of cake,' while she's telling me the Jews are devils. It was beyond belief!"

A week later, she gave Pips bad news: the air raid warden had snooped around and was inquiring about the person going in and out of her apartment. "She said, 'I hate to lose you because I like you so much.' But she knew I wasn't supposed to be there without being registered, so she gave me a day's notice and I was again without a home."

During his various excursions in search of food and cigarettes in the black market, Pips had developed a loose business relationship with the madam of a local brothel that was housed in her ten-room apartment. "Now this madam must have weighed four hundred pounds. She was lying in an enormous bed, and she was really obese. Her arms were as wide as my chest. Every time I came to sell her something, it disappeared under her featherbed—even chocolate, which must have melted. I heard she had a whole grocery store in her bed, which didn't make much difference. She was so big already that another couple of kilos of this or that didn't make any difference."

After losing his latest hideout, he went to the madam with a different proposition. He needed a new place to stay. She knew he was an illegal Jew but, like Communists, he felt that he could count on prostitutes for help because they, too, lived on the edge of legality.

Pips went to her door and the madam came into the vestibule. After Pips explained that he had nowhere to go, she asked him to wait a bit.

"I stepped into the vestibule and after a few minutes she called me back in. One of her girls was there and she introduced me to her. She had a couch in her room, and she agreed I could sleep there whenever she didn't have a john. I was, of course, very grateful. For a number of nights, I slept on the couch—sometimes even during the day, when she had no clients. She slept in her bed, and I never touched her. I wasn't interested in fucking a whore or anybody. We got along and she was very nice to let me be there. They even gave me some food. When the bell rang, I knew there was a customer coming up, and I had to get the hell out of there in a hurry. I walked around the street or stayed in the vestibule for an hour or so until she was free and I could go back. I've been all over the place, to the craziest joints; though that was the only time in my life I visited a whorehouse, not even as a customer."

Following his sojourn at the brothel, Pips was again homeless. He ran into an old girlfriend, Uschi Redlich. They recognized each other instantly. But now, they were both illegal and homeless. A family on vacation had taken Uschi in. Taking pity on him, she let Pips sleep with her in her room. But Uschi threw him out the next morning. Once again, he had nowhere to go.

One night in 1944, in the dead of winter, Pips was walking near the zoo. By now, that area and the nearby Kaiser Wilhelm Church had been destroyed in unrelenting bombing raids. A lurking Gestapo agent seized Pips by his overcoat. Pips managed to wriggle away, leaving the officer holding a coat, but not his prey. A cyclist chased Pips as he ran, but Pips managed to dive into the basement of a bombed-out building. There, he slept on the floor, with rats scurrying over his body. Starved and shivering, coatless, in the freezing cold, he no longer cared.

"My life in a sense ended here. My old life which had included my parents, my friends, my home, and all the things that meant everything to me. Now came an interregnum for a couple of years during which only my strong instinct for self-preservation carried me along. A deeper liberation began, painful in itself. I've really led two lives."

CHAPTER 6

IN THE HANDS OF THE GESTAPO

Pips scurried to get to the apartment of one of his black-market contacts, where he had an appointment to pick up some potatoes. "It was never a big amount. A pound of this or a pound of that." A few minutes after Pips sat down, two Gestapo agents appeared. Perhaps the trader had been threatened with arrest for his black-market activities and he offered to trade his liberty for a Jew. In any case, Pips was dragged away. This time, he was taken not to the Polizeipräsidium, but to Grosse Hamburger Strasse, located in the center of Berlin. Originally a Jewish old-age home, it was repurposed in 1941 to serve as the main *Sammellager*—collection point—for deportations to concentration camps and ghettos. The prison was destroyed in 1943 and its inmates were sent to another prison.

"It wasn't the end of the line. Jews who were arrested because they were living illegally or weren't deportation cases but had committed certain crimes—like me—were taken there. Whenever they had a hundred or so together, a transport was organized. Not everybody was taken to Auschwitz, though. Some people were taken to Lichterfelder, a suburb of Berlin, which had a large SS barracks and was one of their favorite execution sites. If you were taken to Lichterfelder, you were a 'special case,' and you knew you would be dead an hour later. You didn't know why Lichterfelder rather than Auschwitz, and even if they took you to Auschwitz, the chances were that you would be dead anyway."

Pips was again taken to a cellar. It was a large one with a long hallway flanked by cells, originally built as storage rooms. There were steps at the end of the corridor leading down to a windowless, underground bunker—the infamous *Bunker Eins*, Bunker One, for "special cases." But Pips didn't end up there. For now, he was taken to a candle-lit communal bunker.

"During the night, we were locked up, but during the day, it was fairly loose. We could visit each other in the different bunkers—Bunker One, Bunker Two, Bunker Three, Bunker Four. This wasn't a camp that was supposed to run us down or kill us. It was just a transit point."

In the cellar where they were held, the windows were bricked up, except for one brick, at sidewalk level, which was left open for air. Pips gazed out through the hole from time to time. There was a bakery across the street, where he observed housewives going in and out, doing their shopping. "Here I was in prison, with a fate that didn't look too good, because my case had become much more serious since my escape. And just a few steps away, separated only by this wall, were people—people just like myself, of whom I was once a part—walking, living their lives. I was no longer part of that society."

Pips was at the same place—Grosse Hamburger Strasse—where they had taken Ilse. After a few days there, he spoke to a fellow Jew, who had been in the prison for several months as a kind of trusty to help maintain order. Pips sidled up to him and asked whether he remembered an Ilse Rosenthal, who had come through in the spring and was shipped out. He said he had. He took note of her because she had almost immediately started an affair with a man, whom he claimed Pips knew. When the man was deported to Auschwitz on a prior transport, he recalled that Ilse tore her hair and collapsed into frenzied weeping.

Pips was incredulous. He'd never heard of this alleged prison lover, whom he supposedly knew. "Later, when I began to think about this, I said to myself, there are several possibilities: This guy could be honestly mistaken. The name Rosenthal is pretty common among Jews. He may have mixed Ilse up with someone else. After all, this was months ago, and new people came in and went out every day. Or, because some of the people who've been imprisoned for a while become cruel, he was a sadistic son of a bitch who made this up. Or a third possibility: he was telling the truth. But I can't believe that. It doesn't make sense. I was everything to her. For two years we were totally involved with each other and in three days she'd become involved with another man? On the other hand, I said to myself, what if?"

Ilsa had a middle-aged aunt, her mother's staunch ally in trying to separate the young lovers. The aunt worked in the records office of Grosse Hamburger Strasse, where Ilse had been sent. Pips speculated that the aunt had somehow found out about his betrayal of Ilse during the interrogation and wanted to take revenge. "Maybe she told Ilse, 'You see what a bastard he was?' But even if she did manage to poison Ilse's mind, I can't imagine Ilse would turn to another guy. It hurt me terribly."

The weeks went by. Pips befriended a Jew who was in a mixed marriage and, like him, not a deportation case—for now. "He had been arrested and didn't know whether he would be on the next transport. After my various escape attempts, neither did I. We lived from moment to moment." But the friendship came with a bonanza: potatoes! Pips's new pal had been given the job of cleaning up bunkers used to store potatoes. The two never failed to steal a few and find a place to roast them.

The Kommandant of the prison was Hauptscharführer Walter Dobberke. Although a low-level employee, Hauptscharführer was the highest enlisted rank in the SS. A former police officer, Dobberke was tall and stocky, with a short military haircut and pinched face. He joined the Gestapo in 1937 and was stationed at the very Alexanderplatz police station where Pips had first been detained. Initially working in the central card index, he was also charged with processing homosexuals. By 1939, he was moved to the "Confiscation of Assets Department," which was his entry point to the "Jewish Department." His career path there would lead him to be dubbed the "face of Berlin deportations."

In 1941, Dobberke was posted to the Levetzowstrasse collection camp, which had been set up in the Levetzow synagogue. With 2,100 seats, the immense colonnaded structure was one of the largest houses of worship in Berlin. In adapting the sanctuary to its new purpose, the seats were removed and straw was strewn on the floor. Collections at Levetzowstrasse continued, at the rate of up to one thousnd per night, until 1943. Dobberke was reassigned in 1942 and put in charge of Grosse Hamburger Strasse—a big step up in his career.

That's where he and Pips crossed paths, and where Dobberke would become a central character in Pips's story.

As Pips would learn, Dobberke could be at times decent, and at others very violent and almost certainly corrupt. "I'm sure that he helped himself to some of the goodies that came in with the detainees—watches or gold, some clothes maybe. He was doing fine."

A loyal Nazi, Dobberke carried out the instructions of his superiors efficiently and without question, overseeing the deportation of Berlin's Jews from start to end. He was present at the train station as each transport departed for the East. Yet, there was no sign that he exceeded his orders or that he was overtly antisemitic. "Dobberke didn't hate Jews, he didn't care, really. Of course, ten years of the Hitler regime had already imbued him, as much as everybody else, with the knowledge that Jews are vermin, but he wasn't particularly excited about it."

By 1943, the deportation of Berlin's Jews was largely complete and much of the Jewish population had been murdered. But with thousands of Jews in hiding, it was now Dobberke's job to track them down. Using the service of "Jew catchers," fugitives like Pips were on his radar. When they were caught, Dobberke personally conducted many of the interrogations and beat the prisoners to extract the whereabouts of other underground Jews. But Dobberke was unpredictable and wielded his power in such a way that select individuals might be spared deportation or have their deportations deferred. Pips was one of them.

"There was one thing the Gestapo really cared about, particularly the Kommandant, and that was his head count. He was very anxious that no illegal Jews should escape and very anxious that any Jew who stepped off the beaten track should be arrested, even if he was not a deportation case. Jews for the most part were middle-class people; they didn't excel as escape artists. It was a relatively easy chore to keep the bunch together. I was the exception."

Although his family lived only blocks away, Dobberke sometimes spent nights at Grosse Hamburger Strasse, where he was seen playing cards with detainees, and getting drunk on liquor served to him by inmates. On some nights, he dallied with his mistress, Frau Heim, an Aryan woman who worked in the records department in the Gestapo office. Among the files in that office was Pips's documentation.

Dobberke was thirty-six years old when he took the helm at Grosse Hamburger Strasse. At that age, he could easily have found himself on the Russian front. "This job was the softest possible thing that could happen to him. He was a big shot. He had his own little kingdom, and he was left pretty much alone by his superiors—as long as he could show every month how many Jews were arrested and how many Jews deported. At the same time, he couldn't deport all of them or there would be nothing left to do."

One of Pips's fellow detainees was indifferent to the threat of deportation. Rehfeld, a full Jew, was—unlike the Jews Pips knew—poor and uneducated. A strong bull of a man, he went underground when the deportations started. One of his friends, a superintendent of an apartment building, allowed him to sleep in the coal cellar, "which didn't do much for his cleanliness." When he was arrested and brought to Grosse Hamburger Strasse, the other inmates warned him that he would be on the next transport to Auschwitz. He shrugged his shoulders and said, "I don't give a damn. They make me work in Auschwitz, I'll work in Auschwitz." The bystanders replied, "You won't be working. They'll kill you." "If they kill me, they kill me." And he meant it.

Rehfeld was Mr. Fix-It. He could fix anything. "His intelligence was not through the roof, but he could do anything with his hands. Very soon, he made himself useful and came to the attention of the higher echelon. Any time something needed to be fixed, and something always did—whether a water pipe or an electrical wire or a clock—they called Rehfeld. He was kept busy from morning till night. The Kommandant didn't have to get a German to do all these things; he had his own built-in maintenance crew. Rehfeld was a godsend, and they wouldn't send him to Auschwitz for all the tea in China."

During his first stay at Grosse Hamburger Strasse, Pips and another prisoner, Erich Hopp, were sent to the *Juden Dezernat*—Jewish Affairs Department—on Kurfürstenstrasse to clear bomb damage and rebuild a bunker. (Like Pips, Hopp had once found shelter in a brothel.) This massive complex had been the seat of the Jewish Brotherhood before being appropriated by the Gestapo in 1939 to serve as Adolf Eichmann's Central Office for Jewish Emigration. At least three of the apartments had been designated as forced homes for Jews. By June 1942, all those residents had been deported and very few survived.

Now Pips was truly in the belly of the beast and it became the site of his second escape. "It was very easy. Hopp and I just walked away."

The two fugitives spent the first night after their escape with a friend of Hopp's wife. She allowed Hopp to remain there because of their relationship, but Pips was sent away the next morning. That left Pips scrambling for his next hideaway.

The year wound to a close. Max Koppel, a relative of the Blach brothers, was also living in Berlin illegally but had important Aryan contacts and was active on a large scale in the black market. He had occasionally helped Pips with contacts, cash, and ration cards. Now he directed Pips to a place where he could spend a few nights. One of those nights was December 31, 1943. It was the worst New Year's Eve of Pips's life, spent alone, sleeping on a mattress on the second floor of a bombed out building.

Early in 1944, Pips turned to Karl Streckfuss for help, one of his black-market contacts, whose wife had been a friend of his mother's.

Streckfuss was a German deserter who shared a name with a prolific nineteenth-century German writer. *This* Streckfuss had served in the French Foreign Legion and was fluent in that language. He was drafted into the German army in 1939 and, after Germany occupied France, assigned to work in a POW camp. This proved to be a boon because it enabled him to steal Red Cross packages intended for the French POWs. When he was found out, he vanished before he could be court-martialed.

Streckfuss was hiding in a *Gartenlaube*—a hut with a vegetable garden—that was owned by his family. He had taken in a French deserter. Streckfuss had two daughters, and once a week the eldest brought fresh towels, linen, and food to the *Laube* from his wife's apartment. (His wife would later be killed during the Battle for Berlin.) Pips holed up with Streckfuss for a week or two. During that time, Streckfuss made no attempt to hide his nightly forays with an accomplice to rob unsuspecting housewives of their jewelry, ration cards, cash, and anything else that had some value. That was how they made their living. Streckfuss invited Pips to join them in their forays, but he refused. Street crime was not his style. Streckfuss, who was bringing in all the food and cash that helped sustain Pips, told him he had to leave if he refused to contribute by participating as his partner in crime.

Streckfuss was eventually caught and deported to a harsh moorland labor camp, where political opponents of the Third Reich were imprisoned. It's unclear why army deserters would have been sent to a labor camp for political prisoners, if it as even true. "Many of them died in the swamp. They even invented a song there, 'Moorsoldaten' ('Peat Bog Soldiers'), which became a sort of anthem of the deserters who had not been shot right off the bat." The dirge-like song, which moved prisoners and guards alike to tears, spread to concentration camps, POW camps, and even to the United States, where Pete Seeger and Theodor Bikel recorded it in English.

While in the *Laube,* Pips had written a letter pleading with Hopp's wife's friend to take him in. When he went out to mail the letter, he ran into a man and woman who looked familiar, but he couldn't quite place them. After extending his hand to say hello, they tried to put handcuffs on him. Now he realized who they were: Stella Goldschlag, with whom he had gone to school, was now the notorious "blonde poison," a Jewish collaborator who had been recruited by Dobberke to apprehend underground Jews. Her companion was Rolf Isaaksohn, Stella's second husband and fellow collaborator. Pips sprinted away, chased by the couple. Always a good runner, he was able to outdistance them. He tried to evade them by running alongside a funeral procession to Goldschlag and Isaaksohn's shouts of "Stop him! A Jew! Stop him!" The mourners dropped their flowers and piled on top of him. The collaborators handcuffed Pips, and took him back to Grosse Hamburger Strasse prison, where he was beaten. The damning letter was found when they emptied his pockets. Pips averred that it was a letter to a friend of his mother's. But Kommandant Dobberke wasn't buying it. He whacked Pips with his bare hand and broke his eardrum. "Even though he had been very mad at me, and he gave me a beating, he didn't give me a sadistic beating. He didn't beat me just because he could. He beat me because I marred his record. Everyone who escaped would have to be in his report, and that was an embarrassment."

The address on the letter led to Hopp's arrest a few hours later, when he was found at the home of his host.

Hopp never held his capture against Pips. But this escapade confirmed Pips's reputation as an escape artist who needed to be closely watched. Pips's recent escapades made him a legitimate case for deportation to Auschwitz. Dobberke summoned him and warned: "I know you can escape, and you know that we can always catch you. I promise you, if you do it again, we will find you, and I will not let you live another twenty-four hours."

Pips and Hopp were remanded to Bunker One, a grim place that was the last stop for prisoners before they were taken for execution. Hopp, who took his arrest in stride, was less depressed and fearful than Pips. But Pips, having attempted three escapes and broken the code, was sure he was headed to Lichterfelde.

During their two-week stay, he decided he would rather die in this dark bunker deep underground than to be beaten, lined up against a wall, and machine-gunned down. Discovering a drainage pipe under the ceiling and realizing that he was doomed anyway, he tried to hang himself. "I have a very highly developed instinct for self-preservation and suicide is way down on my list. I tried suicide with, at best, half a heart, so needless to say, I failed." He was not alone in his thinking. Between 1942 and 1943, seven thousand Berlin Jews were said to have committed suicide.

During his second sojourn at Grosse Hamburger Strasse, Pips became acquainted with more of his fellow prisoners, especially those who didn't ship out right away. Charlotte "Lotte" Paech, a nurse in her early thirties, became his only trusted prison friend. She was married and had a four-year-old daughter, who remained hidden throughout the war. She never spoke about her husband or what happened to him, but Pips knew he had been killed.

Lotte and her spouse were part of the Herbert Baum group, a small anti-fascist Communist organization, mostly made up of young Jews, half of whom were women. Many had been part of the Jewish youth Bunds that were disbanded by the Nazis in the 1930s. The Baum group had done leafletting and committed small acts of sabotage for at least ten years. But they were best known for their attempt, on May 18, 1942, to blow up the anti-communist "Soviet Paradise" exhibition at the Lustgarten. This formal garden and parade ground, in front of the Altes Museum in Central Berlin, was a principal site for Nazi mass rallies.

As Communists—an identity often more important to them than being Jews—they were infuriated by the anti-communist tone of the exhibition and determined to destroy it. Although only one of several explosive devices detonated properly, the symbolic importance of penetrating this anti-Soviet exhibition in the heart of the Nazi machine was enormous. The Baum group hoped it would instill a spirit of resistance among workers. In the end, very little damage was done and the exhibit opened again the next day. But the Nazi leadership felt threatened by the Baum group's form of resistance because it showed that Jews could be defiant.

Most of the group, including Paech, were arrested the next day and almost all were executed soon after. But it didn't end there. In retaliation, the Nazi high command decreed "Death to the Jews." Within a few days, 258 Jewish suspects were arrested and taken to the Alexanderplatz police station, then transferred to Gross Lichterfelde to be shot. Another five hundred were killed in Sachsenhausen and Auschwitz. Paech, nicknamed "grandma" because she was one of the oldest of the group, was spared execution and ended up in the same prison as Pips.

"She was interrogated many times. They tried to squeeze whatever information they could out of her about the Communist underground. I'm sure she couldn't give them much because she wasn't a big shot in that connection. But she was involved. They kept her in the Grosse Hamburger Strasse—probably because they thought they could get something out of her. She was one of the loveliest people I've ever met in my life—mild-mannered, soft-spoken, very brave, and she always kept her head high. She exuded empathy and friendship. She would hold my hand when I felt like crying. We became platonic friends and did a few things that required guts—including engineering an escape during a fake air raid."

But Pips did have a weak moment. Lotte had been privileged with a commandeered hospital bed. One summer evening, they sat on her bed, touching hands and talking like friends. "Then I got horny and tried to kiss her on the mouth. I told her I just wanted to lie next to her. She realized that I was on the make, and very gently and sweetly let me down. She said it in such a way that I realized my charms, such as they were, wouldn't work. I wasn't physically repulsive. I was skin and bones, but so was everybody else. I assumed that she, like everybody, had a need for warmth, for closeness, to have another naked body next to her. But she made it clear that she loved me only as a friend."

Pips knew to trust no one in prison. But Lotte was the exception. He trusted her completely, and she trusted him as much. He never asked about, nor was he interested in, her communist activities. "And why should I be? I was apolitical. The lives of all my friends were issues, the lives of all the Jews were issues, but what did that have to do with Communists or fascists? Nothing. The big enemy was the Gestapo, the SS."

Nevertheless, he was deeply moved, when he heard the strains of a Communist song floating over the partition one day. It was Lotte's voice, and the melody was what touched him, not the ideology behind it. "Communism never thrilled me."

But escape surely did. "Escaping was my resistance, as long as there was any hope of not being caught. But now, there was no hope."

Unrelenting bombing raids shook Berlin in late 1943 into 1944. The raids that took place on November 22 and 23, 1943, killed 3,000 Berliners and left 275,000 homeless. Among these was Marie Philipsohn, whose apartment had been destroyed in a carpet bombing that leveled an area stretching from Bayerischer Platz to Kurfürstendamm to Kaiser Wilhelm Church.

"Early in the morning I was called upstairs into the visitors' room. There was my mother with a blanket over her head. I could see that her hair and eyebrows were singed. She was bombed out, and our whole section was flattened. The only reason she survived was that, years before, they had broken through from their cellar to the one in the next building, with just a flimsy division between them. If your house fell down on top of you, you could still go to the next house. If you were lucky, the next house hadn't fallen down yet. So, that's what she did. Some were killed and the whole area was totally in flames. Even when she finally got to the street, she had to run through flames."

Marie was now homeless, too. But she had friends in Gera, a small town in Thuringia in east-central Germany. "Knowing that sooner or later her number would be up in Berlin, she had been smart enough to send some furniture, china, and silverware to Gera over the last couple of years. And Gera was small enough that the Allies didn't bother bombing it."

Marie had come to tell her son that she could no longer stay in Berlin and would be taking shelter in Gera. She advised Pips that most of the people who could previously help him on the outside were now bombed out themselves. "Please be reasonable," she pleaded, "and don't try to escape." She reminded him of the Aryanization process she had undertaken on his behalf and didn't want him to spoil it with another escape attempt.

After fleeing Berlin for Gera, she soon settled in with Walter Ranke, a retired printer who was an elderly union man and a Social Democrat. With everything smashed to smithereens in her home, there wasn't much left for her to take. Among the few things that Marie managed to salvage from her Berlin life was a porcelain tea service.

The bombing raids continued in December and January. "At the beginning of the bombing, people would walk a mile to see a building that had been bombed. At the end of the bombing, people would walk a mile to see a building that had *not* been bombed." Despite his mother's admonishment, Pips spearheaded a brazen plot with Lotte and another prisoner.

The detention center on Grosse Hamburger Strasse was well-guarded from the outside, with sentries patrolling both the street side and the garden side. Ten-foot-high lights remained on all night, lighting up the façade from front to back. Despite the blackouts, these lights were kept on, except during actual air raids. But the prison had a big vulnerability: its fuse box. Pips had been assigned to work in the coal cellar, and there he stumbled on the electrical room that housed the fuse box. That inspired the idea for his fourth escape.

The inside guards were positioned in the building's core. At the back of that room was a storage rack for keys. The schemers realized that if they could shut down the electricity for the whole building—especially the high-powered outside lights—the total darkness would lead the guards to assume that an air raid was imminent. And that would conceal their escape.

First, they had to figure out how to find their way without light.

They trained themselves in the dark to find the keys they needed for the door upstairs and then to locate the door to the garden. "We didn't know which lever did what, so we had to take a big chance and test it. We did that in the daytime, just for a second. And sure enough, the lights in the bunker went out. Nobody noticed; it just looked like a momentary disruption of the current. But now we had to do it at night. Next, we found the right fuse for the outside lights and were pretty much set."

Guards patrolling along the façade of the building were brought indoors during air raids, so there was no worry about encountering them outside. But it was still a risky venture. Even if the trio succeeded in getting out of the building, they would have to breach a high fence.

"We set our time for the escape. A day or two before that, a trusty came to me and said, 'You know, I have a feeling you're thinking very hard about escaping. I happen to know you don't need to escape; they're going to keep you here, at least for a while. So, in case you have any funny ideas about escaping, my advice to you is, don't do it.'"

With nowhere to run and nowhere to hide, Pips cancelled his bold plan at the last minute. After all, Grosse Hamburger Strasse was livable, and he was relatively comfortable there. But Lotte and Pips's comrade went ahead with the plan and managed to escape. With escape no longer on the table, the only remaining option for survival was for Pips to be a "good Jew" and stay out of trouble. He knew how to be an upright subject in Dobberke's kingdom. "Every time I saw the Kommandant coming or going, I clicked my heels and stood at attention: 'Good morning Hauptscharführer.' He would give me a glance and walk past me, but it made an impression on him. I didn't feel like doing it, didn't feel like standing at attention when he walked by. I could have acted like I was busy. But I did it on purpose. I was cooperating with the Gestapo, but so was everybody else, in one way or another. If a Gestapo man said to you, 'Go over there and pick up something' you went and did it. You didn't say, 'What do you mean, I'm too good for that, it's not my job.' Yes, I cooperated with the Gestapo to improve my situation, but that's very different from collaboration."

One pay-off from his deference toward Dobberke was that he knew Pips by sight and would even call out to him "Philipsohn!" Unlike most of the inmates at Grosse Hamburger Strasse, Pips wasn't just a number. He also had a name. "When the time came for a transport, everybody who was eligible was put on a truck, and off they went. They were just numbers for him. But I was not just another Jew to be processed."

* * *

It was now early 1944. The Jews from Grosse Hamburger Strasse were moved by truck to Schulstrasse, a Jewish hospital that was partly converted into a prison. Walter Dobberke moved with them.

Opened with 230 beds in 1914, the hospital was a block-long neoclassic edifice with a three-story central structure and two long two-story wings, all topped by attics. The driveway, through which ambulances had delivered patients in better times, was now the entrance to the camp. Both the street side and the garden side were encircled with barbed wire. The ground floor windows, which had been shattered during air raids, were covered in plywood backed by iron bars. The second story windows were left uncovered. On one side of the driveway was a smaller building that housed the Gestapo. Under its small attic was just enough space for one room—a room that Pips would later occupy. The other attics were divided by wooden partitions. The regular floors contained rooms, each with a pile of mattresses to accommodate between eight and twelve prisoners. Men and women were jumbled together and the rooms were left unlocked. In the cellar, there was a morgue, which was now a one-man bunker—much smaller than the one in which Pips had been held in Grosse Hamburger Strasse. The campus was patrolled by policemen who were too old for frontline duty.

"There was a rather large place for the Jewish camp leadership. As in the much larger camps, the Gestapo didn't want to be bothered with all the details. There were a few Jews who worked in the office keeping track of who goes in and who goes out, and they had a former high school principal named Reschke, who was the Jewish camp leader. Of course, the Jewish camp leader had to do what he was told because Dobberke was the camp Kommandant."

There was also a barbershop tended by a Jewish barber who lived in a mixed marriage and was free. He came to Schulstrasse two or three times a week to give haircuts for which inmates paid a couple of marks. If they didn't have the money, he cut their hair anyway. There was also a dentist who was stationed in the hospital, but doubled as a dentist for the prisoners. Finally, there was an infirmary that was run by a nurse. "This nurse, Margaret, was a peculiar case. She had been adopted as a baby by a Jewish family and brought up as a Jew. Even though she was fully Aryan and they knew it, she had somehow rubbed them the wrong way and the Gestapo arrested her. They put her there as a nurse, but she was a prisoner.

"Compared to any concentration camp, let alone the extermination camps, this place was a sanatorium."

In Pips's cohort, there were a couple of dozen inmates who were not being deported, including Pips's roommate, Rehfeld—"a full Jew, so a clear-cut deportation case, but Dobberke wouldn't let go of him for anything." Then there was Jonas, whose job it was to take care of Dobberke's ten rabbits and keep them well fed for the Kommandant's later dining pleasure. There was also Hans Rosenthal, a chauffeur who drove a repurposed ambulance that was used to round up Jews. Of course, Jews were not allowed to drive cars, but he had special permission. His old mother was kept around to make him feel more secure. And then there was Zeitman, a Polish Jew. He and his daughter were prisoners at Schulstrasse, but his wife and son still managed to live illegally in the city. Despite Dobberke's threats, Zeitman never revealed his family's whereabouts. "At that point, these individuals had already been there for a year, so I think Dobberke had given up getting anything out of them."

Tatiana, a handsome, middle-aged Russian Jew, was in charge of Little Kanada, the storage area where confiscated clothes and other goods were kept.

"They took away whatever clothes we had and gave us rags: torn jackets, shirts, sweaters, pants—still a lot better than Auschwitz. They took away my marching boots." Tatiana dispensed what goods the prisoners were allowed.

Pips was free to roam the prison grounds during the day. During his meanderings, Pips met an elderly window glazier. As the Jewish spouse in a mixed marriage, the glazier was free. But he came most days to the prison to repair windows that were shattered in the nightly air raids, including the small glass panes in the prisoners' cells. Being a slow worker and unable to keep up with the demand, he applied for an assistant. Pips was it.

"Of course, I didn't know from putting in glass, but he taught me, and I picked it up very quickly. It became complicated because we no longer got a supply of glass panes. We now had to piece it together from fragments that had broken away from the windows. It was practically done with Scotch tape." The old glazier soon retired, and Pips became the sole glazier for Schulstrasse.

"Slowly but surely, I managed to get out of the prison, off the grounds, through the gate. Usually I had an excuse, like I had to get some glass that was just being delivered. The police guards were easygoing. They knew I had permission to run around the compound as much as I wanted to. I wasn't just one of the crowd; I was someone special. Slowly that became a habit, almost to the point where I could come and go as I pleased. Once or twice, I even had the nerve to go to a movie. I always had to be careful not to overdo it and stay away too long. I had escaped three times. I knew that if I escaped once more, they would surely catch me and then I'm really done for. Dobberke wasn't that good-hearted of a guy! So, I was free but on a long leash."

Although Pips was able to walk down the street, he wasn't part of the society that moved around him. "I was just a visitor, then to the prison I went. And the prison wasn't just physical. It was also a state of mind. There was a time in my life when I longed to be part of the majority, part of the society around me. By then, the immediate society around me was all Jewish."

Marie occasionally wrote to her son and Pips was able to write to her. Even if there was no mailbox on the prison grounds, he could go out and mail his infrequent letters. Every few months, Marie came to Berlin—usually with Walter, her now fiancé, from Gera—to visit Pips and bring food. There was a visitor's area, but Pips could also go out with her. "Sometimes she even sent some traveler ration cards from Gera. It was never enough to still my hunger but at least, once in a while, I had some decent bread. I don't think I saw an egg or meat in two years."

One day, Pips was told to report to Frau Heim's home to replace the windows that had been blown out during the previous night's air raids. Because he was carting tools and bulky glass pieces, Pips was given a ride in Hans Rosenthal's car. It was early in the morning, and he arrived just as Frau Heim was leaving for work. She instructed her elderly mother to give Pips some lunch. "The car departed, and I was left alone with the old mother. I did what I could to the windows. The mother was very friendly. At lunchtime, she brought me a sandwich and a glass of milk, stuff that was normally unobtainable. And then, right before I was finished, she called the prison to pick me up."

Pips also became part of the fire brigade, which consisted of three men. Their job was to go up to the attic during the air raids to intercept firebombs. "The British dropped sticks. One end of the stick was phosphorous. When they fell through the roof, they wouldn't fall all the way down to the cellar because their momentum was spent. But they started fires because the wooden planks in these old buildings were so dried out that they were like tinder, and they burned like hell. Our job was to take the firebomb and throw it out the window. If it was a bigger bomb, we would stick it in pots of sand. By that time, we were so used to air raids that we weren't afraid. I was much more afraid of the Gestapo than I was of any British bomber."

Because the brigade was spending air raids immediately under the roof, they were moved into a one-room attic, where each had a real bed. "We were treated like royalty. Every morning, I would go to the basement workroom where I did my glazing. At midnight or 1:00 am, the British came. As soon as the siren started, I put my pants on, got out of bed, went to the big attic, and stayed there until the air raid was over. Then I went back to bed. We didn't get any extra food, which was one of the really bad things. I had already had bad food for a long time, but scarcity and hunger became a real problem."

One sunny day, Pips was handed another opportunity to endear himself to Dobberke. A building a half block from Schulstrasse was completely flattened by a bomb. With no functioning rescue or fire brigades on hand, Dobberke selected several Jewish prisoners, including Pips, to search for survivors. Because Pips was so thin, he was directed to crawl through the rubble. "Suddenly I heard a voice, as if from miles away. I was startled but surely there was somebody there. I crawled to where I thought the sound came from but there was no human being to be seen. I started throwing the bricks aside and after about ten minutes, I unearthed a head, just a head." The disembodied head was covered entirely in dust and Pips assumed it was a statue. "Suddenly this head opened its eyes and its mouth, and some noise came out. I almost fainted dead away! It was so scary, so shocking, this head with no body. It would have scared the shit out of anybody." Realizing it was a woman, who was alive, Pips urgently freed her body and dragged her to safety.

The Kommandant watched the whole operation approvingly and commended Pips for his good work. "By the time we saw daylight again, I was out of my mind. I said something that was unbelievable under the circumstances—a Jewish prisoner says to the Gestapo Kommandant of the prison, 'Give me a cigarette.' He gave me a cigarette; he gave me a light. And I didn't even say thank you."

In his state of shock, Pips whispered to himself, "If you want to ship me to Auschwitz right now, I'm ready. It can't be worse than this." It took Pips some hours to regain his equilibrium. The woman whose life he'd saved never tried to find out who rescued her. She never made an attempt to visit Pips or bring him some food. "She was a German. I didn't rescue her because I wanted to rescue a German. I was told to do it, and you don't say no, so I did it. That, of course, gave me a big plus with the Kommandant."

Because of his fire brigade duties, Pips was always in the attic during air raids. A few days before one of the air raids, a newly arrived mother and her seventeen-year-old daughter appeared in the attic lodgings.

"They both knew they had only a few days before Auschwitz. When I walked past their compartment, they called me in and started chatting with me about what I was doing and when I thought the next transport would go. After a while, the mother asked that we have sex. She was a good-looking woman, and I hadn't had sex since Ilse, so I said okay. Then she said that her daughter should participate. I had sex with the mother and the daughter—not simultaneously. And it was very exciting. The idea that this was mother and daughter made it even more exciting. It was so, so odd; so weird; my libido was so stimulated that, within a short time, I could satisfy both of them. If these had been normal times, there was no way I would have had that *ménage a trois* with them. These were times when people did crazy things, to hold on to a little bit of life. Everything was topsy-turvy, the rules were reversed, and everything was cockeyed.

"These were perfectly ordinary middle-class people. These women weren't whores. They didn't say now you pay us or give us some cigarettes. These were women who had lived underground—probably under terrible circumstances for a year or more—who had been caught, who knew that their lives were ending in a very cruel and terrible way. They wanted to have sex once more before death, and I was a handy tool. These people weren't depraved. They were looking for some comfort. It wasn't just the sexual titillation; it was human contact, warmth, a body." Pips had experienced the same need with Lotte Paech.

Pips was now working very hard as a glazier, clicking his heels, and throwing firebombs out the window. "I was a very good boy, and Dobberke had sort of forgiven me for my multiple escapes. I only started kissing his ass after I realized that I can no longer escape. I was playing a game to do whatever I could to cement my position—working, getting myself to be important in a minor way. But that doesn't mean he loved me. My hope was that I could live out the rest of the war in this comparative sanatorium. But I still had very, very little hope that any of us would see the actual end of the war. I was convinced, as most of us were, that even if we survived until the minute before midnight, they would still find time to mow us down."

Lotte Paech had managed to escape Grosse Hamburger Strasse, thanks to the fake air raid that Pips had devised. But after Pips had long been in Schulstrasse, she was caught again and brought there. They renewed their friendship, and she stayed in one of the attic compartments, near the mother and daughter whom Pips had bedded.

At 11:00 one bright morning, a policeman came down to the glazing workshop and ordered Pips to stop working. "I didn't know what he wanted. I said, 'I just have to finish this. It'll take me five minutes.' He said, 'Forget about it.' And as we walked out, he said, 'They're coming for you.' I will never forget that sentence."

Pips was given fifteen minutes to get himself organized. He didn't have much to pack, so he grabbed a piece of underwear and put it into a little paper sack. As he was led out, the other prisoners stood around and looked at him knowingly. This was a harbinger of what was in store for them. A couple of them gave Pips a few cigarettes—a generous gesture at a time when cigarettes were gold.

When Pips was taken to the street, there was no car waiting, like the one that had ferried him to Frau Heim's house. Instead, a streetcar was idling on the tracks in front of the prison. Its windows were barbed with wire, but Pips could look out. He was the only passenger, save for two lowly guards in SS uniforms. Pips lit a cigarette, his heart racing. His turn had come, sooner than expected. One of the guards gave him a dirty look. "What was he going to do to me? He could have slapped me and kicked me. It didn't matter at this point." Instead, Pips was stunned to find himself back at Grosse Hamburger Strasse, which was now a transit prison for all kinds of prisoners, not just Jews.

Pips was, once again, put in a bunker—this one, holding twenty men. "It wasn't the homey feeling I had the first time. Most of the people didn't speak German and this time, the cells were locked. There was no walking around in the hallway. There was a bucket in the corner. I went over to the bucket and vomited like crazy. I knew that this was the gateway to Auschwitz, tomorrow or the next day." Pips intuited that, for him, Auschwitz meant death. Now it wasn't just the separation from Ilse; it was the separation from his life. Pips was only twenty-one and a half years old.

There was a French Catholic priest in the bunker. Because Pips spoke fluent French, he approached the priest and confided his sadness, fear, and desperation. "The priest was very understanding, even though he was in the soup too, but not the same soup I was in. He didn't stroke my hair or embrace me or any of that, but just to be able to talk to somebody calmed me down. That was the only time I had a heart-to-heart with a Catholic priest."

Night came and they slept on the floor. Morning dawned. At noon, the bunker door opened and Pips's name was called. He took one last look at the priest and waved. With trembling knees, Pips was led to the office. There stood a half dozen Gestapo officers, some in uniform and the rest in civilian clothes. Pips spied a face he knew, but it took a moment to figure out who he was. It was a low-ranking officer by the name of Tietze. "Tietze was one of those guys who was drafted into the Gestapo, who wasn't volunteering, a very good man. If he had anything against the Jews, he didn't show it."

Pips went up to Tietze and asked what he was doing there. Tietze broke out into a wide grin and said, "I came to bring you home to Schulstrasse." "It was an unbelievable moment. I was saved. At least for the time being, I wasn't going to Auschwitz; I wasn't being shot. He was taking me home. After all, it was the only home I had. I almost fainted and I said, 'My God, give me a cigarette' and he said, 'Not here, outside.' All kinds of papers had to be filled out. Then he took me out and there was the car. I got in, and he finally gave me a cigarette. Twenty minutes later we were back home. A miracle! An absolute miracle! Twenty-four hours ago, I was being picked up for transport with that streetcar."

An hour after arriving back at Schulstrasse, Pips was summoned to Dobberke's office, where he learned who'd saved him. "I clicked my heels and stood at attention. Seeing the relief on his face, Dobberke said, "Philipsohn, you are the luckiest son-of-a-bitch I have known." He then proceeded to tell Pips that Frau Heim thought of him more as a German than as a Jew and felt sorry for him. When she learned that Pips was being shipped out, she took his file and slipped it behind a filing cabinet. She then made some phone calls and pulled a few strings, explaining that there was no file for this prisoner and that he should stay in the Schulstrasse until his case could be clarified.

"Sure enough, they fell for it. And that's how I got back. She was really taking a chance. Dobberke told me, 'What Frau Heim did for you, you will never be able to repay. I believe that you have learned your lesson. I will let you go in and out, but if you escape once more, I give you my word of honor'— and he was grim at that point—'you will not live to see the next day. Will you promise me that you will not escape, no matter what?' A promise from a Jewish prisoner to a Gestapo man wasn't really worth much, but I had no hesitation in promising by all the saints in heaven. And I was honest about it because I knew I couldn't escape, I had nowhere to go."

Although Pips's life was saved by a Gestapo officer, he dared not shake his hand. But he did profusely thank Frau Heim and shake hers. "If I had dared, I would have kissed her. She was quite a good-looking woman, but of course, it was out of the question."

When Pips crossed the driveway to get from the office to the prison area, he was greeted with jubilation by his fellow inmates.

A week later, another transport to Auschwitz was put together. No matter how many of these he witnessed, Pips could never get used it. "I started shivering. I was not going, but to see these people going on that truck was hard. My fellow Jews from Berlin. These were not criminals. They were old people and children. And while they went on the truck, Frau Heim was in the immediate vicinity playing with a German shepherd. She had a wonderful time with the dog. She threw a branch, the dog retrieved it, and she laughed—right next to the truck where these poor, poor people were sent to death. And this is one of those paradoxes. She went out of her way to help me, and it didn't bother her that there were eighty people standing in the truck awaiting a terrible fate."

A few months passed, and Hopp was still in Schulstrasse. One day, Pips was approached by a Jewish prison functionary, whose job it was to convey orders from the Kommandant to his fellow inmates. Hopp had gotten permission to visit his Aryan wife for dinner that evening because, unbeknownst to him, he was to be put on a transport to Auschwitz the following day. Pips was to go with him and ensure his return to prison. "Such a sadistic thing. Dobberke wanted to test me and have his fun with me. It was unheard of that a prisoner, who was going to be on a transport, would be allowed to go home for dinner. And I, who was his friend, was to be in the guard to guarantee that he would be back in time to go to Auschwitz the next day."

Pips was caught on the horns of a dilemma. If he confessed to Hopp that he was scheduled for deportation, his friend would surely run. Although he couldn't return to the woman in whose home he had been caught, he had nothing to lose and had other underground connections. On the one hand, if Hopp fled, Pips would have to go with him. But there was no assurance that Hopp could take care of Pips; he would have enough on his hands taking care of himself. On the other hand, if Pips were to return to prison without Hopp, it would be he who would be on the next transport to Auschwitz.

"What to do, what to do? I decided I had to be a Judas goat, the goat that leads the other goats into the slaughterhouse. So, with great trepidation, I decided to go with him to his house and have dinner with him. He knew that I was supposed to be responsible for him, which was okay with him, because he had no plans to escape. I was sitting at the dinner table with him. We talked and had a nice evening. Of course, I was in terrible shape. Then we went back to the Schulstrasse, and the next day he was deported. It was the only thing to do, at least to save myself, even if I couldn't save him. Otherwise, we would both be finished. It's one of these sins about which I have a terribly bad conscience, even though I say to myself, it was the only practical thing to do."

Pips thought he might be sending his friend to die. But the Soviets were advancing rapidly, and he reasoned that Auschwitz wasn't going to be there much longer. He saw that as the saving grace for many who were sent to that camp at the last minute. "They simply didn't have the means and the time because they had 420,000 Hungarian Jews to deal with."

Hopp survived and remained friends with Pips.

Dobberke continued to favor Pips. There came a time when Pips developed a high fever and was obviously seriously ill. Dobberke again did something unusual; he sent Pips to the remaining medical wing of the Jewish hospital, which was still functioning for half-Jews and those in a mixed marriage. It was in the Nazi's self-interest to keep the remnant of the Jewish hospital going throughout the war because it was inconceivable for any kind of Jew to be treated in the same facilities as Aryan patients. Although many doctors and nurses had fled or gone into hiding, there was enough staff to provide care.

"I was a prisoner, and I had never heard of another prisoner who was given that benefit, so that was pretty decent of him." Pips had free run of the ward, and no sooner had his condition improved, than he returned to his usual antics—specifically, his "thing" for nurses.

He spotted a nurse behind some equipment, which concealed everything but a pair of gorgeous legs. The next day, she was revealed in totality—a pretty young woman in her twenties. "I was beginning to recover and got horny." But his plans were momentarily derailed because the nurse was scheduled to undergo hemorrhoid surgery. However, it also gave him an opportunity to endear himself to her. As she lay in a separate room, recovering from her operation, Pips went to her room and sat at the side of her bed, holding her hand and stroking her. "For me it was the perfect opening. I kissed her and she was with it." After a couple of days, the nurse recovered, resumed her duties, and Pips was released back to the prison.

"But I had my foot in the door, and I wasn't going to let that go to waste. I was free to come and go, and I went to her room, and we did it. A few days later, we did it again, and she was a very good lay." Then one of the most embarrassing things in his life happened. Just as Pips reached orgasm, the door opened and a young man stood there staring at the couple in *flagrante delicto.* He let out a long moan and closed the door. "I said 'Who was that?' 'That's my fiancé.' All this while I was having my orgasm. I just put my pants on and left and that ended our liaison. It was absurd." Later, Pips learned that the nurse and her fiancé, who was a half-Jew, made up and she became pregnant. Someone speculated that it was Pips's child, but by his calculation, it couldn't be his. And although they met as friends a couple of times after the war, no further mention was ever made of their little dalliance.

"There was another very cute nurse in the hospital,. After some weeks of pulling out all the stops on my part—deep voice, a couple of poems—she finally succumbed. But it was uneventful. No fiancé showed up. Ilse was now a memory that I didn't want to come to the fore. I was on the make, in spite of the lousy food. I was twenty-two, and at twenty-two, you can screw up a storm."

Having become Dobberke's pet Jew, Pips was now assigned to yet another job for which he had no training or skill. Dobberke's superior, Hauptsturmführer Krischak, who worked for Adolf Eichmann, wanted to build a summer house on land he had purchased on the outskirts of Berlin. "Not a fancy house but also not one of those shacks that lower class people had." Pips was to lead a work Kommando of ten men.

"On the one hand, I was flattered at being singled out as the boss of a Kommando. On the other hand, I didn't know a fucking thing about building a house. So immediately, there were a million things I had to worry about. I was given some days to prepare, and during those days they put together the Kommando."

Dobberke had another pet Jew. A master black marketeer named Weiss had been caught by the Gestapo and sent to see the Kommandant. He offered to get Dobberke anything he wanted if he let him skip transport. Dobberke agreed and said he would give him his shopping list. Weiss went to work but was forbidden to reveal to his fellow black marketeers that he was a detainee. Dobberke sent an officer to watch Weiss, but not to interfere with his activities.

Weiss became an important part of the building project. Each day, Pips was to give Weiss a list of the building materials he needed.

In the meantime, workers were taken out under guard to gather bricks. "You couldn't get new bricks, but Berlin was full of bricks from the buildings that had fallen down—millions of bricks all over the place. They had cement stuck to them so you had use a hammer to knock the cement off. They had to bring loads and loads of bricks into the yard, which was still surrounded by barbed wire, and there they set up their shop. They hammered away like crazy to get the cement off, which was stone hard."

It took about a week for the pile of clean bricks to grow. While this was going on, Pips turned to Rehfeld—Mr. Fix-It, who shared a room with him—and anxiously asked him how to build a house.

Rehfeld explained that you first have to build a foundation by digging a trench to fit the external dimensions of the house. The trench then has to be filled with cement. The rooms would then have to be measured and space left for electrical lines.

"It was all Greek to me. I said, 'One thing at a time.' Let's first dig that lousy trench. So, these ten guys and I went. We had one or two guards with us on the subway. Krischak was there, and he showed me where he wanted to build the house and its size. I told him that we had to first build the foundation. For that, we had to get pickaxes and stuff like that. The first tour was only an inspection. Krishak said he wouldn't be there going forward because he couldn't afford to take the time. I was responsible, and if I had any problems, I was to report to Dobberke, and then Dobberke would notify him." Meanwhile Weiss had been briefed that he needed to bring in cement, shovels, and trucks. All this was produced and Pips's Kommando started to dig the trench.

"You might wonder, why didn't these guys escape? These were all cases that were not clear-cut deportation cases: mixed breeds, mixed marriages, and they were in for something or other, maybe for not wearing the star. But they didn't fear imminent deportation to Auschwitz. They were in a somewhat similar position to mine, except they were not as free as I was."

One day, Pips had to meet Krishak to go to a bank to withdraw three thousand marks from his savings account to pay for a delivery. As he handed Pips the cash, Pips said, "Don't worry, I won't skip." "He gave me the iciest look that I've ever seen in my life and said, 'I don't worry.' And his look said, 'You lousy Jew, I've got you on a string, you ain't going anywhere.' I felt the ice going through my veins when he gave me that look and I said to myself, 'This guy is still a high SS officer, a Gestapo officer, and I'm a Jew, so I can't kid around.'"

The work on the house proceeded for several weeks. Had it continued, Pips had little confidence that it would survive its first winter. But the work didn't continue, because this project was completely illegal. "No one was allowed to build pleasure houses during the war. This was 1944, and we were using precious building materials and labor."

After work one day, the Kommando and its guards returned to Schulstrasse. But Pips stuck around at the worksite, which was in an empty area with only corn and potato fields in the vicinity. As Pips started heading to the subway, the sun was just going down over the horizon. He made a detour and ambled toward a potato field. "It was a beautiful sunset and here I was all alone on this field and I was alive. It was part of my inner turmoil. Am I living or am I on my way to death, with one foot in the grave and one foot in the world?"

When Pips returned to the Schulstrasse, two guards raced up to him as he walked through the gate. They grabbed him by the arms and dragged him down to the bunker. Pips was terrified. He asked them what was going on. What had he done? "We don't know," they replied, "We were just told to take you down."

This could be the last stop. Had Pips's luck finally run out?

Pips had been put in the bunker to ensure that he didn't take another walk. Soon Dobberke appeared. Pips could see that he was in a terrible state. "Philipsohn, come with me," he ordered.

Rolf Günther, Adolf Eichmann's deputy, had found out about Krischak's project and was in Dobberke's office to investigate. Günther had asked who was in charge. Pips's name came up and he demanded to see him as soon as he returned.

"As we walked up the stairs to the office, Dobberke said, 'Be careful what you say.' I walked into the office and there, behind Dobberke's desk, sits *Sturmbannführer* Günther in uniform. The SS officers had very handsome uniforms, sporting insignia with the death head and the crossbones. He was blond, tall, thirty-one years old, and you could feel the ice that emanated from this guy the moment you entered the room. He was there as the great inquisitor.

He was going to find out what this was all about. And it didn't occur to me right away, but his real interest was Krischak, not Dobberke, nor me. He wanted to know what Krischak had done and how he had done it, because Krischak was part of his command, and he had committed a crime."

At first Pips was so confused that he hardly knew what was happening. Dobberke stood next to him and Pips noticed that he had gone completely pale. Clearly, Dobberke feared that he was going to be arrested and sent to a concentration camp or a punishment battalion on the Eastern front. "They sent them out as cannon fodder, right up front to get killed. Dobberke was scared shitless, and I couldn't stop my knees from vibrating, which was rather embarrassing. I was standing at attention when Günther started: 'You're going to answer my questions, you're going to answer every one of them, you're going to answer in full, absolutely truthfully, or else I will have you shot right away.

"'Where is your father?'

"'My father is in Theresienstadt.'

"'Your father will be taken to Auschwitz. Where is your mother?'

"'My mother is Aryan and lives in Gera.'

"'Your mother will be arrested and taken to Ravensbrück.'

"So for openers, he had told me what's what."

Pips was in a bind. He couldn't say anything that would embarrass Dobberke because, if he had a chance, he would take it out on Pips. He couldn't say too much about Weiss either, because, having kept a Jew to provide him with supplies, would again get Dobberke into trouble. The only one Pips didn't worry about was Krischak. "I knew his goose was cooked anyway." Pips confessed that Krischak had commanded the work. Krischak had come to the prison and appointed Pips as head of the Kommando. He kept Dobberke out of it as much as possible. When asked where the cement and other materials had come from, Pips responded in the safest way he could:

"I don't know." Although the interrogation lasted for only a half hour, it felt like an eternity to Pips. During that endless half hour, he knew that his life hung by the thinnest of threads.

Günther had taken out his revolver and put in on the desk. "If he wanted to shoot me, it would have been nothing, like stepping on an insect. But he was apparently satisfied with my testimony. So finally he said, "*Raus*—out!'"

Dobberke stayed behind for further grilling. Pips was taken back to the bunker and released the next day. "I didn't see Dobberke, but I was told that Günther had settled down and things were going back to normal—except that we weren't going to work on that house anymore. Later on, I found out that Krischak had been assigned to one of the punishment battalions, which was fine with me. Günther was like Eichmann—a man with power over millions of Jews. And I was just a little Jew boy."

So, this time, Pips had saved Dobberke, the Nazi who had saved him.

Time went on, and as 1944 turned into 1945, Pips's hunger grew more intense. By now, part of the camp had been taken over by the German army as a field hospital for soldiers. Pips discovered a pile of coal briquettes in the prison yard. "I couldn't eat the coal but I made a deal with a grocer across the street. Because I was free to come and go, I would go in the middle of the night to leave a sack of coal in front of his door. The next day, I would come and he would give me a bag full of potatoes. I could roast the potatoes and that was a terrific meal. The first time I did it I got away with it. Sometime later I did it again. Sure enough, the next morning I was called to the office. Dobberke wasn't really furious but he certainly couldn't let that go on. So, he gave me hell. 'Are you crazy? You think you can march out of here making deals in the neighborhood? Do you want to go to Auschwitz?' I promised on everything that's holy that I would never do it again and I never did."

Despite their having saved each other, Dobberke and Pips weren't close. "Most of the time, he didn't even look at me. He didn't fraternize with me. Later on, he fraternized with some of the other Jews." But those Jews were doctors and nurses at the hospital, not the lowly Jews in the prison camp.

The Red Army continued to close in on Berlin. The final Soviet offensive began on April 16, 1945. On April 20, Hitler's birthday, the 1st Belorussian Front advanced from the east and north, shelling the city center. Dobberke assigned the Jews who worked in his office to issue release documents to the prisoners. A Soviet soldier entered the grounds of the Jewish Hospital on Schulstrasse on April 24 and reported that there were no Jews; the Jews were "kaput." The SS had evacuated earlier that day and the eight hundred to a thousand Jewish prisoners in the Jewish hospital exhaled a sigh of relief when the Red Army finally arrived. When a hospital spokesperson explained to the Red Army representatives that most of the people at Schulstrasse were Jews, he was met with disbelief. How could Jews have survived in the heart of the Third Reich?

The Battle of Berlin ended Pips's first life. Everyone he loved was gone, except for his mother, whom he deeply resented because she had betrayed his father. The hometown of his youth was gone because Berlin was nearly completely destroyed.

CHAPTER 7

OLGA'S STORY—AN AUSCHWITZ DETOUR

In January 1945, with the impending Soviet offensive, fifty-six thousand prisoners were marched from Auschwitz under heavy guard and moved to camps inside Germany. It became known as the Death March. Olga Horvath, an eighteen-year-old Hungarian, was one of thousands of Jews on that march.

Olga Horvath was born in Dej, a small Transylvanian town, on September 6, 1926. She had an idyllic childhood with parents she adored—and who adored her in return. Her totally protected childhood was shared with a beloved orphaned cousin, Victor Hartmann, whom her parents had taken in.

Her enormous, expressive blue eyes and broad forehead were evident early on and clearly came from her father's delicate features. From her mother, she inherited a refined nose with a gentle bend. In childhood photos, Olga appears to be a serious girl, not prone to smiling. But as an adult, the smile would become luminous, with dainty white teeth and perfectly proportioned lips. An arresting beauty with dark wavy hair and smooth skin, she needed no makeup.

Olga started playing violin at the age of six. As she got older, she traveled from her home in Budapest to Berlin for violin lessons. She didn't think she would have made a great soloist, and she had no interest in playing in an orchestra. But she loved to play chamber music and, by age eighteen, she was ready to embark on a music career. But she never had the chance to try because at that age she was deported to Auschwitz.

German forces occupied Hungary in March 1944. Although Hitler was already losing the war, that's when deportations of Hungary's Jews began in earnest. Pips observed, "Transport was badly needed to get ammunition to the front. Yet, even at that time, preference was given to getting rolling stock together to deport Jews. That shows you what was really important—almost more important than winning the war."

In less than two months, from mid-May to early July, nearly 440,000 Jews were transported, almost all of them to Auschwitz. Olga and her forty-one-year-old mother were among the first wave of deportees. Olga's father had already died in a forced labor battalion in Ukraine.

The mother and daughter spent three days in a cattle car with no food or water. There was one bucket to use as a toilet in the tightly crammed car. When the train finally arrived at its destination and its passengers were herded out of the cattle cars, two lines were formed—one for men and older boys and one for women and children. During the selections on the train platform, a child was crying for her lost mother. Taking pity, Olga's mother took the girl's hand—and that was her death sentence. Any mother with a child younger than fifteen was immediately gassed with her offspring. The SS officer assumed the little girl was hers and with a flick of the wrist, directed Olga's mother and the unknown child to the gas chamber. That placed them among the 80 percent of Auschwitz's Hungarian Jews who were murdered upon arrival.

In the confusion, Olga lost track of her mother. Panicked, she approached a Polish trusty and implored, "I can't find my mother, where's my mother?" He replied indifferently: "I don't know. Did she have a child with her?" Olga said, "Yes, but it wasn't her child." "It makes no difference," said the Jewish trusty. "You see the fire coming out of the chimney there? That's the crematorium. That's where your mother is." The trusty numbly conveyed this news to Olga without a trace of pity. It took a couple of days before Olga could fathom that her mother had literally gone up in smoke.

Pips explained, "Polish Jews and Jews from other areas had been tortured, killed, murdered, slaughtered every which way since shortly after the Germans marched into Poland in 1939. These trusties in Auschwitz were people who had been there two or three years, since Auschwitz had opened its friendly gates. They bore a resentment toward the Hungarian Jews who now came in enormous numbers. Why? Because they said, 'You must be real idiots. This is 1944. Didn't you know what was going on? How could you stick your head in the sand and act like everything's going fine? You could have done anything because nothing could be worse than your fate here, nothing.' They were talking about the Hungarian Jews en masse, including the leadership of the Hungarian Jews."

In Olga's case, she was a protected, slightly timid girl, who would not leave her mother. With no idea of what awaited her, she had declared, "If they deport my mother, I go along." And when she learned the truth about her mother's disappearance at Auschwitz, her mind went into a dreamlike state, as if she was simply going through a nightmare from which she would eventually awaken.

Although shorn of their hair, and deprived of their few possessions, the SS didn't bother to tattoo numbers on the arms of the Hungarian deportees who were destined for the gas chambers.

Olga was assigned to a block in Section 3. Each section was surrounded by electrified barbed wire. There she met Eva Sebestyen, a newly married girl whom she knew from Budapest. Olga and Eva stuck together. They also knew a third girl, Vera, but they weren't particularly close to her, and she remained on the fringe of their small clique.

Together they faced daily selections. All the women had to exit the barracks at five o'clock in the morning. Summer or winter, completely naked, they lined up to be left standing for hours. Then, either the notorious Josef Mengele, or one of his deputies, would amble through their ranks to look over the hapless prisoners. Pips explained, "Anybody who looked under the weather, women whose breasts were sagging too much, anybody who didn't look quite kosher, anybody who wasn't fit, was taken by truck to the gas chambers. The girls knew where they were going, so they pinched their cheeks to look rosy. They were young, their breasts weren't sagging, and they were in good shape physically."

The inmates tried to protect the very sick prisoners by pushing them against a wall and covering them with a blanket so they wouldn't be seen. Sometimes it worked, sometimes it didn't. While they managed to save a few, being so weak, most died anyway. Then the women had to load the corpses onto trucks.

It soon started getting cold. A German Communist, who held a prison post in the men's block, owned a very short cashmere jacket. Spotting Olga, he threw it to her over the fence because, even with her shorn head, she was beautiful. This jacket became her secret possession, which she hid whenever there was an inspection by the SS. Otherwise, she wore the rags that were distributed by the Kommando of Kanada—the sorting center that sorted purloined Jewish booty and gave out the junk. At that point, the inmates didn't have striped uniforms, just rags. Later, Olga received a totally threadbare coat with a big red stripe painted down the back. It was appropriate for her work assignment: *Scheisskommando.*

Every morning, the Kommando had to empty the buckets from the barracks where inmates had toileted during the night. With widespread diarrhea, the buckets overflowed. The buckets were carried to the latrine, a thirty-foot-deep pit with slippery poles to seat as many people at one time as its length would allow. Those who were short had to dangle their legs above the thick brown sea swelling below like a volcano cut short and forced to swallow its own eruption.

Recalling Olga's descriptions, Pips said, "The ditch was near the fence that separated the women's from the men's camp, so the men had a full view of the women's asses. But it didn't matter at that point. Besides, this sight was not particularly enticing. They had a term—not limited to Auschwitz—'latrine parole,' meaning gossip from the latrine. As the girls sat on this thing and did their business, that was the equivalent of a beauty parlor where they exchanged gossip. Shortly after arrival, almost all the girls, including Olga, lost their period, partly because of malnourishment, and partly because of the shock, which was convenient for hygiene purposes."

Eventually, Olga was reassigned to the epidemic hospital. "Why the hell would the Germans have a hospital in Auschwitz-Birkenau where they're burning five thousand people a day?" wondered Pips. "This was only for transmittable diseases: typhus, dysentery, measles. It was run by a Jewish doctor; except she couldn't do much because she hadn't any medication. People had open sores, bleeding, and pus. At best they found a little piece of absorbent paper and that was the best they could do. Olga became a nurse, which was crazy since you couldn't nurse anybody."

The patients were tended to in three or four tiers of bunks that were infested with lice. Lice-ridden blankets had to be taken away. "These poor women were freezing and said, 'Why do you take away my blanket?'—if they could speak at all," described Pips.

Olga futilely tried to feed people who were too weak to eat. There was no bath or latrine, but she helped to the extent possible. Pips continued, "Olga had no medical experience whatsoever, but that didn't matter. For what she was doing, you didn't need it." It was Olga's good fortune that she never caught any of the highly infectious diseases to which she was exposed every day.

By December 1944, the Red Army was closing in and the SS began the final evacuation of the Auschwitz complex. From January 17–21, 1945, fifty-six thousand prisoners were marched under heavy guard from Auschwitz and its sub-camps to camps inside Germany.

Olga was in a group of about a thousand, mostly young women, who were marched to Upper Silesia. "It was a good distance: a hundred miles or more. And the girls were not in the best shape. They wore wooden clogs. Even though they managed to find some straw to soften the clogs, marching ten miles a day with these clogs, their feet became bloody," Pips observed.

The women arrived outside Kurzbach and were put to work digging anti-tank ditches in the forest. Like at Schulstrasse, the SS was now reinforced with regular police because the SS was needed for fighting. "The Germans were scraping the bottom of the barrel as far as manpower was concerned. Many of these police were in their sixties. Olga said some of them were senile," Pips recalled.

The earth was frozen, and the girls could hardly do any digging. The police were charged with watching them, but they didn't pay much attention. When they did pay attention, they were generally respectful. Pips explained, "Some of them were Hungarian. They were all from low-class backgrounds and they realized that these girls and young women were all from middle or upper middle-class backgrounds. So, they called them 'Miss.'"

There was one very talkative German policeman. He would sit on a tree stump, drink hot coffee from his thermos, unpack his wurst sandwich, and eat with great gusto while his starving and freezing charges looked on. He gave them nothing but was otherwise quite friendly. One day he received a letter from home. Sitting on his tree stump, he began to weep. Olga and a couple of other girls wandered over to him and asked why he was crying. He explained that his wife had just informed him that their canary died, and he had been very attached to that little bird.

"This was typical of the so-called good Germans," reported Pips sourly. "This one could cry bitter tears about his canary. He could be respectful to a thousand girls who were in rags, who were destined to be dealt with brutally. But that didn't touch him. It didn't matter; it didn't penetrate. You might compare it to people who step over a body on the street without knowing whether that person is dead or drunk or sick. They just step gingerly over that body and march along. This was the same kind of attitude, only on a much bigger scale."

Some of the girls contracted meningitis. With intense headaches, they screamed in pain all night until they died. Other girls died of the cold. The majority survived.

The SS women and SS commandant of the little labor camp in Upper Silesia weren't as monstrous as many of their colleagues. They didn't go out of their way to beat the women. But the Soviets were again approaching. Under no circumstances did the Germans want any prisoners to fall into the hands of the Allies, especially the Reds. So, the prisoners continued their Death March.

A long line, surrounded by guards, snaked its way out of Kurzbach toward Bergen-Belsen. Some women collapsed, were dumped in a cart, and taken away to be shot. The others marched into the interior of Germany. They approached Cottbus, a town that was the locus of a Nazi prison for women and numerous labor camps. But just before arriving, the group encountered some escaped French prisoners of war. The POWs were supposed to work in factories but most of them had fled and were trying to get home to France. Olga, Eva, and Vera went up to them and, because Eva spoke fluent French, they managed to communicate: "We don't know where they're going to take us, but we know this isn't going to end well." The Frenchmen bade them, "Come with us!" And they did.

The three young women fled from the group, which wasn't difficult. The French gave them kerchiefs to cover their heads, which by now had sprouted crew cuts. But there was no disguise for their rags.

The trio walked with the POWs to Cottbus and got as far as the platform of a railroad station before they were arrested. To protect the POWs who had helped them, they averred that they had nothing to do with the French soldiers, other than saying hello to them. The three friends were relegated to a regular prison, where they remained for a couple of weeks. There, they agreed on a story among themselves: they are half-Jews, and that's why they were released from Auschwitz. "Complete bullshit. But the Germans swallowed it," Pips gloated. "The Gestapo there wasn't very sophisticated, so they didn't quite know what to do. When they have a case like that, they always shove it off to somebody else."

The three were shipped nearer Berlin to a labor camp for men, where they stayed for two horror-filled days. They witnessed prisoners laden with heavy rocks being beaten, whipped, and kicked. The three young women were clearly out of place in this camp, but what to do with them? Olga, Eva, and Vera were brought to Berlin, where they remained in a small Gestapo prison. Had they not been sent there, they would have ended up in Bergen-Belsen—if they didn't die along the way. That's how they found themselves in Schulstrasse. And there began the saga of Olga and Pips.

CHAPTER 8

LIBERATION

The January 1945 arrival of the trio from Auschwitz caused a stir at Schulstrasse. Nobody had ever seen anyone *returning* from that death camp. Even Dobberke was curious enough to come down from his office to look them over. Pips, too, managed to steal a look. One of the girls, Olga, happened to be exceedingly pretty. But Pips dubbed her *Kugelhopf* because she had a round head.

"We looked at them as if they were from outer space. Everybody felt sorry for the girls. If anyone had something to give to them, a piece of bread or whatever they had, they gave it to them. They felt, these poor girls, what they must have gone through in Auschwitz."

After the excitement died down, the new arrivals were assigned to a room. Because they had only rags, Tatiana, the detainee assigned to Kommando Kanada, gave them some clothes. She immediately took to the girls, especially Olga. Because her looks were so magnetic, it seemed that everyone focused on her.

By then, the American air force was raining bombs and incendiary devices on Berlin every day, and the Brits did the same every night. The British planes couldn't be seen unless they were in the crosshairs of the search lights. But the American planes were visible in the clear daytime skies.

"You could see these tiny silvery things going in perfect formation and, after a while, you would see confetti coming down. After twelve years of living in Nazi Germany—and in ever-increasing measure being hunted psychologically, physically—up there were these men from Mars who came from another world. They were up there, twenty, thirty thousand feet up, and they were not Nazis. They did not belong to our world of Nazi Europe, but they were unreachable. You couldn't lift your arm and grab them, which became particularly significant when the Russians finally came. They were there, on the ground. The Americans felt like a mirage."

Schulstrasse hadn't been hit by any bombs so far, and the incendiaries had posed little threat. But then their luck ran out. Pips and Rehfeld were asleep in beds—a luxury in their prison—in their small attic room. Rehfeld's bed was next to the outer wall and Pips's bed was on the opposite side of the room. The air raid sirens sounded, and Pips should have taken up his post as fire warden. But he was too groggy to get up and Rehfeld was snoring in sweet oblivion under the hat he always wore to bed. Because sirens were a daily occurrence, the urgency to respond had long faded. But on this night, the British dropped an explosive bomb that landed under the roof where Pips and Rehfeld shared a room. Below their small space were the Gestapo offices.

"Suddenly this enormous crash! A bomb shaved off part of the roof. The Gestapo offices were hardly touched because of the angle at which the bomb hit. But it took most of the outside wall of our room. I saw a sight which I will never forget: Rehfeld's head was already outside the wall, and it looked like his bed was tipping over and falling with the wall. Rehfeld's back was covered with debris, but he kept on snoring." Pips tried frantically to wake him. But Rehfeld grumbled, "I'm tired, leave me alone!"—and kept on sleeping.

Pips wasn't as sanguine. "I was in my pants faster than you can blink an eye. I was downstairs in a matter of seconds because, this time, I knew it was no joke! I ran into the bunker where the other prisoners were held until the raid was over. I wasn't quite sure what had happened because it was dark." Pips found his way to the steps, and although they were barely maneuverable after the bombing, he managed to make his way back to his little space. Although there was debris strewn all over the attic, Pips's corner of the room wasn't damaged, and he went back to sleep. Just like Rehfeld.

The next day, Olga's friend, Eva, came to help Pips and Rehfeld clean up. "She could do this much better than we boys, and we didn't want to do it. She came for several days because the room had to practically be dug out. So, she and I became friends right away."

During the day, while Pips did his glaziery, he caught glimpses of Olga around the prison—especially during the daily half hour that inmates were released into the fenced-off exercise yard. He noticed right away that every male under sixty was gawking at her and she was quite conscious of it. He, too, was keenly aware of Olga, but decided not to be too obvious about it. By now, Pips had a reputation as a lothario because of his dalliances with several nurses. He had perfected his techniques for attracting women. Accordingly, Pips opted to arouse Olga's curiosity by making sure that he was visible, while paying no attention at all to her. "*Of all the people, why does this guy not look at me?* Eva told me part of their story and I discreetly inquired about Olga without letting her know that I was particularly interested in her. But Eva was intuitive enough to figure that out. So, she became a sort of go-between for Olga and me, even though we never directly addressed each other."

A couple of weeks went by and Schulstrasse was bombed again.

Several types of bombs were used in air raids. Some bombs detonated as soon as they hit a solid surface. Others detonated seconds after they hit resistance. These were more deadly than the bombs that exploded right away. In this instance, a delayed detonation bomb went right through the main building into the isolation bunker. "There was only one guy in the Schulstrasse isolation bunker, which was separate from the general air raid shelter. The bomb went right into the bunker and blew him to pieces. There was some damage to the building, but it wasn't great. The building stood, mainly because the bomb didn't explode right away. It exploded in the cellar and the explosion was contained by the cellar walls."

Pips began to fall in love with Olga. "I said to myself, wouldn't it be wonderful if she and I could be put into a bunker and live the rest of our lives together undisturbed. That was as far as my fantasy dared to go. I just wanted to be alone with her and make love with her around the clock. But it wasn't a sexual thing as much as me just wanting to be with her. Of course, she knew nothing about that, and I didn't tell Eva either."

The Red Army had crossed the Oder River by early February and tension in the prison grew among the prisoners, the SS, police, and Gestapo. "Latrine parole" had revealed that the Red Army was at the border, although no one in the prison understood why they were stopping there. "We knew for years that the Germans were going to lose the war, but now you could almost touch it. It was just a matter of weeks or days. Whether the Gestapo or the SS were going to let us live to see that day and say hello to the Ruskies, that was the big question. But at least the Third Reich was coming to an end. The twelve years were over. Whether that meant we go into the ditch or we survive, we had no way of knowing. The chances in our minds were still much better that they would mow us down. But why didn't the Russians come?"

As they soon learned, the two-week pause at the Oder was the preparation for the final offensive in what became the Battle of Berlin.

Meanwhile, something else happened. "Olga and I finally got together. We started talking to each other. Given her broken

German, we spoke mostly French. It became very quickly obvious that we were in love with each other. We got to a point where we wanted to get physical and the only place where we could kiss—which was as far as we could go—was in the toilet."

In Auschwitz, inmates were relegated to open air latrines. But Schulstrasse, as part of a hospital, had real toilets. "There was no division between men and women. Every time you went to the toilet, you would hear the farting. But we were past being bothered by such things. So, she and I met in the toilet for our first kiss. Now we knew we belonged together."

It had been two years since Pips had lost Ilse. But Pips was a young man and Olga was a beautiful girl. "It didn't mean that I stopped loving Ilse, but my life was not over."

It was now March, and Dobberke was spending almost every evening playing cards in his office with a couple of doctors from the Jewish Hospital. "Obviously, he was preparing for the end and wanted to soften the blow, so he got chummy with some Jews. He couldn't do it with the prisoners; that would have been too obvious. There was also a strong rumor that he screwed the head nurse in the Jewish Hospital."

At the same time, the Gestapo started wearing uniforms, whereas—except for the top command—they had worn civilian clothes throughout the war. That was because, as a secret police force, they needed to blend into the population. But as the allies advanced, the Gestapo was needed as a fighting force, which meant distinguishing them from civilians.

"Otherwise, nothing much changed. The air raids continued day and night. Then came an amazing day: April 16, 1945. It was early afternoon. The sky was blue, not a cloud in sight. We began to hear faraway rumbling. At first, we thought it was a thunderstorm somewhere. But the thunder didn't stop. In fact, it began to come a little closer, a little louder. Some hours later, it suddenly dawned on us:

this isn't thunder, it's artillery, Russian artillery. You have no idea how that made us feel. I could hear them! I could hear the liberation. I could hear the end of my life, from the age of ten to twenty-two in the Hitler world!"

Despite their elation, Pips and his fellow prisoners gradually started to doze off after midnight. At 6:00 a.m. the next morning, they woke up to the realization that there were no SS or police around.

"I'm sure they had orders to kill us—that was routine."

Indeed, Dobberke was ordered to liquidate the remaining Jews. But he didn't do it. Like his prison guards, he took off—with his rumored mistress, the hospital nurse. But first, hoping to avoid prosecution by the allies, he allegedly made his prisoners sign a statement, attesting that he had spared their lives. The Gestapo had earlier incinerated incriminating documents.

With no one left to stop them, the dazed prisoners drifted to the gate and just walked out.

"For the first time I could remember, I was not in Nazi Europe. However, we weren't off the hook just yet. There were roving bands of SS looking for deserters. Anytime they found somebody on the way home, they shot him. They may not know that Schulstrasse was a Gestapo prison. But if they found out, they would make short shrift of us. The Russians were on the outskirts of Berlin, but not yet where we were in the north. The remnants of the German armies—there was more than one army—were marching through Berlin. But they were not supposed to defend the city; they were supposed to make another stand west of Berlin. Most of them got stuck in Berlin anyway.

"Hitler and his entourage were in the *Führerbunker*, which was about two miles away, but we didn't know that. There were still bombings by the British and Americans for another few days. Russian artillery of all calibers hit us, but nothing serious. The streets were full of shrapnel. Then Russian planes came to support the ground troops. I'd never seen Russian planes during the whole war. Now they came very low and machine-gunned everything that moved in the streets. We went back to the cellar because that was the only place that was halfway safe. But the water was now shut off and we had no food. The days dragged on, so a couple of fellows and I volunteered to find something edible."

They found a pile of turnips, of which they had eaten plenty swimming around in watery soups throughout their incarceration. "We had it up to here with turnips, but the only thing we had to eat now were turnips, raw turnips for a change." The volunteers brought arms full of turnips into the cellar for its hundred occupants to eat, but they still needed water. Berlin had tall pumps on alternate street corners from the days of horse carriages. Equipped with buckets, the former prisoners ventured out to the pumps.

That was tricky because it meant going out to the street with machine guns firing and shrapnel flying. When they got to a pump, which was a block away, a crowd was already gathered there, standing in line for water. "Because the water works had closed, nobody had water, not even the Germans. Once in line, some of the people would be killed right in front of our noses, and we stepped over their bodies, to get closer to the pump. We ran back and forth to the cellar with the full buckets and had to do this about once a day. We found some tinny air raid warden helmets. But we were warned not to wear them because we would be mistaken for soldiers 'and the Russians will make a special point of firing at you.'"

The Soviets came closer and closer to Schulstrasse. Pips and a couple of his fellows went on the roof of the army hospital that had recently been set up in the Jewish hospital. From that aerie, they could spot the Russians. "It was a fascinating sight. We saw them from a distance—it was the first time we saw them and didn't just hear them. We could see the tanks, fighting vehicles, even regular automobiles. They used everything they could find, racing back and forth and firing like mad. But it took about a week for the Russians to reach our place."

More than two million Soviets, coming from all directions, were deployed to Berlin for the final battle. "Can you imagine what an army that was? And the Germans had close to a million to defend, so it was a very spirited time. Of course, the closer the Russians came, the more intense became the fire from both sides. As the German machine guns started opening up, it was pretty hairy. But we were euphoric!"

The cellar was dark. The Jews didn't have light of any kind. Whatever candles they might have found had long since burned out. But some people still had matches. "In this pitch-dark cellar, I suddenly hear a big commotion a few feet away. Somebody lit a match, and I saw a Russian soldier surrounded by Jewish prisoners. He was pretty filthy, but they kissed him and hugged him. The poor fellow had no idea what this was about. He thought he was in a nut house, and I could see how panic-stricken he was. He was alone with a hundred people converging on him. A short while later, the first unit arrived, one of many thousands. They had field artillery and howitzers, which several men pushed manually. They set up their little cannon in our now open gateway and fired point-blank across the street into the German machine gun."

The free residents of Schulstrasse emerged from their cellar and saw a dozen Soviet soldiers. "Young fellows, red-cheeked, smiling, having a wonderful time, firing their submachine guns. We came up behind them and they looked at us and didn't know what to make of us. As we came closer, a couple of boys and I had piled up ammunition for the camp and we felt we had to do something to help them. They must have thought we were Germans, but we're helping them. They fired the cannon by pulling on a string and after we saw that a couple of times, we used sign language to indicate that we wanted to pull the strings—to get at least one lick in."

The Jews jubilantly shot the cannon a few times and felt the joy of payback coursing through them. A couple of hours later, the Germans across the street had been cleared out and the Reds moved on.

"This little group had been an advance group, and now came the bulk of the field armies, swarming all over the place. Marvelous! Vera and a few others spoke Russian. We found an officer and started to explain who we were. The one thing I had learned to say in Russian was '*Ya yevrey*,' which means 'I am a Jew.' (Then I learned a few other Russian words like '*trakhni tvoyu mat*,' meaning 'fuck your mother,' which was used all the time; '*khleb,*' bread; and for me, the all-important '*sigarety*,' for cigarettes.)"

The officer told the eager crowd to wait for the imminent arrival of the NKVD—secret police—to explain their situation. "Then came a few officers who were introduced to us as political commissars from the NKVD. One or two of them were Jews. We could speak to them in German because they spoke Yiddish."

A hospital representative explained that Schulstrasse was a prison camp for Jews. The Soviets were stunned. They were aware of the industrial scale massacre of Jews and that the Third Reich had declared Berlin *judenrein*. The Soviets couldn't believe that there were any Jews left. *"Nichts Juden. Juden kaput!"* declared one of the first on the scene. But there were, in fact, about 8,000 Jewish survivors, most from mixed marriages, and another 1,700 who were in hiding.

"Many of the Russians had never seen a Jew, didn't know what a Jew was. They came from Kazakhstan, Uzbekistan, Eastern Siberia. Some were Muslims. Some were from the Caucasus, Tartars, Georgians. The political guys started interrogating us, wanting to know who was in command here. We gave them the names of Dobberke and others. The next day, the front again began to move slowly, street by street, further into the interior of the city. When

Eisenhower had considered conquering Berlin, he and Bradley figured it would cost a hundred thousand men dead to conquer Berlin. And they were right on the button. The Russians later announced that they had lost a hundred thousand. And we were smack in the middle of the damned thing, but we were ecstatic. We were free!"

Now came the second wave of Soviets. These were supply units and reinforcements. They were much more unruly than the front troops, which were very disciplined, primed only to fight. "But these guys didn't fight. They set up field kitchens and looked around to see what there was to take. And slowly the raping began." It is estimated that at least one hundred thousand German women were raped in Berlin. "Many were raped by three or four guys. There were cases of Russian soldiers, twenty years old, who raped eighty-year-old women. What they saw in them I don't know. It was just a matter of principle: the enemy had to be raped to establish their power and revenge. The German women tried to hide and blacken their faces with ashes to make themselves look ugly. But the Russians weren't particular. These guys hadn't seen a woman for God knows how long. They had come all the way from the Volga to Berlin, into the lair of the beast. Now was their last chance to get their licks in and the raping went on and on. What they didn't do, which we had fully expected them to do, was to kill everybody in sight. They killed nobody, unless they were fighting. And when they teased children, they gave them chocolate or a piece of bread. They loved children. That was completely different from what the Germans had feared. Germans were sure that they would mow them down, every one of them.

"One of the things they coveted were watches. They said to anybody who passed *'Uri, davai'*—*davai* means "give me" and we saw some of them with watches up and down their arm, ten, fifteen, twenty watches. Some of these people came from wild areas—the middle of Turkmenistan, or Baluchistan or Central Asia. They had never seen a toilet. They thought it was for washing potatoes; they had some potatoes and threw them into the toilet and then flushed. Another thing was the love of alcohol. Practically all the Slavs were big drinkers and they didn't have enough vodka in their supplies, so they liberated drug stores that had cologne and drank that. They were so used to alcohol it didn't hurt them. Their stomachs were like iron."

The NKVD men declared Schulstrasse off limits. They hung warning signs and posted soldiers to guard the Jews so they wouldn't be bothered. But when the remnant went outside, they were vulnerable.

One day, Pips looked around for Olga and Eva and didn't see them. Someone noticed that they had gone out of the gate. In dread, Pips ran out into the street. "There was more steel in the air than oxygen. I ran around the next corner and there they were, the two of them, Olga and Vera. It was a beautiful April day, and they were having a little promenade, enjoying the spring air. Overhead, Soviet planes were firing like crazy. With the artillery and the machine guns, it was total chaos. And they were oblivious. I ran up to them and dragged them back into the cellar. They didn't understand what I was so nervous about."

A day or two later, Pips and another resident took Olga and Eva out for a walk in the hospital yard. They strolled for a few minutes, but Soviet soldiers were everywhere. Two drove up with a horse cart, tommy guns slung across their backs. They took one look at the girls and grabbed them. Pips and his chum yelled, "Act sick!" Olga and Eva started moaning and groaning and the Russians didn't know what to make of it. "In desperation, I became a hero for a moment. I grabbed Olga and Eva away from the Soviets. The Soviets were swearing and screaming and wouldn't let them go. But I couldn't let something happen to them, so I managed to pull them away and the other fellow came forward and also started pulling. The Soviets finally let go, waving their machine guns at us and threatening us with holy murder. Of course, we didn't understand a word. But we got the girls back and to the relative safety of the prison."

Pips admonished Olga to stay put in the prison. Obediently, she contented herself to sit by the window—or the hole in the wall that passed for a window—and look out. Wanting to be friendly, she smiled at the Soviets teeming all around. "They took this for an invitation, thinking this was some kind of whorehouse. They wanted to come in and were just barely held back by the signs and the couple of guards that had been posted."

Pips ran into the room where Olga was sitting and warned her not to smile. "By a hair's breadth, I managed to save the girls from being raped."

Then came May Day, the day to celebrate workers and showcase Soviet military might. A few blocks from Schulstrasse, there was an electrical factory with battery-powered carts. The soldiers commandeered the carts and careened up and down the streets. Directly across from the former prison, an entire block lay in ruins. But one house stood intact. "In order to have a real celebration, they set fire to that house, and it burned like crazy. They danced in the street and had a wonderful time. We had to watch, because if the wind changed, the fire might come over to us."

Even before the Gestapo left, Pips, along with a few other men and women, had moved into the room where Olga, Eva, and Vera were housed. The room had only mattresses, but they now managed to bring in a couple of beds and some big European duvets from the abandoned Gestapo quarters.

"We had not known privacy for years and were not particularly shy about parading in front of the girls naked. When I undressed, the girls fell into hysterical laughter because I had layer upon layer upon layer of clothes on. I had three pullovers on, and each pullover had a big hole. But the three together made one complete pullover. I had newspapers stuffed under the sweaters because, even though it was already spring, I was still cold. I weighed only about a hundred pounds; I was skin and bones."

Olga and Pips had started sleeping together.

"Sex didn't work out too well because she was a virgin. I wasn't all that experienced with virgins, except that Ilse had been a virgin, and it took a few days to penetrate. Olga was totally innocent and childlike, but I didn't rape her."

That evening, a horde of Soviets showed up at the door of their room with a load of vodka and a gramophone. Already a bit drunk, they saw the women and were ready to party. They turned on the gramophone and wanted to dance.

"The moment they came in, I put Olga under a feather bed, so she wasn't visible. Just behind the rowdy Soviets were two Jewish officers. One of them said in Yiddish, which of course the other officers didn't understand, 'Get out of here. Once they really get drunk, there's no telling what they might do. They don't mean you harm, but they're wild.' One of us said to him, 'Can't they go into another room so we can stay here?' He said, 'They won't go upstairs because the German artillery is still firing. You go upstairs.' So, we went. I had to take Olga, and I didn't want them to see her, so I grabbed one side of the feather bed with the sheet underneath. Thinking it was only a feather bed, the Yiddish speaker wanted to help. 'My God, how heavy that thing is!' So, we went upstairs and bedded down, and the Russians had to have a party without us. They didn't come after us, but we heard their hollering and laughing and dancing.

"Outside, the whole city looked like one mass of fire. It was so lit up, the night was like day. There was chaos on every street, dead animals, burned out vehicles, dead bodies burned in tanks."

On April 30, Hitler committed suicide. On May 2, Berlin's depleted garrison surrendered. The war ended on May 7 with Germany's surrender in Reims, France. A second signing took place in Berlin on May 9.

For the Soviets, conquering Berlin was the ultimate prize. Getting there before the Americans or the British was their key to gaining control of Eastern Europe.

"For two or three weeks, total chaos reigned. Here is a major city—the capital of Germany, which in normal times had a population of four million people—without any law and order. No police, no military patrols, nothing. Everybody could do anything they wanted to—or anything they could get away with. That goes for the civilians as well as for the Red Army soldiers. Everybody looted. Everybody stole from everybody. They went into the factories where there were still stores of goods. They went into the banks, broke open the safety deposit boxes. As I walked into one of those banks, there were millions of Deutsche Marks strewn around. They figured if the bills had swastikas on them, they wouldn't have any value, so nobody bothered. Then they went into the villas on the outskirts and took away Persian carpets, chandeliers. They felt it was their right, and I felt it was their right. They conquered this bastard who had burned half their country and killed twenty million people, so both Russians and Germans looted in perfect harmony, shoulder to shoulder, except that the Russians could afford to take heavier things because they had trucks to cart them away. The Soviet high command gave them free rein for a couple of weeks; after that, finished. It was a time of total freedom, total chaos, total anarchy, wild. And for us who had been under the thumb of the Nazi regime for twelve years, this was unbelievable."

Pips and his fellow inmates looked for Jewish officers among the Soviet soldiers. Most were found among the higher ranks. These were the only ones from whom they expected a little help. But you couldn't go up to a Russian officer, as a German civilian, and ask, "Are you a Jew?" That might be perceived as an insult. But if they suspected that he was a Jew, they would go up to that officer and test out some Yiddish. If the officer was Jewish, he would react; if not, he wouldn't understand.

Sometime in the summer of 1945, Olga and Pips went with another half-Jew and his girlfriend to swim in one of the many lakes that surround Berlin. It was in the Russian sector, and they stayed in a tent on the beach overnight. The next morning, Pips noticed a middle-aged Russian couple sitting nearby whom he sensed were Jews. He ambled over to find out. "The Germans didn't generally approach the Russians. They were cocky but not that cocky. So here I march right up to them and said, 'Am chai.' They understood, and they spoke Yiddish, so I could speak to them. I told them who we were and what we had gone through, and they told us they were in the occupation army and were going to stay there for a while. He was a colonel and she was a major, so they were high-ranking guys. We parted good friends, and he gave me his telephone number. He said, 'If you can find a phone give us a ring and we'll get together.' We hoped they would come up with cigarettes and food, and he brought us some food. Then they invited us to dinner. The area where they lived was closed off with fences and there was a gate with Russian sentries. She said, 'I'm going to meet you at the gate at six o'clock, and I'm going to tell them that you are my cousins, so keep your mouth shut.' She met us and took us to their apartment—small, but nice. Of course, Germans had lived there before. She had cooked borscht and some meat—a real healthy and strong meal, better than what we had seen in many a moon. We ate to our heart's content and drank a little vodka. They treated us like you would treat dinner guests. We managed to converse quite well. They asked us what we planned to do in the future, and we said we wanted to get out of Germany as soon as possible and go to America. 'But it's not that easy,' they countered. "You have a wait list number and you don't even live in the American sector where people got preference.' They said, 'Look, if you ever have to wait, why don't you come the other way? Why don't you come to the Soviet Union?' We almost choked. The last place we wanted to go was the Soviet Union. We politely declined the invitation.

"They didn't think being Jewish held a special significance, which made me want to probe a bit. 'You both picked a Jewish partner to get married and I don't believe this was a coincidence. Also, the moment I came to you as a total stranger and identified myself to you as a Jew, you didn't say, go away. You took us into your arms practically. Why? Not because of any other reason except that we were Jews. So don't tell me that you had no Jewish feelings left.' I wanted to prove to them that their negation, their standoffishness about being Jewish, was only skin-deep. Down at the bottom, they're still Jews, and they finally sort of admitted it."

Another highly educated, middle-aged colonel ventured into Schulstrasse speaking perfect German. He took one look at Olga, lying in bed, and was deeply affected. He sat at her bedside and stroked her hair in a fatherly way, speaking to her partly in French and partly in German. Noticing that she had only rags to wear, he sent an aide de camp to find some clothes for her. That didn't mean buying them; it meant liberating them, which was what everybody was doing. A couple of hours later, the aide came back and proudly displayed what he had brought. "We were peeing in our pants, laughing our heads off, and the colonel did, too. He came with the two things that Olga needed the most at that moment: an evening gown and a bathing suit. But she did wear the gown. She cut off the long part of the evening gown and used that for handkerchiefs."

The starving ex-prisoners were hoping that the Soviets would give them some food. A few did, but the food they offered was mostly lard. "Our stomachs hadn't made the acquaintance of fat for so long that we got queasy."

It wasn't the only food that starving stomachs could no longer accommodate. Pips spotted a crowd of Germans and Russians running through a factory gate and milling around. Pips walked over there, assuming there must be something worth stealing. It turned out to be a winery and the cellar shelves held millions of wine bottles.

"In their greed to get the stuff, they tore the racks off and the bottles would fall on the floor. Some Germans had gotten so drunk, they couldn't stand up anymore and drowned floating in the wine. That was probably their idea of a perfect death. The smell of the wine was overpowering. There was nothing else, so I grabbed a couple of bottles and got the hell out of there. It was the last thing we needed."

Pips and his cronies also discovered a condensed milk factory with bottles of a strange fatty concoction. "We grabbed as much as we could because it had some nourishment. We drank that stuff out of a bottle and almost all of us got sick. Our stomachs weren't used to fat."

The home of Pips's youth was no longer recognizable. Half of all residential buildings were damaged or uninhabitable. Four thousand acres of Berlin were reduced to rubble. Twenty blocks in any direction from the city center were destroyed. But the seeds of a new life had begun with Olga's arrival at Schulstrasse.

CHAPTER 9

LIFE IN A DP CAMP AND AN INTERREGNUM BETWEEN LIVES

The Battle of Berlin had finally ceased, but fires were still burning three weeks later. There was a network of three thousand forced labor camps in Berlin. By the time of Germany's surrender, there were still thirty-seven thousand slave laborers in the city. "Now a great exodus began. Many forced laborers from Western Europe wanted to get home. The Eastern Europeans were not that anxious to get back. They were afraid of what might happen to them in the Communist countries to which they would return, and some of them were collaborators with the Germans."

Among these were 1.5 million Soviet POWs who had volunteered to work for the Germans—as drivers, cooks, front-line soldiers, and enforcers in extermination camps. These collaborationist Soviet soldiers were an essential cog in the wheel that perpetrated the Holocaust. Many took on these roles to escape the atrocities Germany committed against POWs. Others did it in opposition to their Communist government. Whatever the motivation, it would have been foolhardy for them to return to the USSR.

Schulstrasse was no longer a prison. It was now a displaced persons camp, and it was Olga and Pips's temporary home. Olga still wore the tattered coat with the red stripe down the back. "At that time, it didn't matter. A red stripe or anything that denoted her as an ex-prisoner was nothing to be ashamed of."

In the face of mass repatriation, it was now time for Olga, Eva, and Vera to consider their futures. There was nothing left for them in Hungary, except painful memories of loss. They decided to make Paris the first stop in their new lives. Packing up their sparse belongings, they prepared to board a train under the auspices of the United Nations Relief and Rehabilitation Administration, a newly established agency to support victims of war.

Olga hesitated. "I was standing there and Olga looked at me. I didn't say anything. I was very, very sad but I didn't beg her to stay. If Olga stayed, that meant that we would get married. I was torn between my desire to have Olga stay with me—I loved her—and my feeling that maybe, by some miracle, Ilse would come back. Then what? Two wives? That was why I didn't encourage Olga, and she took my silence for great sensitivity, not begging her to stay with me for my own selfish reasons. That was partly true, but only partly. I never told her what actually went through my mind at that moment."

But Pips did share other memories related to Ilse. "Olga was not my first great love. I never said it in so many words, but she knew that I loved Ilse very much. She knew that I went underground with Ilse without needing to, that I was arrested with Ilse, and that I'd made Ilse pregnant. When I told Olga about it, she would tighten up."

Olga had known Pips for only a short time and knew very little about him. She had heard from other prisoners that Pips was a no-good ladies' man. But another factor had also given her pause: She hated the idea of staying in Germany and letting go of her best friend, Eva, to enter a totally uncertain future with a near stranger.

"She found herself in Berlin, the capital of the German Reich that had invaded her home, killed her mother, killed her family, sent her to Auschwitz. She found herself living in the heart of the enemy's country, in a city that was in a state of ruination, surrounded by Germans, hearing nothing but German all day long, having to communicate in German. She was a fish out of water." Still, Olga stayed.

Eva implored in Hungarian, "Olga, are you sure you want to stay?" But nineteen-year-old Olga had made up her mind. With that, Olga gave up Eva, the last connection to her previous life. She and Pips bade a difficult farewell to someone who had become a dear friend to both. "I had already fallen in love with Eva, not as an erotic object, but because she was a wonderful friend. And I've loved her ever since."

Eva boarded a train with American soldiers standing guard. The train wound its way through the Soviet zone out of Berlin. "It was an adventure to get to Paris, and it probably took the better part of a week. Many of the railroad bridges were down. Sometimes the soldiers, just to get a little exercise, walked next to the train. That's how slowly the train moved in certain spots.

"So, Eva and Vera left. Olga was now stuck with me."

After the war, as the protective cocoon wore off for the survivors, the mourning started. "We didn't allow ourselves to mourn while we were still at the edge of death. Once the Soviets came in and people were liberated, many Jews committed suicide because now it sank in with full force. It hit us all tremendously, and Olga especially, since she knew she would never see her hometown again. And if she did, there would be no one there who had made up her life. She had a tough time."

And Pips was now responsible for taking care of her.

Pips came across a Russian soldier, whom he was certain was a Cossack. "I wasn't afraid of Russians at all, even a Cossack. Of course, I didn't tell him I was a Jew, I could have said '*Ya yevrey*,' but with a Cossack you don't do that. The Cossacks have a long history of killing Jews."

The most famous restaurant in Berlin was Horcher, which during the war was restricted to Nazi bosses, serving food that was exempt from wartime rationing—pâté, foie gras, game meats, the finest champagnes, cognacs, and Armagnac from France. Knowing of the Russian passion for alcohol, Pips reasoned that there must be some leftovers in the Horcher wine cellar. The Cossack had a tiny truck-like car. Through makeshift interpreters, Pips told the Cossack that he could find him some great booze at Horcher, but he would need a ride there. Pips assured him that he was interested only in the food and the Cossack could have all the alcohol he wanted, if it was there. The Cossack was skeptical at first, but Pips convinced him to take a flyer.

"I went into the car with him, and it was very complicated getting there because all the bridges over the river had been blasted by the Germans before the Reds came. We managed to get there in a roundabout way, ending up in the neighborhood where I used to live. The whole Hocher building was on the sidewalk, destroyed. That didn't deter me. We cleared away debris and found the cellar, but it was a big washout. Someone beat us to the wine. And I didn't do much better. There was no real food at all. The only thing I found was a small barrel with ice cream powder. The Cossack was mad as hell, but he drove me back. When I got back, I liberated a spoon, and we all started eating this stuff."

A few days later, a cow bizarrely came ambling down the street. It dawned on the starving prisoners that this was food! While the idea of killing an animal was repugnant to them, they couldn't pass up the opportunity. But how to kill a cow? Pips and his pals convinced a Russian soldier to shoot the cow and promised him a piece. "Sure enough, the guy takes out a revolver and shoots the poor thing's brains out and it falls. Now came the next project: How do you get to the meat? Cutting up a cow requires sharp knives, and we had no carving knives. All we had were regular dinner knives that we had liberated from the Gestapo or the hospital. Two or three guys started to saw away. We knew nothing about getting through the hide and we worked until the sweat was running down. We worked and worked and sawed away and made hardly a dent. The Russian soldier stood there waiting for his piece. After a couple of hours, he walked away. It must have taken a day or more of very hard labor to get the hide off that poor thing and then to carve it into pieces. We took the pieces across the street to the prison and found a pot. There was no gas or electricity, but we made a bonfire in the yard and started cooking that thing. For two weeks, we ate the poor cow—the first meat we had seen in years. We didn't have salt or anything else to go with it, but we ate the cow, and it was delicious!"

Pips then had a visit at the prison from a thirty-year-old man who introduced himself as the fiancé of his cousin, Irmgard. Her mother, Pips's aunt, had died of cancer a year or two before, and Irmgard lived nearby and knew that Pips was in Schulstrasse. "I don't know how she came to that. Maybe it was just a shot in the dark because it was the only place where you could find some Jews. It turned out her fiancé was a *Mischling*, but of Christian religion. He was a doctor and told us how they survived the onslaught. Irmgard used ashes from the stove so she looked ugly and put on old crap for clothes so the Russians wouldn't rape her. I told Olga that she was so homely, she needed no ashes. But we offered our guest some ice cream powder. He ate a couple of spoons full and then just couldn't eat another thing. Of course, they were much better fed than we were."

It was now spring—a month after liberation—and the time had come to look for a place to live. "As cozy as Schulstrasse was, it was no place to hang your hat." The two fake cheese merchants, whom Pips had earlier warned away from Schulstrasse, now showed up with their girlfriends. They, too, were searching for a place to settle. They had in mind Erkner, a lower middle-class suburb in the District of Brandenburg, southeast of Berlin, where they guessed there would be good pickings. "A lot of homes that were still standing were empty because a great number of Berliners fled to Hamburg or Bremen or Frankfurt before the Soviets came in. They were afraid the Soviets would slit their throats from end to end."

For Pips, who had always lived in west or southwest Berlin, it was alien territory. But the sixsome agreed to meet a couple of miles from Schulstrasse to venture together to Erkner. Of course, there was no transportation. "Olga and I set out early in the morning. A few blocks away was one of Berlin's major arteries. There, as far as the eye could see, were horse-drawn wagons going eastward—thousands of them loaded with furniture, carpets, anything you could imagine. We heard that some of the more primitive Soviet boys took unscrewed light bulbs because they figured that the light is in the bulb and by taking bulbs, they would have electrical light at home. Some of them tried to take toilets, too."

Olga, with her small feet, was never a good walker. After a half hour of trudging alongside the caravan, she complained that her feet hurt. Using sign language, the couple gamely tried to thumb a ride. One of the wagons rolled to a stop and Pips helped Olga on to the bench. But when Pips tried to climb up, the seemingly congenial driver took off without him.

"He wanted Olga but not me. It was quite obvious what he had in mind. I may never see her again. She may end up somewhere in Ukraine with this guy! I ran next to the wagon. Boy, did I run! I didn't want to lose track of them, and I kept yelling to Olga: 'Act sick, act sick, do something!' Sure enough, she started moaning, groaning and grabbing his arm and making all kinds of faces. Finally, this guy figured this is no good. That was a close shave, but it worked," just as it had with her earlier encounter with Soviet soldiers.

Now Olga had to go back to trekking again. She and Pips met up with their friends at the appointed place. The other couples had with them wooden children's carts. Pips had the bright idea that Olga could sit in one of the carts and be pulled to Erkner. "The rest of the day, we spent walking eleven miles to Erkner with Olga sitting in the cart like a queen."

The house hunters arrived in Erkner just as it got dark. They came across an empty house. Although it had no electricity, they plunked themselves down to a makeshift meal, made up largely of the ubiquitous ice cream powder Pips had secured earlier. Afterward, exhausted, they stretched out and went to sleep. The next morning, in the light of day, they noticed that they were in the living room of a small house. They roamed around the house to see whether they might find something to eat or to pilfer. They opened the door to the bedroom and were confronted with a gruesome sight: a man and woman of late middle age, dead of suicide and already putrefying the air. This squelched their appetite for that house, and although they looked at some other houses, nothing appealed to Olga and Pips after their encounter with the corpses. As for the others, "They were more easygoing and from a lower social class, so they were less snobbish than we were. We decided to go back to prison and try something else."

The others stayed behind, along with their carts. So how would Olga manage the walk back? Pips found a bicycle in good working order, except for one minor detail: it had no tires, only rims. Pips directed Olga to sit on the bar. "She sat down on that thing and thank goodness she had a well-upholstered behind. Since I was a terrific bicyclist—for me, bicycling is an extension of my body—I had no trouble riding that tireless bicycle for ten miles on pock-marked streets."

On the way, the riders encountered clusters of Soviets who scanned the bicycle. But when they looked more closely and saw that it had no tires, they lost interest. "If that thing had had tires we would have lost it in no time."

Olga and Pips were then stopped by some Polish soldiers manning a roadblock. "We didn't know whether we should let them think we're Germans or Jews. We knew they hate Germans, but almost all Poles hate Jews, too. They spoke a little German from the good old days when they were occupied by the Germans, so we managed to get through and go back to the Schulstrasse."

With the Erkner debacle behind them, Olga and Pips focused on Berlin for their house hunting. "I couldn't go into the neighborhood where we used to live in Münchener Strasse. That was destroyed. Even in the middle of the street, you walked over mountains of debris, bricks, wooden beams—everything was mixed in. It was a total no-man's land. But not too far from there was the Kurfürstendamm, which was, in prewar times, the Champs-Élysées of Berlin. I thought, if I must pick, I may as well try that."

Getting there was a problem. Schulstrasse was in northern Berlin, close to the edge of the city. The Kurfürstendamm was in southwestern Berlin. The bridges were down, and many roads were impassable. Some street signs were still there, such as Grosse Hamburger Strasse. Pips had discarded his bicycle, realizing that it was impractical to ride it in Berlin's rubble-choked streets. On foot, the trip to Kurfürstendamm took three hours. The only food he had to sustain him through his daily excursions was the ice cream powder, with which he had filled his pockets. When he got hungry, he dug down and swallowed a fistful.

The first few times he ventured to Kurfürstendamm, he found nothing and returned to Schulstrasse empty-handed. Going back there one day, he wandered through the Tiergarten, near Brandenburg Gate. With its lush trees mostly fallen, it looked as if a hurricane had decimated Berlin's central park. About five hundred yards west of Brandenburg Gate, he spied a group of people working at the edge of the thoroughfare, surrounded by Soviet soldiers. As Pips walked by, one of the soldiers motioned him over. He took Pips across the street to where the men were working and handed him a shovel. Pips quickly realized that the Soviets had rounded up a couple of hundred Germans and given them shovels, spades, and pick axes with which to dig a hole to lay the foundation of a battle monument to the Red Army's great victory over the city of Berlin.

"I said to myself, damn it, I don't want to work shoulder to shoulder with Germans. I'm an ally and should be treated like one. It was more a matter of principle than anything else. I saw an officer. I went up to him and told him '*Ya yevrey*,' I'm a Jew, and I don't want to work here. I have to go back to the prison and my wife is expecting me.' Sure enough, I got out of that one. He told me to 'Get going' in Russian."

On another excursion, Pips came to a plaza right off the Kurfürstendamm. There, he came across an apartment block arrayed around a large rubble-filled court. "It was built twenty years before in imitation of American buildings, which didn't mean skyscrapers; it meant low houses, three or four stories tall. They didn't have gas; they only had electric kitchen appliances, which was the *dernier cri*. Most of the people who lived there were somewhat Bohemian—not your average citizen. Rumor had it that orgies and wife-swapping had gone on in this place."

Despite the debris, these buildings were still habitable, at least on the lower floors. Pips spotted a door six steps above the ground floor. It was blocked, but he shoved it open and found himself in a one-room apartment with a large living room and an alcove separated by a filthy, half-burned curtain concealing the sleeping area. It was obvious that the former residents had fled and were unable to take their furniture but took everything else. Pips peeked in the alcove and saw a big splotch of blood on the wallpaper. Other than someone having been shot there, the place was in pretty good shape. A couch and coffee table made it serviceable. There was a big window with the glass blown out. But it was late spring, and the weather was warm, so who needed glass anyway?

"I figured, okay, let's make that our home. This was a time when you just took possession of whatever was available. The problem was how to move in as quickly as possible before someone else came along and took possession."

Pips returned to Schulstrasse and excitedly shared his news with Olga. They decided to move the very next day but needed to find essentials to make the apartment livable. They scrounged mattresses from the hospital, the bed from Pips's little attic above the Gestapo offices, pots, pans, blankets. The Gestapo had set up a room for those times when officers had to stay overnight. From there, Pips grabbed big feather beds and pillows. He also took a shaving brush that had belonged to a Gestapo officer. "One of my few souvenirs from the good old days." Pips went on to use that brush for the rest of his life.

They couldn't transport the housekeeping booty on their own. A former Jewish inmate, who was still at Schulstrasse and had a little money, offered to help. He knew a German with a horse and wagon and paid him to come the next day and pick up the "liberated" household goods and transport them to Olga and Pips's new home.

"We unloaded our stuff, set up housekeeping, and settled in our own apartment. There was no talk about leases or landlords, no authority. We wouldn't have recognized German authority anyway. There was only one major problem—we had nothing to eat. We had no meat left from the cow we'd slaughtered. Aside from the remainder of the ice cream powder, turnips were all we had. We had to cook the turnips. We had a pot, but I had to go two blocks to pump water with which to cook. We couldn't cook in the apartment because there was no electricity. So, we did what everyone else did: we built a little fire on the sidewalk. There were a lot of fires with people cooking their food, except most of the others had much more food than we did. The second day, a woman peered out the window and asked, 'Is this all you have to eat?' And we explained that we had just come out of the prison and had nothing else. She and her brother brought us some vegetables and introduced themselves. They said they were half-Jews but not of the Jewish religion, which meant they had been left alone during the war."

During the following weeks, Pips managed to find a filthy, broken-down bicycle. Unlike his previous ride, this one had tires. But he had to now make a serious effort to look for food. The only way to get enough was via the post-war black market, through people who knew each other and had something to either buy or sell. Pips contacted the Zeitmans, who had been his fellow prisoners, and Max Koppel, who had helped him with money, ration cards, and a place to stay while he was in hiding. Now Pips again found himself engaged in a form of trading that he hated and at which he was never very successful. "I was on the lowest rung of the ladder as far as business acumen goes, and commerce of any kind was not my cup of tea. But because we were so hungry and had to eat, I became a sort of go-between for the people I knew."

In August 1945, the Allies carved Berlin into four sectors. Olga and Pips found themselves in the British sector. "To our disappointment, the Allies—particularly the British and the Americans—didn't show any interest in us as survivors or feel any obligation to treat us differently from other civilians. You were either a civilian or a soldier, there was no other distinction. That was a terrible blow to us. Whenever we had any contact with the Americans and the British, we demanded to be recognized as allies. They looked at us like we were crazy. We were bitter because we had fantasized that these were the angels who had come on their wings to liberate us."

Yet, there were instances in which British or American soldiers wanted to be photographed with a pretty *Fräulein*. Olga had several offers to pose in exchange for a few cigarettes, which she brought home to Pips.

"Since I was always desperate for a smoke, I would often walk behind a soldier, usually an American, who was smoking on the street and wait until he threw the cigarette away. I never stopped being amazed that they smoked the cigarette only half-way through and just threw it away. I would pick up the cigarette, still burning. In some cases, I just smoked it to the end right there or I put it out and collected tobacco to roll my own cigarettes at home from the left-over cigarette butts."

Another source of wonder was the enormous size of American military automobiles. "We had seen no private automobiles for years, and the few that we did see after the war were Volkswagens."

By summer, chaos ceased, and the Soviet occupation brought some order. They enlisted Germans because they needed a civil administration for the city. German police, operating under the auspices of the Soviets, were retained to keep the civilians in check. The Soviets restarted the electric works, gas works, and water works. They opened the spigots and food flowed into Berlin from the countryside. There were small quantities of butter, bread, and meat to be had, even sardines imported from Norway.

"One could actually survive without the black market. And these foodstuffs were sold at normal prices, not the kind of prices you paid at the black market. Cigarettes were not available, which for me was quite uncomfortable, but I somehow managed."

The food was accessed by way of five categories of ration cards. Non-workers got the lowest ration card; white collar workers got the next lowest. Those who did the heaviest physical labor got the best ration cards, with the most food—as did Hitler's former victims.

Although German Holocaust victims may not have been treated as allies in personal encounters, official actions did recognize them as a distinct category. ID cards were issued in four languages to victims of fascism, i.e., former concentration camp inmates and prisoners. "We were allowed certain benefits, one of which was not having to stand in line. There were queues lined up at every store and you had to wait an hour or two to get whatever your ration card allowed. We were allowed to go ahead of the queue, which we tried once or twice. Each time, we barely escaped being beaten up. The Germans were so furious: 'How do they dare getting ahead of us in the line? The Jews again, always pushing themselves ahead, always taking advantage.' And the constant refrain: '*Wir haben auch gelitten*,' we suffered, too. The invective was so vile, they made it impossible for us to skip the line. We felt we had every right to go to the head of the line, but we didn't dare."

Churchill said before a joint session of the US Congress in May 1943: "The Hun is always either at your throat or at your feet."

"That was very true. When the Soviets first came during this interval of chaos, they raped a lot. The Germans were afraid of the Soviets. Then they noticed that the Russians were not bent on the kind of revenge they might have taken. They were the victors, but when law and order started up again, normalcy of some kind returned. Now the Germans were no longer crawling."

There was electricity for cooking and to turn on the lights at night. But the power came on only during certain hours. One had to schedule oneself so as not to miss the flow of electricity. Consumption was limited to a small number of kilowatts per month, which was checked on a meter. "We did go beyond it, partly because we felt we did not want to live up to the German rules, but also because our block was unique in that you had no gas; we had to cook electrically. That was originally meant to be a great convenience, but for us it meant we had to go above the ration for electricity."

A couple of months after Olga and Pips moved in, a man appeared who introduced himself as the general manager of the entire development. He advised them that, since they had been living there, it was time to pay rent. In black market terms, the amount was the equivalent of one pack of cigarettes. But Pips was furious. "How dare this fucking German tell us we had to pay rent? The least they could do was let us live in these half-destroyed apartments. I told him to go to hell and then he threatened to sic the police on us. I told him I'm going to get the Russians after you. After a month or so, I gave in—it was not worth the fight and I paid the fee."

During this time, Pips and his mother exchanged letters, even though the mail was unreliable. From those, the mother learned that her son was planning to marry a girl from Auschwitz. Wanting to see her son, her Aryan friends, and her future daughter-in-law, she came from Gera for an extended visit in the fall of 1945. She insisted on staying with the young couple, taking over the couch that was separated from the sleeping alcove by only a flimsy curtain. "We were young honeymooners. We had a lot of sex. And we couldn't do it with my mother just twenty feet away.

"I never really got along with my mother. We loved each other but we also hated each other. It didn't take any time at all for me to get into arguments with her. From the very beginning, she resented Olga."

Marie had assumed that she would have her son back after the war. Now the end of the war had come, and he had instead taken up with Olga, who was not even a German, and Maria felt left out in the cold.

"As soon as we started talking about Olga's experiences in Auschwitz, my mother came up with a magic phrase, '*Wir haben auch gelitten*, 'we also suffered.' She had suffered, her eyebrows and hair were singed that night when her apartment was smashed to smithereens. She had only a few things to take with her to Gera. She didn't have it easy, and she worried about me, no question, and she worried and felt guilty about my father. But that was nothing compared to what we had gone through, and particularly what Olga had gone through. To have the nerve to say '*Wir haben auch gelitten*! Yes, Germans suffered, but they voted for Hitler. Not that my mother was guilty of anything; she didn't vote for him. In fact, she helped save my life with that Aryanization crap. But to compare whatever she went through with Auschwitz—what this innocent eighteen-year-old had suffered—was totally inexcusable. It portrayed not only a total lack of understanding and empathy, but also her jealousy and anger, which she directed at both of us."

After a couple of weeks, Pips inveigled his mother to stay with one of her friends who still had an apartment in Berlin. Having lived her entire life there, Marie was no stranger to the city. But Marie exploded. "A mother can always take her child in. You always had a room with me. I always gave you shelter and took care of you. Now you have no room for your mother?"

As soon as she saw that Pips was embarrassed because of the noise, she stationed herself in front of the unglazed window to make sure that her rant would be broadly heard by neighbors. "She carried on at the total strength of her very healthy lungs. That didn't improve the situation at all, and I didn't think she was justified. When I lived with her, I was a child. As soon as I had to go underground, I was gone. During the war, during my incarceration, she sent me a little food. It was wonderful but it was not a sacrifice. She wasn't that hard-up, particularly in a small town surrounded by farms that were never bombed. To compare this to Auschwitz and to have no sensitivity that she was intruding on us—not only intruding with her presence but stirring up trouble—was too much. Olga, who was the mildest person at that time, said 'I can't stand this.' And Olga couldn't hurt a fly."

Pips felt torn between his mother and his fiancée. He felt he owed his mother something, but he owed more to this girl who, because of her devotion to him, was living in a painfully strange country. In the end, Marie stayed put and Pips had to find a way to support himself and Olga.

"We knew that this can't go on forever. Now that we are free, I should look for a legitimate job. I told Olga that, ever since I was a little boy, I wanted to be an actor. I can't be a doctor or lawyer. I don't have the education for these things, but for acting, what do you need? Nothing much. The only problem was there were no theaters open. They were either gone with the wind or there was nobody around to put on a play. That was also true of most movie theaters. But there were still some buildings in which everything above ground was burned out, but the theater itself was still hanging together."

Pips came across a man who owned a movie theater only a few blocks away from Kurfürstendamm. He had received a permit from the Soviets to show films—but only Russian films—and these were neither dubbed nor subtitled. Pips was offered the job of interpreting for the German-speaking part of the audience. "I didn't speak Russian, so he got me a Russian interpreter. The interpreter explained what the film was about, including some of the dialogue. The film ran three times a day, seven days a week, so I saw every movie twenty-two times—once with the interpreter and twenty-one times with the performance. I sat on the aisle next to a knob that controlled the sound. Every few minutes, I would turn down the sound, give a running commentary on the action, and then put on the sound again. There were two types of films; one was political, a deadly bore. A guy in a leather jacket standing on a soapbox on a street corner in Leningrad berating the crowd by the hour. It would put anybody to sleep. I hated those films. Other films I enjoyed tremendously. These were war films, lots of action, lots of anti-German stuff, and great Red Army songs. I was already inculcated from my Bund days in Cossack songs and have always had a weak spot for

Russian music. I did another thing; I improved the anti-German parts: 'And now Ivan comes home to his village after having beaten the Huns and he finds that the Huns have burned and raped and murdered and killed. The women are crying, they were raped by ten men or twenty soldiers.' I really laid it on thick."

This turned out to be a dangerous job. Half the audience were German and the other half were Soviet soldiers, who were still required to carry their tommy guns. "I said nothing good about the Germans and they got very angry. The Reds were even more dangerous because they were enjoying the movie and, suddenly, the sound disappeared and a disembodied voice came out of the darkness and spoke in German, which they didn't understand. At first, they couldn't figure out what this was all about. Then they saw me sitting there next to the knob. So, this is the son of a bitch who's taking all the sound away! Many of them threatened me with their guns but nobody really touched me. In between my tours, I went up and down the aisles to look for cigarette butts. This, my first career in the theater, lasted until the end of the Russian occupation of that section of Berlin."

Pips had a second career as an actor. He had seen many films that featured Hans Stiebner, a German character actor, whose extensive filmography spanned from 1934 to 1958. Stiebner was building up a repertory company in the auditorium of a school near Pips's home. Pips sought him out and Stiebner immediately signed him up for his nascent troupe. "I didn't read for him or audition for him; he couldn't care less. It didn't take me long to realize that my acting ability or lack thereof was not the issue. At that time, any German store or company that reopened, if they had a Jew on the premises, that was helpful. They thought it took some of the Nazi taint off. That was his reason for wanting me."

Of the dozen or so troupe members, the oldest was a paunchy character actor, Alfred Beierle, in his sixties. "He called himself a victim of fascism because he had been in a concentration camp for a short while. He claimed that it was his heroic resistance to the Nazis that got him there. Later, I found out that he was very active in the black market, and they had caught him for that. He was not a victim of fascism, but he rode that for all it was worth."

There were tight restrictions on the kinds of plays that could be put on. Anything that was nationalistic was *verboten*. The first play put on by the troupe was *Pit unter den Piraten,* "Pit Among the Pirates," about a boy's adventures with a group of pirates. It opened to paltry advance sales, with a spartan set. Pips played one of the supporting roles, but no one had coached him on how to apply makeup. So, he went on stage looking like a clown with his bright red cheeks. The audience was divided into those who fell asleep and those who laughed. The play ran for only a few performances.

The next play was Pirandello's *Six Characters in Search of an Author*. Pips was promoted to assistant director, which meant that he was a gofer. "I didn't know how to direct anything. Stiebner directed the whole thing. From time to time, he would stretch out his hand, which meant that I had to get cigarettes on the black market. That was my main attraction for him."

The actors had trouble learning their lines because the script was so convoluted. Beierle, Pips opined, was in the early stages of dementia and seemed to be only interested in eating and drinking. He had a male servant who cleaned his apartment and who was dispatched to do errands. Pips was tapped to help Beierle learn his lines and he complied, coming every other day to coach him.

"I had the text in front of me. He played the father, one of the main roles. After one or two sentences, he got stuck, so I had to read them for him. He would say, 'Next,' so I read him the next sentence. Then he got another two or three sentences out and got stuck again. It was like pulling teeth! I did the best I could and before our opening he seemed to have gotten the gist of the thing."

Six Characters in Search of an Author opened to a full house. Everything went smoothly until the middle of the first act when the Beierle character started reciting lines from the third act. The female lead playing his daughter managed to coax him back to the first act. He later got stuck again. But he was hard of hearing. When he was fed his line from off stage, he couldn't get it. "We managed to muddle through. But since that play was very hard to understand under the best of circumstances, the audience didn't know what the hell was going on anyway. But I had a chance to act a little bit."

Summer turned to fall, and it got cold. "It was October, and we needed windows. We got in touch with a glazier and made a deal. I would pay him a pound of butter, and he would put in the windows. I could have put in the windows myself, but I had no tools. We were in touch with other people from Schulstrasse and one gave us a very good present, an electric heater."

The couple spent a good deal of time that fall sitting on the couch, huddled under a blanket, with the heater warming them. Within a few hours, the heater consumed two months' worth of their electricity allotment. Pips's experience in using a fuse box to enable an escape from Schulstrasse came in handy. The meter that recorded consumption was just outside his entrance door. "I looked this thing over and decided to go for it: I cut the wire just next to the red seal, bent it over, opened the box, and used a piece of wood to turn the dial back. I did this once a week. We lustily used electricity like there was no tomorrow and didn't feel guilty about it at all."

One of Pips's former black-market contacts came by with a radio to sell. Before the war, the Germans had developed the *Volksempfänger* radio, the kind that Pips had before his first arrest. It was important for the Nazi regime that every German have a radio set because that was one of their main propaganda tools. Wanting a radio, Olga and Pips purchased the one on offer for a few cigarettes. A short while later, the seller was arrested after the body of a woman was found hacked to pieces in a suitcase that had been tossed into the ruins of a building. The victim was his wife. "Why had he killed her? She ate too much, depriving him of his ration card. Can you imagine such a thing? This was the kind of craziness that went on."

Along with the craziness, there came a glimmer of justice. A former Schulstrasse inmate informed Pips that Walter Dobberke had been arrested by the Soviets and put on trial. Making a last-ditch effort to demonstrate his humanity in the event of arrest, Dobberke had declined to execute Schulstrasse's prisoners. Frau Heim, who had saved Pips's life, was hoping that he would testify on Dobberke's behalf. Frau Heim never contacted Pips directly, although she probably could have found him through one of the Jewish organizations that had been set up to register the few surviving Jews. Pips, who was hearing this thirdhand, had no idea whether it was true. Even if it was, he had no appetite to testify for Dobberke. "He had certainly helped me and treated me decently. He also beat me up at one point. Considering the circumstances, I did owe him something: he contributed to my survival. But I could not forget that he was in charge of all the deportations from Berlin; he had deported all my friends; he had deported my father; he had deported Ilse. I'll be damned if I give anybody the impression that he was a humanist."

As for Dobberke's fate, he would die of diphtheria in a Soviet prisoner of war camp in 1946. "It didn't interest me anymore. I felt no real gratitude or relief. I just didn't want to hear anything that had to do with the SS or the Gestapo."

Pips wanted to focus on getting married and putting the war behind him. Some German civil institutions had reopened. Olga and Pips went to the registry office to get a marriage license. Nothing doing: Olga was underage and needed parental consent to marry. Where are the parents? The parents are dead, courtesy of the Germans. Well, then she must have a guardian, but she didn't have one. Then the court must appoint a guardian. But the court cannot appoint a guardian because she is not a German citizen and not under German jurisdiction. Her last citizenship was Hungarian. "On paper, I was a German citizen, but we considered ourselves stateless. I, of course, could get the papers, but I didn't need them because I was over twenty-one." They made repeated visits to the registry.

On November 26, 1945, Olga and Pips were finally married and Marie finally left. They found an open print shop and sent out formal invitations. UNRRA had set up a Central Tracing Office for Jewish survivors to facilitate reuniting families and friends. Sooner or later, all Berlin's surviving Jews ended up there, and that's how Pips was able to find friends like Max Koppel and others who were invited to his wedding.

"My mother gave us a present, gold wedding rings, which she of course didn't buy. They came from a Jewish couple she had been friends with for years and who were about to be deported. They knew wherever they went that jewelry was not going to stay with them, so they gave her these rings. These people never did come back and so my mother gave us their rings."

On the appointed day, Olga and Pips somehow got hold of some wedding clothes and went to the synagogue, Olga in white lace and Pips in a tuxedo. The sanctuary held eighty people, and every seat was taken, mostly by Schulstrasse alumni. "We had a chuppah and a glass for me to step on. The only gentiles in the bunch were my mother and a flower girl." The flower girl, Ute, was the youngest daughter of Karl Streckfuss, the deserter who had hidden Pips in his Laube during the war. He and his wife were in attendance, as was Lotte Paech and Erich Hopp. Following the ceremony, the group went to the wedding feast, such as it was. The featured item was potato salad; there was no meat at all. But there was some alcohol—beer and a bottle of vodka donated by a soldier.

The venue for the feast could not have been more incongruous: Hitler's half-brother, Alois, had a beautiful apartment in Berlin that had been "liberated" by some Polish Jews from Schulstrasse. And that's where this postwar Jewish wedding was celebrated.

Despite the festivities, Olga was melancholy throughout. Her unhappiness about being in Berlin had not abated.

Their kitchen window overlooked a large, empty plaza, beyond which was the Kurfürstendamm. Twice a week, a bustling black market operated on that plaza. "All the Allies came—the Russians, the French, the Americans, the British, with their trucks, jeeps, whatever vehicles they had, and the Germans came en masse. Very lively trading went on in the open. Nobody intervened. The Allies had chocolate, butter, cigarettes, which the Americans bought in the PX (Post Exchange) for pennies. The Germans had cameras: Zeiss, Nikon—some of which were liberated from France and other places—paintings—though not the top stuff—and oriental rugs. They traded lustily back and forth."

Olga looked out from her tiny kitchen and started sobbing. "It galls me," she wept. "Here are these Germans, and the Allies are handing them cigarettes and chocolates. I'm dreaming of chocolate. I haven't seen chocolate in years, and here the Germans are getting it from the Allies while we get nothing because we have nothing to trade."

Olga's misery hit Pips very hard. He frantically looked around for something he could trade. The only thing he could find was his Jew star. "I figured that some allied officer might want to have a Jew star as a souvenir and trade me some chocolate for it." He took the Jew star and went out. Seeing a small truck with British soldiers, he walked up to the truck and showed them the Jew star. Perplexed, they looked at it, not knowing what it was. Pips explained, "Jude, Jude." Suddenly, a British soldier grabbed him by the shoulders, turned him around, and was about to take a swing at Pips when Pips blurted out, *"Ich bin ein Jude."* "He stopped. He was a Jewish boy. He was going to hit me because he thought I was a fuckin' German

Ernst Philipsohn, Pips's father, a proud German veteran, in his World War I uniform. *Photo credit: Photog. Atelier, Waarenhaus Hermann Tietze*

Gerd "Pips" Philipsohn and Ilse Rosenthal, the great love of his life.

Destroyed prison at Grosse Hamburger Strasse, where Pips was an inmate after his second arrest.

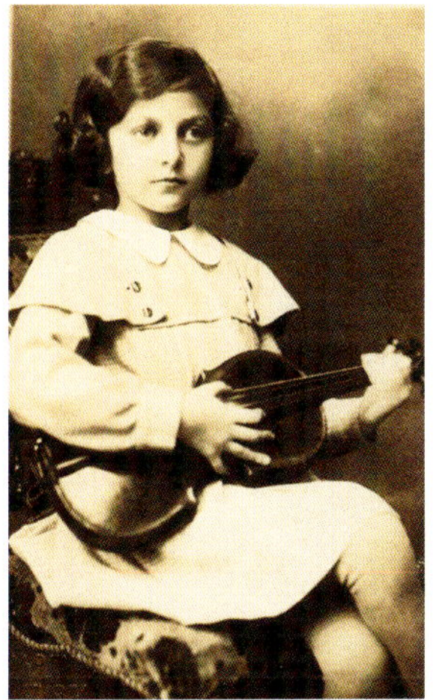

Olga, as a child, with her violin.

Olga Horvath and Gerd "Pips" Philipsohn on their wedding day, November 30, 1945—one of the first Jewish post-war weddings in Berlin.

Marie Vollbrecht Philipsohn, Pips's mother, 1946. *Photo credit: K.L. Kaemchen, Berlin*

The Jewish star that Pips refused to wear but was eventually forced to wear in prison. After Germany's surrender, he tried (and failed) to barter it for chocolate for Olga.

Olga and Pips soon after their arrival in the US.

Pips at United Service for New Americans (USNA), one of his first jobs in New York.

Olga Phillips and the author, as a child in Forest Park, Kew Gardens, New York, ca. 1954.

Pips on one of his daredevil hikes, undated.

Pips with his ubiquitous cigarette.

Pips in a *Playboy* magazine layout. The desperate photographer urgently phoned Pips to fill in when the male model failed to show up for the shoot. Undated.

Pips at the Globe Photo office.

Olga with her "adopted" son, Orlando "Jerry" Perez, ca. 1970s.

Pips walking the author down the aisle during her wedding to Rabbi Marc Tanenbaum, June 6, 1982.
Photo credit: Valeche

Pips, working on Marc Tanenbaum's papers and playing with newborn Joshua-Marc Tanenbaum, October 1992.

Pips and the author, September 1994.

Pips with the author and Joshua-Marc Tanenbaum at the 2005 Tanenbaum Center for Interreligious Understanding Gala.

Pips in his 1968 Cadillac Coupe de Ville—the car that he kept for the rest of his life—in 2002.

Pips, the serial kisser, bussing a friend, Nancy Sandmael, 2005.

Pips at the Western Wall in Jerusalem in 2004.

Pips at the Holocaust Memorial in Berlin, 2005.

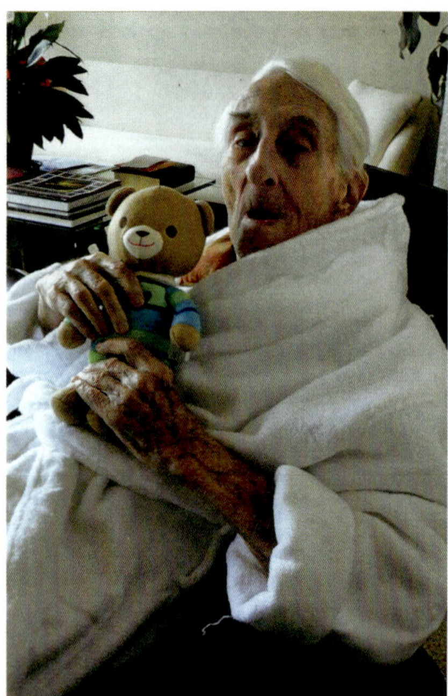

Pips in 2015, several months before he died. He had long stopped bothering to put his dentures in his mouth.

Olga and Pips's gravestone at White Plains Rural Cemetery. Pips enjoyed visiting his grave and did so many times.

who was making remarks about Jews, and he was going to let that bastard get it, rip his nose off. He said, 'Jew, yes?' I said, 'I don't speak English.' The soldier responded in Yiddish.

"'Where do you live?'

"'Right here.'

"'Let's go.'"

The two went over to the apartment to be met by Olga who was stunned to see Pips with a British soldier in tow. The soldier kissed her on the cheek and immediately emptied his pockets. Players cigarettes, chocolates, everything he had, toppled on the table. He didn't take the Jew star. He wasn't trading; he was giving, and that touched the young couple deeply. The soldier explained that he was posted in Berlin as part of a tank unit stationed near the Havel River on the outskirts of the city.

"He didn't have much time, so we embraced him, and off he went. We thought we'd never see him again, but sure enough, within a week he showed up again. And again, he brought something. The British didn't have much at the beginning of '46. They weren't like the Americans who swam in goodies. The British still had rationing so he got packages from his mother in London. Whatever he got in the packages he brought to us. We learned that his parents had come from Poland and had settled in England. He was born in England and joined the army, but his parents spoke Yiddish. English Jews don't normally speak Yiddish, but he had learned it from his parents."

The beneficent soldier came at least once a week. During one of his visits, he announced that he was going to take Olga and Pips on a boat trip the following Thursday. Incredulous, they couldn't imagine where he would get a boat. "Oh, we have liberated a number of motorboats. We have some petrol and we're going to have a wonderful cruise up and down the Havel. You be ready at eight in the morning, and I'm going to pick you up by jeep and we're going to have a great day."

He wasn't alone on the boat. Three other British soldiers came along for the ride, one of them steering the vessel. "It was a beautiful sunny day. We ate and I smoked. It was lovely. We went down the Havel River. I had seen it before when my mother took me on a big boat to Werder, where all the trees were in flower, on Hitler's birthday, years ago."

Sometime later, Olga and Pips were awakened early one morning by banging on their door. Pips went to the door bleary-eyed and there stood their friend in full battle-gear. Their benefactor sheepishly said, "I'm sorry to disturb you so early in the morning but we just got orders to pull out of Berlin, the whole tank battalion. I talked my comrades into leaving the formation. We're double-parked and I have no time, but I brought you something." He ran back, and with the help of one of his mates, he dragged in a big sack stuffed with corned beef. Olga and Pips never saw him again, but for months, they feasted on his parting gift.

On a later day, there was another knock at the door. When Pips opened, he was greeted by the sight of a Canadian officer, who introduced himself as Klaus Goldschlag, the notorious Stella Goldschlag's cousin. He had come to track down and arrest Stella for her collaboration with the Gestapo in apprehending underground Jews. She had engaged in these activities after being arrested and tortured. Walter Dobberke had promised to spare her family, and he paid her for each Jew she caught. The promise was broken. Her family was deported and murdered in Auschwitz. But she converted to Christianity and became an open antisemite. Klaus later became Canada's Ambassador to Bonn.

The next call came from the American Joint Distribution Committee. "They had a list of all the Jews in Berlin and they had received two or three thousand packages with personal supplies. We were invited to their offices and Olga picked up a package for herself, and I picked up a package for myself. When we got home, we could hardly wait to open the package and see what was inside. The first things we ran across gave us cause for hysterical laughter, which reminded us of the Russian officer who had sent his man out to bring Olga some clothes and had come back with a long evening gown and a bathing suit. The first thing we saw was toothpaste and toilet paper. In other words, it should be clean when it goes in and it should be clean when it comes out. We were totally used to using newspaper as toilet paper. We hadn't seen regular toilet paper in years, and in Auschwitz, they had nothing. Toothpaste wasn't exactly high on our list either. There was also food—not a helluva lot, but it was something—and some blankets, which were really welcome. We brought them to America; we wouldn't let go of anything."

The Immigration Act of 1924 had set strict quotas for immigration to the United States. In 1946, President Harry S. Truman signed an order approving a quota of nearly twenty-six thousand immigrants from Germany. This cleared the way for Olga and Pips to register for US visas at the American consulate. It would take a few months, so they were admonished not to pack their bags just yet.

Marie, who had left Berlin after the wedding, invited her son and daughter-in-law to visit her in Gera for a couple of days. Train service was still erratic. When the couple went to the train station to embark on the 150-mile trip, they saw thousands of people waiting to board a train headed for Leipzig. They managed to squeeze in, but Olga was already fatigued. "The train hadn't even left the station. We had at least a three-hour ride to Leipzig, so what could I do? I noticed that one car was empty. It was reserved for Soviet officers; no German was allowed in. There was a guard at either end. The Germans were like sardines in the other car. With my chutzpah, I said to myself, 'What have I got to lose?' I don't have the faintest idea how I got past the guard. I went slowly along the gangway and looked into each compartment. In one, I saw a colonel sitting alone, and he looked Jewish to me. I was always sniffing out Jews if I could."

Pips opened the door. The officer looked up, startled. Pips gambled with *"Ya yevrey"* and hit it right. The colonel was a Jew! "Come on in, come on in!" he said. Pips explained that his wife was suffering in the crowded car, and the colonel invited him to bring her along. Pips went to get Olga, squeezing through the crowd, and both returned to the colonel's compartment. He immediately embraced Olga. "We were like family. We spoke Yiddish, we spoke German too, and it was like we had known each other for years. In those days, Jews understood each other. We spoke the same language, and we were rare birds because we had survived. He and all the other Russian Jewish officers felt a certain obligation to treat us well. He sat us down and unpacked some chocolate and cookies and fed us. He had several watches on his arm. Apparently, they were hard to get in the Soviet Union. He took one of the best watches and gave it to Olga, which I found hysterical because the Russians were always taking the watches away from the Germans. He was traveling to Leipzig and wanted to know who we were and what had happened to us and, ach! Olga was in Auschwitz! In no time flat, he opened his wallet and showed us family pictures: this is his wife, this is his grandmother, his daughter, his uncle, aunt, niece and nephew, and we admired all the pictures. Then he said, 'Listen, how much time do you have until you catch the train to Gera from Leipzig?' We had a couple of hours, so he invited us to the Russian officer's club in Leipzig for lunch."

The three arrived in Leipzig and set off for a luxurious restaurant that had survived the bombings and which the Soviets had taken over for their officers. "We went in with him as his guests, sat down to a white tablecloth and silverware. Everything *comme il faut.* We ate our fill, thanked him, he kissed us, and we said goodbye. He was a darling. I have no idea what his name was." Olga and Pips boarded the train to Gera to visit Marie, who took them to see an operetta. It was an otherwise uneventful interlude.

Pips had ignorantly persisted in using the rhythm method of birth control, despite its previous failures with Ilse. This time, it was Olga who found herself pregnant. "There was no question in our minds that she couldn't have a baby at this juncture. She had very little to eat. Our future was tenuous at best, and we had no idea when we would get out of this country. We didn't know what awaited us in America, a continent away, a world away, so there was no question, she had to have an abortion. To start a new life in America with a newborn would have been too much for us."

Abortion was still illegal in Germany, except in cases where the mother's life was at risk. Pips managed to find a sympathetic woman surgeon who certified that Olga needed a legal abortion. Olga was admitted to a hospital for the termination of her pregnancy. She remained in the hospital for ten days but kept bleeding for three months. She was examined by another doctor who could find no physiological reason for the bleeding. Olga, who was depressed to begin with, became even more depressed after the abortion. She spent most of the time in bed, but eventually she improved.

"As usual, I wasn't much of a help, I loved her, I kissed her and slept with her, but I was not as patient or supportive as I should have been, just like with Ilse."

The depth of Olga's despondency was evident when Max Koppel gifted Olga with a violin—an instrument that had been such an integral part of her life only a few years before. She touched it for an instant and never picked it up again. In his self-absorption, Pips never encouraged her to resume playing the violin.

In 1947, emigration became more of a reality, and Olga and Pips began to make plans for their exit from Germany. They made a deal with Margaret, who had been a nurse in the Schulstrasse. "She was a rather lanky, tall girl who had, not long before Olga came to town, come to my room and seduced me. I'd screwed a lot of nurses, but she wasn't on my list. Not my idea of a great lay, but a nice girl and we kept in touch with her. After the war, she married a half Jew, who practiced the Christian religion, and although she had been adopted by a Jewish family, she was a Christian, too. She and her husband were looking for an apartment. We said that once we get out of here, you can take over our apartment with all the furniture. It wasn't really our apartment to sell, but they paid us something. Now things were a little easier to buy, and we purchased a few things, mainly for Olga. She still had that damned coat with the red paint stripe on the back, but at least her new coat was halfway decent. Somebody gave us a steamer trunk with drawers on one side and hanging space on the other. We slowly got ourselves ready to leave."

Then came the question of an affidavit from a US citizen, vouching to take financial responsibility for them so that the new immigrants would not become a public charge. Pips had written to *Aufbau*, the American German Jewish weekly, in the hope that they could provide an affidavit. The response came on April 10.

> *Unfortunately, we cannot provide a visa since this can only be granted by an individual. Do you not have any relatives or friends in the United States, who would be able to do this?*

Olga and Pips knew no one in the US. But the Hebrew Immigrant Aid Society—HIAS—stepped in to help them, as it did for three hundred thousand other Jewish DPs in the aftermath of the Holocaust. HIAS also paid for passage on the ship that would take them to America.

Finally, in early March, their number was coming up. They needed to be ready to leave on the spur of the moment. Olga and Pips declared themselves stateless and were issued a certificate in lieu of passport. "I could have said, I'm a German citizen. But screw them. I'd rather be stateless." Then a message came, alerting them to be at a staging area in Berlin in two days. There was a makeshift camp where they could sleep. But, of course, they were too excited to sleep.

They met some people they knew who were going on the same transport. This time, the word "transport" was no longer ice water in their veins.

After a sleepless night, on a bitterly cold day in another freezing winter, they were taken to the railroad station and put into a sealed passenger train with American soldiers standing guard. Unlike the cattle car that took Olga and her mother to Auschwitz, this was a heated passenger train with comfortable seats and a welcoming packet of biscuits for each person. The train arrived in Bremen, a port on the North Sea, and its passengers were disgorged into a holding camp. "There was now a constant flow of emigrants. There were Ukrainians, people running away from the Soviets. Many of them had collaborated with the Germans—people with all kinds of checkered backgrounds. The only ones who were clean were the Jews."

Olga and Pips stayed in the camp for two weeks. During that time, they were assigned spaces with ten or twelve people to a room. "We were fed. In the morning, we got powdered scrambled eggs. The food was lousy. The whole internal operation of the camp had been turned over to Germans. Americans ran the camp on a higher level, but didn't want to bother cooking. The Germans stole the food en masse, so we got the worst part of the food and little of it. Another guy and I took a streetcar and went to the city to see if we could do some black-market business and get some cigarettes. We made some contacts but nothing to speak of."

One day, the two took their wives into Bremen as a diversion from the boredom of the camp. While coming back on the streetcar, they heard a man mumbling something and getting louder and louder. Suddenly, everybody heard him saying, "It's a shame that not all of you were gassed, that some of you slipped through the net, you should have all been gassed." Apparently, he had recognized the visitors as Jews from the camp. "I reacted like a pistol shot and jumped at this guy's throat. He was much stronger than I, but at that moment, reason was not a factor. As long as he was holding forth, the conductor did nothing. But the moment I lunged, the conductor practically threw us off the streetcar. That was our farewell to Germany, a fitting farewell."

A few days later, on February 27, 1947, the call finally came. Olga and Pips were put on a bus that took them to the harbor, where a liberty ship, *Marine Flasher*, was waiting to take them to America. These liberty ships had been used as supply ships by the Allies and were manned by merchant mariners and armed naval guards. As such, they were outfitted for soldiers with narrow, hammock-like bunks and thin mattresses. Olga was ushered to a cabin with only three other women, which had likely served as officers' quarters in the ship's prior incarnation. The men were assigned to five tier bunks and Pips's bunk was close to the front of the ship. A gong announced dinner in the cafeteria-style mess. Each passenger was handed a tray with different compartments—something he had never seen before—and they moved down an assembly line in which one worker ladled potatoes, another meat, and the next, an apple.

"This was the first square meal we'd seen in a long time. As soon as we finished, we stood in line again for seconds. When we couldn't possibly eat anymore, we still got in line and took the whole tray full of stuff just to get the apple. We had two or three apples in our pockets. We were still psychologically starving. We never knew what will be tomorrow; we may need the apple. We couldn't believe that we wouldn't starve anymore. We still had some cookies left from the train to Bremen and we brought them to New York. We were given four dollars each as board money to do whatever we wanted. Between Olga and me, we had eight dollars. They had cartons of cigarettes for a dollar apiece, and I could finally smoke as much as I wanted. We spent four dollars, mostly for cigarettes."

That first evening, Olga started getting seasick, and the ship hadn't even left the harbor yet. She warned Pips before boarding that she would be seasick, and he retorted that she was priming herself for it. As for himself, he insisted that, never having experienced motion sickness in his life, he would be immune to seasickness.

The ship sailed the next morning, heading to the North Sea through the half frozen English Channel, with ice blocks smashing against the hull. In the rough seas, Pips sought out the geographical center of the ship. There, he stood as long as he could, with legs spread, to counter the movement of the ship. "I did it for a couple of hours and felt very proud that I was fine. Came the next morning, I got out of my bunk, close to the bow where the toilets and wash basins were located. Since this was the bow, as the ship moved up and down, you would one moment be pressed on the toilet and nothing could make you stand up; the next moment you would be practically floating in midair. I wanted to shave and went to the area where the basins were. I lathered up and looked in the mirror and saw that my face was whiter than the lather. I dropped the brush and my razor and could barely make it back to my bunk. For the next forty-eight hours, I was the sickest man on board. The headache and vomiting were so bad that they allowed my wife to come and hold my head."

The *Marine Flasher*, the first ship to bring DPs to the United States under the Truman Directive, made a stopover in Antwerp. There, eight years earlier, the ill-fated *St. Louis* returned its doomed cargo of German refugees trying to escape Hitler's Germany. But this ship was greeted by crowds of Belgians waving and tossing oranges at the refugees arrayed on the decks.

The ocean crossing from Europe took two weeks. Pips had a feeling of weightlessness. No more ties to Europe and none to America. He was leaving the past behind and didn't yet have any history in America.

PART TWO

FROM A NIGHTMARE TO A DREAM AND BACK

CHAPTER 10

GETTING STARTED IN AMERICA

After sailing out of Antwerp, its passengers laden with oranges, the *Marine Flasher* took two weeks to arrive in New York. As it came through the Verrazano Narrows—long before that waterway was spanned by, what was for a time, the longest suspension bridge in the world—the Statue of Liberty came into view. It was smaller than Pips expected. Because the *Marine Flasher* dropped anchor overnight in the Narrows, he had plenty of time to contemplate that icon of welcome and freedom.

The ship left Europe in bitter cold; it arrived in America in bitter cold. But Pips still went to the top deck to get his first glimpse of New York. Ahead of him were well lit skyscrapers. To his left was Lady Liberty and to his right was the Brooklyn-Queens Expressway. Pips was mesmerized by the glimmer of white headlights and red rear lights as the cars whizzed by all night.

He had never seen so many cars. Nor had he ever owned or driven one. That would change in the United States, where driving became an abiding passion. The trajectory of his progress up the ladder of the American dream would be marked by the successive cars he owned.

When morning came, the *Marine Flasher* was tugged into port on the West Side of Manhattan. The passengers were ordered to disembark. Olga and Pips didn't have much luggage—only the trunk with which they had been gifted before departing Berlin. When they got to the bottom of the gangplank, Pips was startled to see two familiar-looking men—brothers—waiting for them, both wearing Eisenhower jackets. He had last seen one of them in Berlin a decade earlier. The other was Pips's childhood friend and Krummhubel companion, Karl Weirauch, now Americanized to Charlie Wyle. Charlie had managed to escape Berlin for Palestine in 1938, from where he and his large family emigrated to America. He and his brother, Bert, were subsequently drafted into the US military.

Pips, unaware that he knew anyone in America, was perplexed. How did Charlie and Bert know that he would be on the ship that had just docked? They regularly scoured *Aufbau*, the German-American newspaper to which Pips had earlier turned for help to get an American visa. *Aufbau* featured a weekly list of DPs from Europe who were due to arrive in New York. Having seen the name "Gerd Philipsohn" on the list, the Wyle brothers headed to the pier.

"We had expected to be completely friendless. But when we got down, they saw Olga and me and embraced us. I noticed that their German—I spoke only German—was a little shaky, a little hesitant. I thought it was a put-on to prove they were Americans, but I didn't hold it against them."

The reunion didn't last long. A social worker from HIAS approached to take charge of the newly arrived DPs. "You go with the social worker," urged Charlie. "We'll see you tomorrow."

The social worker took Olga and Pips in a taxi to HIAS headquarters on Lafayette Street in Greenwich Village. That building would later house Joseph Papp's renowned Public Theater, where so many Broadway hits were spawned. But in 1947, it was a shelter for newly arrived Jews.

On the way to Greenwich Village, the taxi passed through Times Square. "I couldn't believe it. Such a place like that, lights all over. There was one sign, an advertisement for Camel cigarettes. It was a block-long face of a man with an open mouth. Every second, a puff of smoke came out of his mouth. The eighth wonder of the world! We couldn't believe that we weren't dreaming!"

But there was also shock and disappointment. "Even though we had always known it was unrealistic, we had visions of New York—and particularly of Broadway—as nothing but tuxedos, Fred Astaire, Ginger Rodgers, and everybody dressed up. There was a movie series called 'Broadway Melody of 1936, 'of 1938,' '1940.' We had seen at least one of these 'Broadway Melodies,' and of course it was all bullshit. We knew it couldn't possibly be that people spent their time waltzing along Broadway. But somehow this had stuck in our heads. Now we see little crummy buildings, filth, paper. We had come from Berlin, which was not exactly a city in full bloom, but that was war, and those were honest-to-goodness ruins. We were used to them. But New York, the shining city on the hill, looked so dirty."

The couple finally alit at HIAS headquarters, a building that had been completed in 1881 as the Astor Library—a gift from John Jacob Astor to the City of New York. Their cohort included several couples, each of whom was assigned one bed. "That was okay. We were all married and we weren't used to privacy anyway. It didn't bother us."

The Wyles came to the HIAS shelter and squired Olga and Pips around New York. Henry, the youngest of the Wyle brothers, took them to Radio City Music Hall. "I had never seen something like this before. The ninth wonder of the world! It was a gigantic place, and I still remember the movie I saw there in 1947: *The Late George Apley*. I couldn't understand why this guy was late. I didn't know that 'late' also means dead."

Olga and Pips remained at the HIAS shelter for three weeks. A case worker helped them find an apartment: a fifth-floor walk-up on the corner of Jerome Avenue and 181st Street in the Bronx, along the route of the Jerome Avenue elevated train. "Every couple of minutes, you had to stop talking because the train would go by and make a tremendous racket. At my age, a five-floor walkup was not much of a problem, but Olga was still weak from her time in concentration camp, and it was difficult for her to manage the steps. Still, the apartment had two bedrooms and two living rooms, with one kitchen and one bathroom. That was too big for us alone and HIAS wouldn't pay that much. So, we shared it with another family whom we had known, fleetingly, in Berlin. Their name was Wertheim, and they had owned one of the largest department stores in Berlin for several generations."

When the Nazis took power in 1933, Wertheim, a beacon of modern retailing, was Aryanized and the Jewish owners forced out. At least five members of the Wertheim family were deported to concentration camps, with only two having survived. Guenther managed to escape to the US with his wife and two children. They eventually settled on a small chicken farm in New Jersey.

"There were the four of them and we were the two of us. We got one bedroom and a living room, and they got one bedroom and a living room, and we shared the kitchen. We were not particularly fond of them, and I don't think they were particularly fond of us, but we got along. Of course, it's not easy to get along with one kitchen and one bathroom, but we managed. The apartment was furnished, probably by the Salvation Army, and it was pretty crappy. The rent was $150 a month, which in those days was quite expensive, especially for this neighborhood and for a five-floor walkup, so it was $75 apiece. HIAS paid the rent, and they also paid us a weekly stipend to buy groceries. They didn't give us any riches, but we still had money left over to go to the movies—in those days the movies cost fifty cents. Loew's Paradise on Grand Concourse. It was like a palace. We went to the movies at least once a week. That was our big thing, and we learned a little English."

The Philipsohns and the Wertheims now had to shift for themselves. None of them spoke English but the two families didn't shop together or cook together or team up in any way. With a Jewish grocery and a butcher shop a couple of blocks away, the newcomers were able to make themselves understood in German. "If I wanted a piece of salami, I would point. The humor of the situation didn't escape me. It was kind of funny, finding yourself in a strange country where you don't know any of the life rhythms and don't speak the language. But I thought it was adventurous and interesting, and we had very simple needs—groceries and that was about it."

They had been in the apartment for a couple of months, and just barely settled in, when they discovered bedbugs. "Every day we went hunting for them. It was a slaughter and everywhere on the walls were blood spots where we had killed the damned things and the blood they had sucked from us splattered out. It took us the better part of a year, but we did finally manage to eradicate them."

Olga and Pips kept in loose touch with some of the other refugees who had come to New York and whom they had known from Berlin. One of them got a job as the personal chauffeur to George T. Delacorte Jr., founder of Dell Publications. Among other things, his company published *Inside Detective* magazine with which the driver kept the Philipsohns copiously supplied. "Olga would read them from morning to night and that's how she learned rather quickly to read in English, but she wouldn't speak in English."

Eva, Olga's friend in Auschwitz and Schulstrasse, had earlier married Aurel Sebestyen, a Hungarian from an elite Jewish family. Both were deported to Auschwitz and separated there. They survived and lived in Paris after the war. But Aurel went to Geneva on business and contracted polio. For two years, until he died, he was in an iron lung—from head to toe—completely paralyzed. That, after surviving Auschwitz.

Aurel had a cousin, Renee, from Bucharest, who married Joe Vogel, a Hungarian Jew from Budapest. Renee and Joe lived in Paris at the start of the war but managed to escape to Cuba to await their American visa. Joe was a medical doctor, a general practitioner. Before being felled by polio, Aurel had written to Renee Vogel to alert her that Eva's best friend, Olga, was coming with her husband to New York from Germany, and he suggested that they meet.

The Vogels lived in Astoria, Queens, and Joe ran his practice in his apartment. Two rooms were set aside as a waiting room and an examining room. The two couples quickly became close. The Vogels had a car, an Oldsmobile, and Renee insisted that the foursome get to know their new country. Olga and Pips had no way of getting around and were delighted with weekend excursions to a lake in New Jersey or upstate New York. Renee adored nature and loved having a captive audience to whom she could direct a running commentary on the scenery—but only English was permitted to be spoken in the car. The fact that Joe, who was earning a living, always picked up the tab in restaurants was an added fillip. Pips's early childhood lesson from his mother, "When one gives, take; when one takes, scream," had stuck.

"We did a lot of traveling with them. Renee loved marathon rides, four or five hundred miles a day. In the middle of winter, she announced that the group was going to Niagara Falls. What a stupid idea! It was so cold up there and half the falls were frozen. We couldn't even go over the bridge to Canada because we weren't citizens and had no papers. The next year, they took us to the Blue Ridge Mountains, where we stayed overnight in either New Market or Harrisonburg. Renee and Joe both had an *idée fixe* about hiding their Jewishness, even though he went to synagogue regularly. He called himself Dr. Fogel instead of Vogel, and they did a couple of things that we hated. When we went to Virginia, Renee asked the desk clerk at the hotel for the schedule of services at the church the next morning. Of course, she didn't want to go to the church, but she wanted to appear as if she was a churchgoing Christian. Another time, they took us to the Vermont side of Lake Champlain, where we went to a restaurant. When the waitress came, I asked whether she had chopped chicken liver. Joe and Renee were beside themselves.

"'Did you have to ask for chopped liver?'

"'Why not? I like chopped liver.'

"'Do they have to know you're a Jew from New York?'

"'I don't know why that means I'm a Jew from New York. But if they want to know, then I'm a Jew from New York.' The waitress came back and sure enough, they had chopped liver, and I ate it. But the Vogels— particularly he—were both upset when I asked for what he considered a Jewish dish. But what the hell? I didn't ask for matzoh balls!"

The memory of starvation hadn't left. In their early days in New York, Pips was never able to feel full, no matter how much he ate. One time he was sitting in a deli and the manager came over to him. "I will pay you to sit in the window and eat the way you're eating now!" A friend observed, "He was a really thin guy just trying to fill himself, which he couldn't do," because the hunger was psychological, not physical.

Through the refugee pipeline, Pips learned that he and Olga would need to go to court and file a declaration of intent to become eligible for American citizenship in five years. They duly went to the courthouse on Grand Concourse. A court clerk asked whether they would like to change their name, which was common among immigrants.

"We hadn't seriously considered that and said we didn't know yet. The clerk advised that this was the only time we could do it without charge. If you did it later, we would have to pay for it. I was always interested in bargains, so I couldn't resist. I said to Olga, 'Let's do it. Why pay later?' We were under the impression that everybody in America had an Anglo-Saxon name: Jones, Smith, Williams. We felt that Philipsohn was too complicated, and people misspelled it, so we decided to make it Phillips. Also, I was uncomfortable with my Germanic name *Gerd*. I saw a couple of movies with Gary Cooper, and while I wasn't crazy about him, I always liked the name Gary. But I thought Gary was a nickname for Gerald, so I couldn't just name myself Gary. My middle name was Louis, after my grandfather, who I never met. I wasn't crazy about the name, but they told us we could have a middle initial. In that way, I became Gerald L. Phillips. Our metamorphosis happened just like that."

Pips never stopped feeling guilty for having dropped "sohn" from his surname. "Sohn" means "son of" in German. And although he didn't think about it at the time, he later came to feel that he was negating his father. But the deed was done, and he and Olga now had a fully American name.

Even so, he realized that Americans often shorten "Gerald" to "Gerry"—the disparaging name by which the US forces referred to Germans during the war. That was anathema to him and so "Gerald" became "Gary" henceforth.

When the Phillipses later came before the judge as Displaced Persons, he kindly rebuked them, "You're not displaced persons; you're delayed pilgrims."

June arrived, and the Philippses had now been in New York for five months. The time had come for Pips to find work. Through the same refugee pipeline, he heard that there were waiter jobs at Fleischmann's, a "Borscht Belt" resort village in the Catskills—a favorite of Jews looking to escape to the country in the summer. It was rumored that waiters could make a fortune on tips.

Pips went to an employment office for German Jews and was asked whether he had any experience as a waiter. Given the various jobs for which he had absolutely no preparation in Berlin prisons, he didn't hesitate to lie about having worked as a waiter.

A car was arranged to ferry a group of eight workers to Fleischmann's, where the employment office had a branch from which new hires were distributed to the area hotels. It was July 3, and they were to begin work that night. Pips was assigned to Pitts Mountain Lodge—just him, not Olga. The only job they could offer Olga was playground supervisor at the Pine Hill Country Club, three miles from Fleischmann's.

"We were shell-shocked to be parted! They gave us no time to mourn and said, let's go, no time to waste here. They took me up the road to the Pitts Mountain Lodge, and it turned out that the owner was one of the few non-Jews in Fleischmann's. He was Swiss, and his little hotel had about a dozen rooms. He was very serious, not friendly, but not unfriendly either."

The owner asked the inevitable: "Do you have any experience?" Pips again lied. "Good!" exclaimed the owner, "You have to work with two other waiters who don't have experience, and you have to teach them."

Came dinner time that night, the restaurant was full of German Jews. Pips met the other two waiters, and he prepared them to set up the tables with cutlery. "I had no idea how you do this. I ordered, 'Show me how you do it,' as if I wanted to supervise them. So, they showed me, and I just moved things around a little bit and said okay. Then I was given a big tray. Of course, I didn't know how to hold a tray like this. When dinner started, I held that tray in front of me with all the dishes on top. I must have looked like a real idiot. We served helter-skelter. I had trouble remembering this guy wants chicken with the skin, and the other guy wants all white meat."

Early one afternoon, Pips was called to the telephone. Olga had managed to call from Pine Hill Country Club. "I can't stand it! I can't stand it! Please come and pick me up, you must come and pick me up," she implored on the edge of hysteria. "The kids speak only English, and I don't know how to tell them things. They run wild and I can't handle them. It's terrible and I feel so lonesome."

After dinner service that night, Pips trudged to Pine Hill to find Olga in her room, sitting on the side of the bed, sobbing. Pips calmed her down and assured her that he would find a way to bring her to Pitts Mountain Lodge. "The next day I went to my boss and told him about my wife and said she must come here. He had no job for her. I said that she would sleep with me in the same bed so she won't be in the way, and she can do light stuff to make herself useful. He was already impressed with me, and it was still Fourth of July weekend. He didn't want to be shorthanded and didn't want to let me go. He agreed, and Olga and I were together again.

"But all the guests were poor people: tailors, shoemakers, crafts people who didn't have a pot to pee in themselves, and the hotel was cheap. I got a salary of ten dollars a week. I was supposed to get rich on the tips but, after a week, each couple would give me a grandiose gesture of two dollars for serving three meals a day."

Pips calculated that he was earning ten or fifteen cents an hour. After three weeks, he quit, and the couple returned to New York.

He was now an experienced waiter. He learned of a Jewish restaurant in Washington Heights (in northern Manhattan), which was not far from the Bronx. As a German Jewish neighborhood in the 1940s, it was known as "The Fourth Reich." Pips got the job. But he was clumsy and poured chicken soup on a customer's lap. He was fired within the week. But he was immediately hired as a bicycle messenger for United Service for New Americans (USNA)—a perfect fit for someone who always felt most at home on a bike.

USNA had been founded the year before, in 1946, to help Jewish refugees from Europe. "At that time, it was a big outfit. There were social workers, office workers, medical workers who helped immigrants find jobs, learn English, and get them on their feet. The first year or two, I was a messenger. I got thirty dollars a week minus taxes. There were about a dozen boys who were messengers, a few Americans, and a couple of black guys. The rest, like me, were refugees."

USNA was spilling out of its space at 15 Park Row, across from City Hall Park. They rented more space on lower Broadway, just below Canal Street. Toting a big bag and making his rounds of the in and out baskets on each desk, Pips's daily routine was to shuttle memos and mail from the main headquarters to Broadway.

"I got along very well with my fellow messengers, our supervisor, and the social workers. Although I came from an upper middle-class family, I had no feeling of inferiority because I was a lowly messenger. I dealt with the professionals as equals and they dealt with me as an equal because, if I had been a born American, I would never have been a messenger. I would have gone to college."

Pips joined the union, a part of the Congress of Industrial Organizations, CIO. "The CIO threw out our union because it was Communist dominated. Despite having been liberated by the Soviets, I was not a Communist. I was one of the founders of the new union we started, which was non-communist."

The Wyles continued to onboard their friends to life in America, including bringing them to a political rally. In 1948, Henry Agard Wallace, who had served as vice president under Franklin Roosevelt, campaigned for president as the nominee of the left-leaning Progressive Party. Running against Democrat Harry Truman and Republican Thomas Dewey, Wallace opened his New York campaign with a massive rally in Yankee Stadium.

Holding forth near second base, Wallace's rousing words resonated deeply with Pips: "I had seen the victims of mass prejudice in a DP camp. I had seen and felt—as any decent human being must feel—for the Jewish orphans interned in Italy. . . . To me, fascism is no longer a secondhand experience . . . I have tasted it. . . . And in tasting it, I have reinforced my solemn resolution to fight it wherever and whenever it appears so long as I live!"

"It was the first political rally we ever attended. We had seen the Nazi rallies on news reels, but we had never attended one. And we had never seen a place like Yankee stadium. It was packed!" The *New York Times* projected seventy thousand attendees and *Time* magazine reported forty-eight thousand. "At the end, they sang the 'Battle Hymn of the Republic' with different words: Henry Wallace leads his army against destruction, fear, and hate, the people marching on. The whole fifty thousand people sang, and we were enormously impressed. But when I began to know a little more about America, I became less leftist influenced."

In 1949, Gerd "Loki" Hoffnung, his mischievous classmate from the Lachmann school, made an unexpected appearance in New York. His parents had managed to emigrate with him to England. By the time of his visit, he had become a famous cartoonist. "When he walked in, he looked like John Bull, a typical portly Englishman with a beard and pipe in his mouth. 'I say,' he said. 'So good seeing you!' Just seeing him and hearing a few words, we were practically on the floor with laughter. He told us he had a very strange housekeeper who drank the bathwater. Things no normal person would ever think of, he said with a straight face. We said 'Maybe she just opens the drain and it runs down. 'Oh, that's a thought, why didn't I think of that?' He was terribly amusing." Hoffnung died only a few years later at the age of thirty-four.

Still at USNA, Pips was eventually promoted to stockman, and later to clerk. When he was given his own desk, he felt like an executive. His salary increased with each promotion, but in 1949, he was still earning $30 a week. Even so, he and Olga jumped at the chance to move out of their Bronx walk-up to Brooklyn.

Bert Wyle had been living in a basement apartment in Brooklyn but was preparing to move to the Midwest to take a new job. The apartment was in a modest row house on Gerritsen Avenue in a beachfront neighborhood. There was an oil burner in the basement and a small garage next to the apartment. When Bert told Olga and Pips about the impending vacancy, they immediately rented his former abode for $50 a month.

"The only problem was we had no furniture. The one time in my life I ever borrowed money was from Charlie Wyle—two hundred dollars to buy a sleeper sofa. After a while the mattress was shot, and we slept on the bare springs. Somebody gave us some chairs. We were slightly below street level, and we had a window out to the tiny little garden, if you can call it that. It was a pretty miserable place. We ate next to the oil burner at a little fold-out table that opened off the wall on a piece of plywood, and Olga had a small gas range there. From there I had to commute by subway to my job in downtown New York. It was a long ride—forty-five minutes to an hour—but from the Bronx, it was a long ride, too. I made very little money, and we couldn't swing our rent on thirty dollars a week."

A second cousin of Olga's from Hungary, also named Charlie, came to the rescue. They had made contact shortly after moving to Brooklyn. A middle-aged family man, he took the young emigres under his wing. His wife was a very good cook, and the couple visited them once or twice a week for real chicken soup with matzoh balls and great boiled beef.

"He introduced us to the joys of television, which we saw for the first time in his home. The highlight was Milton Berle."

More importantly, the cousin gave Pips a weekend job at Tropic Isle, the catering hall he owned in downtown Brooklyn. He would be paid $20 a night, no tipping. “It was a large rundown old building with two ballrooms, each with a bar, a place for Italians who didn’t have much money but had a big family. They had a small band and served pre-packed sandwiches. One kind was ham on white bread and the other was cheese on white bread. We piled the sandwiches on the table and served beer in big pitchers. I was the only male and the only Jew besides eight waitresses. Of course, they knew I was related to the boss, but I didn’t pull the ‘I’m-a-cousin’ kind of shtick. I was one of them and worked just as hard as they did. They had a manager who was Italian. Cousin Charlie had a good heart but could be very nasty. When he got mad at his manager, he called him a lousy banana peddler. With my minority complex, I felt that if this guy wasn’t already an antisemite, he would surely become one with this lousy Jew calling him a banana peddler.”

Pips’s waitering pratfall days were not yet over. In one instance, beer had been spilled on the floor. Pips, carrying two pitchers, walked across the puddle, slipped, and landed flat on his back. The pitchers he was holding both decanted on his head. “I was doused with beer, but I was lucky that I didn’t get hit in the head with glass pitchers.”

Pips was now working seven days a week. He had to arrive at Tropic Isle in the mid-afternoon on Saturday to set up and then serve and clean up until the early morning hours on Sunday. He repeated the drill on Sunday to Monday. “I had one advantage: when we were all finished, Cousin Charlie would drive me home in his enormous Chrysler. Sometimes he would take me to an all-night diner, where he treated me to bagels and lox.” This went on until 1951. The extra forty dollars a week helped, and after a time, Olga and Pips were able to buy a television set.

After the night’s programs were over, they watched the infomercials. Americans were just starting to learn about the link between cholesterol and heart disease. But Olga and Pips found Americans’ attitudes toward food bizarre. The commercials they watched touted low calorie counts and low-fat content. For Pips, who had endured five years of starvation, this was inexplicable. He recalled the cow that the Soviet soldiers had slaughtered for him in Germany. He and Olga couldn't get enough of the fat on that animal!

As mean as their lives were, Olga and Pips made their first American friends in their row house basement. For several evenings, Pips heard hammering late in the evening from the basement in the next house. He finally decided to knock on the door and nicely ask the neighbors to stop. That visit led to a lifelong friendship with Frances and John Cameola and their growing family.

"John was a dark-room man. He was unsophisticated but intelligent. He couldn't speak very coherently but he was a wonderful guy. His wife was an angel, a charming woman who had love in her heart. We loved to go to them for dinner even though they were also pretty poor. Their parents came from Sicily, so John knew how to cook, and he loved to eat. Just to be at his table, with his gusto, increased our enjoyment of the food."

Pips stayed with USNA for four years. "During these four years, they retrenched. They fired people every weekend." In 1951, Pips was also let go. But a former Schulstrasse connection led to an introduction that launched Pips's lifelong career.

Ellen Epstein, a fellow inmate in Schulstrasse, was the same age as Pips's parents. After liberation, Olga and Pips met her daughter, Sonia, in Berlin. Sonia had worked as a press photographer in the 1940s. In 1944, she married Tim Gidal, born Ignaz Nachum Gidalewitsch, a pioneering photojournalist, who had begun working in Germany in 1929. During the war, he served in the Jewish Brigade and was chief photojournalist of the Eighth British Army. His renowned photos would find their way to *Life* magazine, Britain's National Portrait Gallery, and countless other outlets and venues. Pips recalled that Gidal had also unearthed previously unknown photos of Abraham Lincoln's funeral. Matthew Brady's civil war photos were the ones that became icons, but they were all posed. Gidal, on the other hand, found candid shots of Lincoln's funeral cortege. He sold them to *Life,* where they were published in 1946. Later, Sonia and Tim co-wrote *My Village, a* popular series of twenty-five photographic books, each featuring a different country through the eyes of its children.

The Epstein-Gidals moved Stateside in 1948, one year after Olga and Pips. Both Sonia and her mother were very fond of Olga, and the two families remained in touch in New York. When Sonia and Tim heard that Pips was losing his job at USNA, they offered to help him find a new job and directed him to contact Mrs. Leonhardt, the owner of a photo agency, Camera Clix. She immediately hired Pips as a salesman.

Pips had never heard of a photo agency and didn't know what it was. Nor had he ever owned a camera. "I knew nothing about photography. I knew nothing about magazines. But, at the agency, there was a guy from Berlin who had been in the newspaper business before the Nazis. He took me under his wing and explained to me what to do. He sent me out to see editors to sell them photos. I spoke English pretty well by then, but I didn't speak the language of the photo agencies. Yet the editors and I became friends. They told me jokes and I told them jokes. I didn't do much business, but I always had a good time."

The editors with whom Pips hobnobbed were the likes of Lawrence Sanders, Clay Felker, and Hugh Hefner, among others.

Sanders was managing editor of *Mechanics Illustrated.* When his editor died, Sanders assumed he would be promoted, but he was passed over. Sanders quit and went on to write blockbuster crime novels, including the "Deadly Sins" series.

Felker had a similar story. He quit *Esquire* to start a Sunday roto section that became *New York Magazine.*

Hefner went on to start *Playboy*.

At the time, "these were hundred-dollar-a-week guys."

With his solid job at Camera Clix, Olga and Pips could leave their basement hovel. They relocated to an apartment in Kew Gardens. A leafy area in Queens with a vast park, Kew Gardens was home to many Central Europeans and Holocaust survivors. The neighborhood became a national symbol of indifference when Kitty Genovese was murdered, allegedly under the eyes of many witnesses watching from their homes. (This later turned out to be inaccurate.) It was also a neighborhood that boasted a disproportionate number of success stories. Among its many bold-face residents were Burt Bacharach, Ralph Bunche, Charlie Chaplin, Rodney Dangerfield, Anais Nin, Dorothy Parker, Will Rogers Jr. and Sr., Robert Schimmel, Jerry Springer, and Dick Van Patten. A film, *Last Stop Kew Gardens*, was made exploring what accounted for so many notables emerging from this small enclave.

Kew Gardens was also a stop on the way to Idlewild Airport, which later became JFK International Airport. As such, it was a convenient place to house airline personnel. Olga and Pips found themselves next to apartments shared by noisy stewardesses. They weren't happy, but it was certainly an improvement over the Brooklyn basement they had left. And even though they were now in another borough, they still visited the Cameolas at least once a week.

Among the editors with whom Pips worked was Jack Podell. "One late afternoon, I went to see an editor at Fawcett Publishing, which published a lot of magazines, including *True Confessions*, *Mechanics Illustrated*, *Motion Picture*, *Fan*, and *Cavalier*, which at that time covered outdoor men's stuff like hunting and fishing. The managing editor was Jack Podell, and I had some ideas I thought he might be interested in. Nothing came of the picture story, but he picked up on my accent and asked me where I'm from. I started telling him and he was fascinated. He really wanted to know: Olga had been in Auschwitz, my God! We sat for two hours, and he couldn't hear enough. We each called our wives to say we'd be late. Since he also lived in Queens, he drove me home. He wanted to meet Olga and she came downstairs. From that moment on we became friends."

One day, Pips got an idea for a picture story: a woman wearing a hat that looked like a manhole cover. He hired a photographer, and they found a spot for the shoot. Now they needed a model. A press agent proposed his client, Shari Lewis, a ventriloquist with a sock puppet named Lambchop. Her father, Abraham Hurwitz, was a founding professor at Yeshiva University of New York City, who also taught magic tricks. His career was devoted to using play as a tool to encourage children to learn. His influence on his daughter's career was clear: she used her famous puppet as an educational tool. Shari, who would later have her own TV show, was already on her way to celebrity, and she did the shoot. A magazine ran the story, and she became friends with Olga and Pips.

In May 1952, Olga and Pips again found themselves at a Westside pier in Manhattan. This time, they were there as American citizens, waiting to meet newly arrived refugees. Olga's cousin, Sidonie Horvath Beitscher, a fellow Hungarian Holocaust survivor, was arriving on the *Ile de France* with her husband, Ignatz, and their five-and-a-half-year-old-daughter. That daughter, named Georgette, is the author of this book.

Sidonie's father and Olga's grandfather were brothers and Olga and Sidonie were both born in Transylvania. But Sidonie grew up in Sopron, a picturesque medieval town near the Austrian border. Valedictorian of her gymnasium class, she left her parents' home at age eighteen to pursue a trade in Budapest. Living there with her older half-sister, she learned to design and create custom-made lingerie and undergarments. She pioneered the use of lacy material that could provide support without using sharp stays that dug into the skin.

Like Olga's parents, Sidonie's mother and father also perished at the hands of the Nazis, both murdered in Auschwitz; her brother-in-law was shot and thrown into the Danube, while her brother fled to join the French Foreign Legion.

Ignatz was a native of Krakow. When his wife refused to be separated from her children, she and two daughters were shot in front of him in the Tarnow ghetto. He later escaped concentration camp and fled to Hungary with his sister using false papers.

Sidonie was running a corset and lingerie salon illegally in Budapest at a time when Jews were forbidden to own businesses. The glamorous blonde took a daily coffee break in a café across the street. One afternoon, a Polish man—Ignatz—and a woman came into the café and expounded on the horrors they had experienced in their country. The patrons of the café pegged them as alarmists. But Sidonie believed them and took them in. During one of the air raids, when the residents of her apartment building took shelter in the basement, a fascist neighbor noticed the strangers and denounced her to the Gestapo for hiding Jews. Sidonie was subsequently arrested and sent to prison. She was later sent to Kistarcsa, a concentration camp in Hungary.

After being captured, Ignatz was put on a train headed for Mauthausen, a concentration camp in annexed Austria. He jumped off the moving train and escaped. With his Aryan looks and fluent German, which he had mastered as a boxer in Berlin during World War I, he was determined to save the woman who had taken him in. As he wended his way back to Hungary, he encountered a German officer, killed him, and stole his uniform. Now dressed in full Nazi regalia, he brazenly approached the Kommandant of Kistarcsa. "I have a girlfriend in this camp, who happens to be a very good seamstress," he confided. "Perhaps you should have her work for your wife in your home." The Kommandant liked the idea, and Sidonie daily trekked from the camp to work in his home. It was from there that Ignatz engineered Sidonie's escape.

He found a hiding place in a Budapest mansion—the very site that the Soviets took as their headquarters when they later liberated Hungary. As they moved in, the Soviets found Jews hiding in the basement, including a man who looked very Aryan to them. Given the hatred of the Soviets for Germans, Ignatz might well have been shot on the spot. However, he quickly dropped his pants to show them his circumcised penis—and that's what saved his life.

For his many heroic acts, including his attempt to save her parents, Sidonie was in awe of Ignatz. They married in 1946 in Budapest, which is where I was born.

Sidonie, Ignatz, and I escaped to France from Budapest in 1948, soon after the Iron Curtain had descended on Eastern Europe. We lived variously in Paris and Lyon while awaiting our emigration papers for the US. Ignatz's cousin, Eugene Beitscher, provided an affidavit that allowed us to enter the country. And that's what led to the moment when Olga and Pips met us at the pier to welcome us to America.

After a two-week sojourn in Brooklyn with cousin Eugene, the new arrivals moved to Kew Gardens to be near the Phillipses.

Unbeknownst to anyone, Ignatz, who was sixteen years older than Sidonie, was riddled with metastasized lung and pancreatic cancer. After a five-year wait to get to America, he died only one year after arriving in New York. Sidonie, now a thirty-six-year-old widow with a six-year-old child, had to make her way in a new country alone. She got part-time jobs at DePinna and Tailored Woman—fashionable stores of their day that no longer exist. She ultimately opted to go into business for herself and support her child by making custom-made corsets, bras, and nightgowns from her innovative designs. Her clients would come to include Margaretta "Happy" Rockefeller, the New York State Governor's wife, and other denizens of high society. After her death, her pieces would be in the fashion collections of the Museum of the City of New York and the Fashion

Institute of Technology Museum. But, for now, she was just another traumatized refugee trying to restart her life. And Pips came to think of me as his "virtual daughter."

"Georgette was now fatherless, living with her mother. They had no family, and we had no family. We were close to them physically and as relatives, so Georgette latched on to me as a sort of father substitute. I spent many afternoons and evenings with her and tried to teach her geography and things like that. She had a big crush on me, and as sometimes happens with older people and little kids, I took to her, too."

Jack Podell was now managing editor of *Motion Picture* magazine, and he tried to throw Pips some business. But Camera Clix, which also sold reproductions of paintings from world-famous museums, had very little material for movie publications. One day, Jack phoned Pips to tell him he'd arranged an interview with Judy Holliday—an A-list star under contract with Columbia Pictures. Podell was going to spend the day with her at Christie's, the Metropolitan Museum of Art, and other locations. He needed a photographer to cover him, whom Pips provided.

They arrived at Holliday's apartment at The Dakota on Central Park West, where a limousine was waiting to take them around for the day. Pips rang her door bell several times before hearing some shuffling feet and a sleepy voice asking, "Who's there?" Holliday opened the door in her robe and said, "You woke me up. Come on in, boys. Give me a little time to get fixed up."

Holliday's mother came in and invited Pips, Jack, and the photographer to sit down in the enormous living room with a grand piano that had layers of cardboard under the legs. The mother asked whether they were hungry and offered them homemade chopped chicken liver sandwiches. After a half hour, Holliday entered and was ready to leave for Christie's. It was a warm day, but she wore a mink coat. Jack quizzically asked her why. "I gained twenty pounds in the last six months and I'm going to platz right out of my dress so I'm covering myself with this coat. This bastard, Harry Cohen, who's head of Columbia Pictures, told me 'You slob. You either lose twenty pounds or you can go to hell!'"

Pips immediately thought of Sidonie and her custom-made corsets, which could slim down the body a couple of sizes without being unduly constraining. Pips told Holliday that Sidonie's garments could make her look twenty pounds slimmer. Jack was mortified but Holliday was intrigued. She eyed Pips suspiciously and asked, "How much does she charge for those things?" "Seventy-five dollars," Pips responded. She looked at Pips like he was crazy. He later learned that Holliday was famous for being a tightwad. Although Pips didn't convince Judy Holliday to spring for a Madame Sidonie original, Mrs. Leonhardt, the owner of Camera Clix, became an enduring customer.

Rita Gam, a stunning beauty with dark wavy hair and light eyes, needed some color publicity shots and came to the Camera Clix studio. She had been a roommate of Grace Kelly, whose Cinderella story led her to marry the Prince of Monaco. Rita, herself a movie star, was married to director Sidney Lumet, but they were in the throes of divorce. She asked Pips to bring the photos to her home when they were developed, which he did. "She had such sad eyes. She was heartbroken because her husband had left her. I spent a couple of hours there, she served me some coffee, and we talked."

Pips remained with Camera Clix for four years. Then in 1955, Jack Podell introduced Pips to Globe Photos, one of the largest picture agencies in the world. Globe held the world's largest collection of celebrity photos—more than 2.5 million—and three million photos of other subjects, along with 26,000 picture stories. Their archives included the last pictures of Marilyn Monroe on a movie set, including a nude scene, which Globe sold to *Life* magazine and later to *Playboy*. Globe hired Pips as a salesman, and there began Pips's next step up the ladder of the American dream.

CHAPTER 11

MOVING UP IN THE NEW WORLD

Eight years had passed since Olga and Pips sailed through the Verrazano Narrows to get their first glimpse of America. It was now 1955 and they still didn't have a car. Jack Podell, who had become like a brother to Pips, had met the Vogels and badgered Pips to get his own car. "You can't always rely on the Vogels. It's not fair to them and it's not fair to you because you have to dance when they whistle and go where they want to go." Pips, who had saved one thousand dollars, finally gave in. With John Cameola providing expert guidance, he bought a used Oldsmobile.

John and some other friends taught Pips how to drive. "I never paid for a driver's course. When I took my driver's license test, everybody said they never pass you the first time. But I passed right away."

Now Pips had to figure out where to keep the car. The apartment building in which they were living in Kew Gardens had a garage. For $50 a month, his problem was solved. "That was a lot for us, but we managed."

The new used car got quite a workout that first year.

Their first outing was to Bar Harbor, Maine, where Olga and Pips feasted on lobster and booked a stay at Range Pond State Park. But hordes of pesky flies drove them away from the waterfront to an inland resort where flies were less of a nuisance. They were shown around a spot with rustic cabins. At the end of the tour the host confided, "I think you'll enjoy it here. We don't have any Hebrews."

"Later, I kicked myself. Why didn't I tell that son of a bitch to go and stick his head in something?"

On the way back, they stopped in New Hampshire and stayed in a large hotel for two days. Going up Mount Washington, they overheard some very WASPish tourists make cracks about Jews.

With a car in the garage, and his new independence, Pips reached out to Rita Gam, hoping to ease her melancholy. "I called her up and said, 'Rita, I'm taking my wife on Saturday to a beach in Connecticut. Would you like to come along?' She didn't sound terribly enthusiastic, but she agreed. We picked her up and drove on the Merritt Parkway up to the beach and plunked ourselves down on a blanket. Rita sat between Olga and me. We swam and, after a while, we got tired. She lay down and fell asleep on the blanket and so did I. When I told the story to friends, they kidded me and said, "Ah, Gary, the guy who slept with Rita Gam!"

Pips was infatuated with Rita and the two kept in touch with occasional phone calls. Once, when she sounded very down, Pips asked if she'd like him to come over to hold her hand. Rita declined. "She must have smelled that I had a crush on her, and even though I had no specific idea of making a pass, I wanted to cozy up with her a little. That ended our relationship." The following year, Gam married Thomas Guinzburg, co-founder of *Paris Review*. The marriage lasted for seven years, but she and Pips never saw each other again.

The Phillipses, both of whom loved nature, wanted to find a weekend getaway that was closer to home. Exploring the Catskills, they came to Lexington, a small town in the southeastern corner of the mountains, along the Schoharie Creek. On the way to Lexington, they saw a billboard for Shangri La Lodge. The creek flowed nearby, and the hilly terrain made for beautiful scenery. The building itself was a shack. It was just before the busy summer season and the couple knocked on the door. A man opened and Olga and Pips immediately noticed his Polish accent. "That didn't sit too well but, although he was not a Jew, we noticed that he had the tattoo from Auschwitz on his arm.

"'Were you in Auschwitz?'

"'Yes, I was in Auschwitz.'

"'Well, Olga was in Auschwitz. How come you were in Auschwitz?"

"'I was with a partisan group in the woods, and we were caught and sent to Auschwitz.'

"The proprietor had the impression that all Jews were Communists, so he claimed to be one. I would say to him, 'I'm not a Communist and I have no intention of becoming one. If you want to be a Communist, I don't give a shit. You be a Communist but not me. I'm a bourgeois through and through.' Later, we got to know him better, and we were sure his partisans were a fascist group. Polish partisans hated the Germans, they hated the Russians, and they hated the Jews more than anything. But he was very friendly and said, 'Oh, we'd love to take you. Come on weekends. We have a nice crowd here.' They had six rooms, if you can call them rooms. They were more like wooden partitions, so you would hear the guy snoring from three rooms away. But it was only seven dollars and fifty cents a day for the two of us and they had good food."

All the patrons were Poles, including one Jewish woman who occasionally stayed there. She warned Olga and Pips, "You think they're nice to you because they like you, but when they speak Polish with each other, you should hear what they're saying. Oh, this guy was 'jewed' by so and so and 'don't behave like a Jew.' 'You know what the guy just said about another Pole? You play like a Jew.' That was not meant as a compliment. Don't kid yourself. This is how they were brought up. It's inbred."

The Phillipses took it all in stride and were summer weekend visitors for a good number of years. "Saturday night we usually would sit around the bonfire and sing. Most of the songs we sang were Polish songs. We sang the 'Marseillaise' and some other French songs, Russian songs, American songs—anything but German songs."

"And then came the Six-Day War in Israel, and the Israelis knocked the shit out of five Arab armies. I remember the Polish proprietor saying: 'Oh, those Jews, nobody ever thought they had it in them.' They all thought the Jews were cowards just because they didn't want to fight for the Czar. I almost said, 'you lousy bastard, the fact that we gave you the Bible; the fact that we have, throughout history, contributed more than any other people numerically to what's called Western civilization; the fact that we have won ten times as many Nobel Prizes as any other group of the same size—that means nothing to you Poles.' To him, intellectual or cultural achievement meant nothing. But to shoot straight, that meant something."

Eventually, Shangri La Lodge was sold to a Ukrainian family. "Now, if anything is worse than Poles, it's the Ukrainians, as far as the Jews are concerned. These Ukrainian owners had fled to Australia when the German armies were pushed back. They were nice people, and we kept coming for two more seasons, even though it wasn't the same anymore. All the other guests were Ukrainians, and they even built a Ukrainian church not far from there."

The weekend forays to the Catskills didn't quench Pips's thirst for driving. The year he bought the used Oldsmobile was also the year he took the first of several cross-country trips, this one to Estes Park, Colorado.

"I loved driving through Nebraska. People asked me, 'What's there to love about Nebraska?' It was so different. You start out with the flat Middle West, the flat prairies. Then rolling prairies, up and down like a roller coaster, and in those days we didn't have the interstates yet, it was just highways. We have the flatland and as you come toward the western part of Nebraska you get a foretaste of the West. You see a low butte here and another one there and then suddenly, when you get to the western edge into Colorado, you see this string of snow-capped mountains in summer. For me, this was all a discovery."

When they arrived in Estes Park, Olga and Pips stayed at a small cabin-style resort with a fireplace and raccoons scurrying under the floor. The owner had been a safari enthusiast, who did big game hunting in Africa. "One thing I didn't like about this place was that, in the main hall, there were trophies on the wall—head of a lion, antelope. I like to see these animals alive, not hanging on somebody's wall, and I don't like the idea of guys behind high-power rifles shooting animals."

In Estes Park, the Phillipses met a family by the name of Schultz. As they got into conversation, Pips asked Charles what he did for a living. "He looked at me and thought I was kidding. Charles Schultz was already famous for his *Peanuts* cartoons. But I had never looked at a comic strip and had not heard of him. The only thing that impressed me was that he had a German name."

Pips, who always loved hiking, trekked deep into the mountains. But Olga, who had trouble walking on the way to Erkner in 1945, still couldn't walk well. Pips put her on a horse, so she could comfortably navigate steep and narrow trails while he held the reins of the horse. That was the only way that Olga could have accompanied him.

Happy with their car and the freedom it brought, but unhappy in their noisy Kew Gardens apartment, the Phillipses came across an ad for an attic apartment in Kew Gardens Hills. Unlike the attic Pips inhabited at Schulstrasse, this one was in a private home, and it had a terrace. Privacy was ensured by the separate entrance that led directly to their habitat. "It didn't look like an attic. It had a corner cut where the roof was, but it was cozy—a small, comfortable, apartment with a living room, bedroom, kitchen with a breakfast nook, a bathroom and an undeveloped part of the attic which served us very well as storage space." There was no air conditioning, but the house had a two-car garage, which included a space for the Oldsmobile. Pips paid $150 a month rent for the entire package and he and Olga were finally together in a real home.

I could see their house from the window of my room and, over the ten years that they lived there, I frequently took the short walk across Queens Boulevard to Union Turnpike to sit in their Danish modern living room to confide whatever teenage angst I didn't feel able to share with my mother. Pips always called me Georgie.

It was now 1959—twelve years since Pips had last seen his mother—and he prepared to return to Europe for the first time. He and Olga booked a group flight through the Westside Democratic Club. It was close to 100 degrees on the day of their departure, and their unchilled attic apartment was unbearable. In order to cool down, they took showers all through the day. They made a resolution: the first thing they would do after their return from Europe would be to buy an air conditioner.

Finally, the moment came to leave for the airport. When they got there, they learned their flight was delayed until the following morning. As a result, they slept in air-conditioned comfort in a Manhattan hotel, courtesy of TWA. Their plane finally took off and stopped in Newfoundland to refuel. It then crossed the Atlantic with another refueling stop in Dublin before finally landing in London. Although TWA initiated its first international jet flights to London in 1959, this was still a propellor plane. As Olga looked out the window, she thought she saw flames shooting out of the engine, but these were just the normal exhaust fumes of the rotors.

Globe Photos had agents all over Europe, and its London agent had made arrangements for their arrival. But because their flight had been delayed, they had to immediately take off for Berlin with a stopover in Hamburg. As soon as they disembarked, Olga got sick. "With my warped sense of humor, I said, 'Welcome back to Germany!' and she almost fainted. The last place in the world she wanted to be was Germany. We didn't want to go to Germany; we wanted to go to Europe. But we agreed on a stopover for three days in Berlin to see my mother."

Marie, who lived in Thüringen, was now in her seventies. She was married to Walter Ranke, the printer with whom she had lived in Gera. She and her husband arrived at the Hilton Hotel just as Olga and Pips were finishing a bountiful American breakfast.

"Instead of 'Hi, Sweetheart, I'm happy to see you!' the first thing my mother said as she walked in the door was: 'Your nose has become so long!' That already pissed me off. It didn't take her long to start complaining that we hadn't sent her enough food packages. I wasn't making a lot of money. But we sent her packages at least once or twice a month. Then she told me, 'If I were a Jewish mother, I would know how to get more out of you.' Well, that did it! I said something to Olga in English, which I knew my mother wouldn't understand. My mother didn't like that either. 'You don't have to speak English here! You don't have to play the big American.' 'Mother, I'm a little rusty. I haven't spoken German for many years. Even though I will never forget it, conversational German is a little tough for me.' She didn't believe a word of that and thought I was just putting on airs. Then they ate all our leftovers. We spent three days there and barely managed to keep the peace."

While in Berlin, Olga and Pips got in touch with Nurse Margaret, who had seduced Pips in Schulstrasse and to whom they had sold their apartment before leaving for America. She had completed her medical education and was now a practicing physician. On the last day before leaving Berlin, she and her husband hosted Olga and Pips for dinner. They had barely arrived when the telephone rang. It was Pips's mother.

"I understand my son is there and I'm feeling really sick," she whined. "Can you come over to where I'm staying?"

"My mother had known Margaret while we were still in Germany and Margaret knew my mother could put on a good act. 'Oh, Mrs. Ranke,' she advised, 'just take a couple of aspirins and call me in the morning. If it really gets bad, you should go to a hospital.' Margaret got rid of her because she knew this was fake. My mother was jealous and angry that she hadn't been invited to this dinner, and that we went without her. This, after we had gone out of our way to spend three days with her. The next day my mother came to the airport to see us off and that was the real start of our vacation."

Despite the sour experience with his mother, Pips felt nostalgia for Berlin. West Berlin had been his home for more than twenty-four years and he had deep roots there. But it was still in ruins. East Berlin, which was under Communist rule, was in even worse shape. "All the people who had made my milieu, my life, the whole context of my life—it was all gone, except for Margaret."

Olga was horrified to be in Berlin and hated every minute of their stay. She still hated to hear German spoken and she certainly didn't like Marie. Olga could barely breathe. When they arrived in Rome, she could finally exhale.

Globe's Rome agent had made reservations for them in a modest hotel off Via Condotti. The next morning, Pips awoke with a terrible migraine, a malady that would plague him for much of his life. But, this time, it was cured with his first ever espresso.

"Our Globe agent, who was Italian, had a charming wife. They showed us around Rome and took us to a restaurant with a lot of outdoor seating. It was very colorful, and we loved the food. Then we went to St. Peter's, just Olga and me. As soon as we walked in, we saw stalls inside the church selling souvenirs and exchanging money to lira. The Catholic church made a big fuss about Jesus chasing the moneychangers from the Temple. Yet here, in their prime real estate, their holiest of holies, there were literal moneychangers. They sold T-shirts and crap like that right inside the church. We spent quite some time going to various churches to see the magnificent art. But I wondered how they could have religious services in a place where your eyes are diverted by art. I always liked the feeling of synagogues, particularly Orthodox synagogues, which are totally unadorned—nothing, just benches, Torah, and that's it. You're supposed to concentrate your thoughts and feelings on the prayers."

Pips didn't understand Catholicism's approach. In its ornate churches, one is witnessing and being inspired by the beauty of God. As such, it's less of a concentrated exercise and more of a sensory exchange. To Pips's mind, this was a form of paganism—especially after his visit to Castel Sant'Angelo.

"A guide took us to a large room where the pope spent a lot of time. All around the low ceiling are frescoes of these fauns screwing like there's no tomorrow. And the guide explained that, for many of the popes, this was their pornography. I appreciate pornography; I have nothing against it, as long as it's not too stupid. I felt vindicated that even the popes appreciated pornography. We loved Rome!"

The following year, Olga and Pips again returned to Berlin. They walked through the Tiergarten, which had been replanted after being destroyed by incendiary bombs and the fallen trees had been chopped up for firewood. When they came to the east-west axis, there stood the Soviet War Memorial for which Pips had, fifteen years earlier, been summoned to help dig the foundation. With its six soaring arches and a center column topped by a Soviet soldier in full battle gear, the memorial was one of three sites in West Berlin that East Berliners were permitted to visit. "We just looked at it and remembered that I was partly responsible for this. There were at least two spadefuls of earth I had excavated for this thing. We stood at the barrier opposite the monument and could see the soldiers. We waved to them. But we didn't want them to think we were Germans, so we yelled, 'Amerikansky!' They couldn't wave back because they were standing at attention, but we could see broad grins on their faces. We just wanted to let them know we don't all hate you."

In 1960, Pips's used Oldsmobile was succeeded by a new white Ford Thunderbird convertible with red leather seats. That car took them cross country again—this time all the way to LA via Las Vegas. Long vacation trips and the weekends in rustic towns were the highlights of Pips's year. In 1961, they were again in Europe. When a teenage Pips had planned a trip to Zermatt, his love for Lucienne Levy derailed him. But this time, he was in his thirties and he arrived at the mountain resort, as scheduled, with Olga. Always an avid hiker, he ogled the four-thousand-meter peaks.

"After our arrival, I went on a hiking trip with a group guided by a little old Swiss guy. He led us uphill until we came to the bottom of a glacier. The first part of the hike lasted six hours. We were ready to run. But the guide walked very slowly. He knew what he was doing. He knew you had to pace yourself to preserve your strength."

On their second Zermatt visit, in 1965, Pips decided to tackle the glacier on his own. He managed to get up about one-third of the way to the Matterhorn. "Maybe with a guide, I could have done it. To go without a guide is suicide." Not to be deterred, Pips put on his heavy paratrooper boots and set out toward the glacier, taking two cable cars. There was no one in sight and he started walking on the glacier.

"It had been fairly warm on the days before that. When it gets warm, crevasses open. During the night, they freeze over and, if there's light snowfall, which there usually is during the night, you don't see the crevasse. To go alone and fall into a crevasse of twelve or fifteen feet, you've had it. You can't get out by yourself. By the time they find you you're a frozen corpse. But this was a beautiful sunny day. I got to the top and, to my surprise, I saw a cable car on the Italian side, with young people jumping out to ski on the glacier. There was no cable car on the Swiss side. I sat myself down on the tip and ate my lunch sandwich. As I was eating, clouds began to gather. My stomach began to bother me and I started to get a headache. This wasn't the first time that I had a problem with the altitude, so I took two Excedrin. When I finished my sandwich, it began to snow. I thought I might as well make my way down. Within minutes, the snowfall became a blizzard, and my headache became the migraine to end all migraines. I was practically blind. I was in a whiteout and I couldn't see more than a couple of feet in front of me. I knew I had to make it down the glacier because the only cure for this kind of altitude sickness is to descend. On either side of the glacier, there were precipices going down a couple of thousand feet. I walked like a dying man in this whiteout trying to find my way back to the cable car at the foot of the glacier and after a couple of hours—miracle of miracles—I got there, half unconscious. It was just five minutes before five and the last cable car was leaving. There was nobody else there except the conductor. As I walked into the cable car, I realized I had to puke. I didn't want to puke in the nice cable car, so I walked out of the cable car and started. The conductor waved me into the cable car because it was going to leave now and he couldn't stop it. There was a trap door at the bottom of the car and the conductor opened it up. Visualize this: I am standing at the edge of this trap door puking my head off, under me is two thousand feet of thin air and I'm still nearly unconscious."

At this lower altitude, the blizzard became a thunderstorm with lightning bolts shooting out of the sky. The cable car paused, and swung in place with Pips fearing that he would fall through the trap door. When the car finally arrived at the way station to connect with the next cable car, Pips stumbled into the car. There were a few stragglers on this second leg of the descent, and one gave Pips Baldrian, a German tonic, that revived him. He walked back to the hotel and after a brief rest, he and Olga headed to dinner. Pips could easily have died in the whiteout, but Lady Luck was with him again.

He tested her again, as he had always been wont to do, on another Swiss hike. "It was wonderful weather, and I started out with my little satchel. I had some sandwiches and a first aid kit. After a couple of hours in higher elevations, the trail was no longer visible because it was solid rock. But it wasn't terribly steep, so I thought I could make it. Metal bars were drilled into the rock as trail markers but after a short while I got lost. I found myself on a very narrow ledge with a sheer drop beside me. It wasn't even a good place to stand. I thought if I went to the edge of the ledge, which was only about thirty feet long, maybe I could find something further. But the ledge just petered out. Having gotten there, I should have been able to get back. But I couldn't go forward, and I couldn't go backward. Then I noticed another ledge, which seemed broader, but I couldn't pull myself up to it. The little satchel was in my way, so I let it drop until it sailed out of sight into the trees below. It occurred to me that, maybe five minutes from now, I'd be following the satchel. Then I saw a couple emerging from the woods at the beginning of the rock ledges. I called, casually, 'Could you help me?' They didn't hear me. Now, to hell with it: 'Help!' I wasn't sure he heard me. Then my last trick. In German, I yelled: '*Hilfe*!' I yelled at the top of my lungs and was embarrassed as hell but it's better to be embarrassed than dead. They heard me and shouted back in German, 'We're coming.' He got out on the ledge with me and his wife had a rope, which she tied around him. He helped me on to that higher ledge and from there I could get out. On the way back, I found my little satchel."

That satchel would accompany Pips on many hair-raising hikes, which left Olga alone and anxious about whether her husband would return in one piece, if at all. His chronic risk-taking and her chronic anxiety would take its toll on their marriage. But that was later, much later. For now, they were still basking in their emergence from terror and starvation into newfound freedom and glamour.

In 1966, on the recommendation of Renee Vogel, they made the first of twenty-eight annual pilgrimages to Caneel Bay, the exclusive Rock Resort on St. John, the smallest of the US Virgin Islands.

Caneel Bay was developed by Laurance Rockefeller in the 1950s. He had purchased five thousand acres—nearly half of the pristine island—which he later donated to the US government as a national park and on which he built his exclusive resort.

On their first stay at Caneel, Olga and Pips met a welcoming couple on the beach who immediately chatted them up. Herb Hahn was a senior public relations executive, and his wife chaired the French department at an exclusive private school in New York. Later in the day, along with another couple, they chartered a fishing boat. "I wasn't interested in fishing; I was interested in boating. I don't enjoy killing animals, any kind for any purpose—unless I need to. I was being fed well enough; I didn't need to fish for myself."

Later in the day, Olga, Pips, and Herb walked around and discovered Turtle Bay, which was more secluded than other parts of Caneel. "We saw a cottage up there—Room 99—which was different from all the units in the old main house. Olga and I both said, 'This is for us.' So next time—we'd already decided there was going to be a next time—we will ask for Room 99." And that became their room for the next twenty-seven years.

But the friendship with the Hahns lasted even longer. For forty years, Olga and Pips were hosted for black-tie Thanksgivings by the Hahns and their four daughters. Because Thanksgiving coincided with their anniversary, Olga and Pips were always feted with gifts and a cake. It was a sacrosanct tradition, with which nothing was permitted to interfere. The four Hahn girls served the bounteous meals and sometimes entertained. Licia Hahn wrote:

One year, I had planned to play a Chopin prelude and have my sister Alexandra accompany me on the violin. Now the violin was Olga's turf and I suppose she could tolerate poor piano playing. But Alexandra's squeaking finally got to her. And when we asked her to play instead, it was one of these moments none of us will ever forget. Olga picked up Alexandra's beginner violin and played it magnificently. We were all riveted and teary-eyed and extremely moved. This was an Olga we had never seen. We felt so privileged to share a moment when she reconnected with a happier time in her young girlhood. After finishing the piece, she put down the violin and then told us that she could never play again. It had taken too much out of her.

In between Thanksgivings, there were weddings, meals at the Harvard Club, hospital visits, and all the quotidian events that mark a close relationship.

Vice President Hubert Humphrey was another of Caneel's visitors. During one of their stays, Olga and Pips met him and his wife, Muriel. Upon learning that Pips was a Jew, Humphrey mentioned that his tailor was also Jewish, and he invited Olga and Pips to come to Minnesota. Caneel Bay extended special privileges to Humphrey, including a reserved boat and car. The Humphreys happened to be leaving for the airport the same day as Olga and Pips, and Hubert invited them to join him on the VIP boat. Pips observed that it must be wonderful to travel so much and get VIP treatment everywhere. The vice president replied, "Yes, but you have no time for yourself." The Humphreys had just lost the presidential election. Pips quipped, "It could have been worse," to which Humphrey retorted, "It could have been better."

During another stay at Caneel, the couple met the actor Howard Da Silva. Pips was sure that he was a Sephardic Jew. He approached the actor and asked, "Mr. Da Silva, I hope you don't mind, are you

Sephardic?" "Hell, no," he replied. "I'm a Litwak and my name is Rabinowitz."

Secretary of State Kissinger also made an appearance at Caneel with a retinue of Secret Service agents. Like all dignitaries, he was given Cottage 7, which was at the end of Scott Beach. Pips, who had become an avid snorkeler, decided to go there to try out a mask he had borrowed. He dove into the water and when he came out, a man materialized from the bushes with a scuba tank and bomb detection equipment. He dove into the water from which Pips had just emerged. Bemused, Pips watched him. When the Secret Service agent came out, he asked, "Did you find anything?"

During one of their early stays, Olga and Pips met a handsome young couple, Tony and Myrna Bloom, on the ferry from St. Thomas to Caneel. Pips was certain they were Jews, but their accent was South African. Before they had exchanged three words, Pips, who loved to shock people, immediately queried them on how Jews were faring there.

Pips's guess was correct. The Blooms were, indeed, Jews. Tony's family had fled Lithuania to escape persecution, and then founded the Premier Group in the early 1900s. Starting as a small business, it grew into the one of the largest industrial conglomerates in South Africa. At the time they met, Tony was chairman and CEO of the business his family had built.

"He was very rich but not stuck up at all, a regular fellow. We became friendly and, since he had no trouble noticing my interest in Jewish things, one day he came with a paperback book which he had bought in the gift shop: *The Joys of Yiddish* by Leo Rosten—and some of it is very funny."

Myrna and Tony divorced a few years later. Tony phoned Pips from Johannesburg to announce that he had remarried and would be passing through New York on his way to Caneel. As it happened, they would arrive the night before Olga and Pips were departing for Caneel, and they would all be on the same flight the next morning.

A lifelong opponent of apartheid, Tony's was one of the few companies that hired political detainees after they had been released. The Harvard-trained lawyer went on to earn numerous recognitions, including the Teddy Kollek Prize for his philanthropic contributions to Jerusalem—which made it even more shocking when he turned up in New York with his second wife, Gisela von Mellenthin, the daughter of General Erwin Rommel's chief military advisor in Africa. Mellenthin had fought with the Panzer Army Afrika in all of its battles from the Siege of Tobruk to El Alamein.

Tony had gone to school with his new wife, but Pips was outraged when he heard about her father. "Tony, you may not like to hear this, but I'm absolutely shocked to the bone! Not only did you marry a *shiksa*, you married a German *shiksa*. You married the daughter of a Nazi general, who, if he had been successful, would have cost the lives of hundreds of thousands of Jews in Palestine." He looked at me and said, 'You always were a swine.' And he wasn't kidding. He was angry. I didn't give a damn. I was so shocked, and I was hurt. By that time, they already had two children, and she had two children from her first marriage, and he had two children with his first wife. I said to him, 'I can just imagine your children sitting on grandpa's lap, saying 'Grandpa, what did you do during the war?' 'Well, I was a general.' 'Did you succeed, were you victorious?' 'No, unfortunately I was not.' In other words, he would tell them, in effect, that if he had been victorious, that would have cost another few hundred thousand Jews their lives. And here are the children of a Jew sitting on Grandpa's lap."

Tony was in love with Gisela and was deeply offended by Pips's remarks. "I didn't insult his wife, I insulted him. He got over it, at least superficially. So, we spent a week or two with them in Caneel. A couple of times when we met them, I clicked my heels, and she was very sore. I'm such a practical joker, I can't resist—I know it's an insult."

There were other, more pleasant encounters, with conductor Leonard Bernstein, actor Fritz Weaver, and several of the Rockefellers. But mostly, Pips enjoyed the company of the Virgin Island natives who staffed the private resort.

"We met so many people and got friendly with so many because we were relaxed. In New York, when I came home at night or on weekends. I didn't want to talk to anybody because all day long I had to talk, talk, talk, see editors, and talk my head off. I wanted quiet. But at Caneel, my natural tendency to talk came up again."

There was a magical evening, which was one of the highlights of Pips's life. One of their waiters, Conrad, was very friendly with Olga and Pips. He was going to a concert one evening and invited them to come along. "That shows you the relationship we had with these people. He didn't hesitate to ask for a social get-together, and we were happy to go. We went to a little building on top of a hill, with a large area where people were dancing to a steel band. There were maybe thirty, forty people, a mix of black natives, mostly men, and white, young girls who were tourists from a nearby campground. The men came to dance with the girls. There was this interracial thing that pleased us no end. They danced beautifully, and there was a full moon. You could see the shimmer of the moonlight deep in the water. The trade winds gently fanning you, the steel band playing, and these pretty young people dancing. It was wonderful! These unexpected, unplanned events—that's something that made us happy."

But the unannounced appearance of Georgette—me—at Caneel one evening didn't make them happy at all. I had married my high school sweetheart, Warren Sandler, in 1968, after graduating from Vassar College the year before and after completing our first year of graduate school. We had been dating since my junior year, and his senior year, at Richmond Hill High School. Warren was popular, handsome—a Bobby Rydell lookalike—a great dancer, and he played in a rock band. What teenage girl would not have swooned over those credentials! But my mother never thought that Warren was quite up to her standards, despite his being a member of Arista and a top student. Warren and I often confided our problems to Olga and Pips. So, it was a blow to me when my closest relatives decided not to interrupt their annual sojourn at Caneel to attend our wedding.

It was just as well because, four years later, unbeknownst to them, Warren and I separated. While I got my PhD in Sociology, he got his in Clinical Psychology. But I received my doctorate first. That, along with the success of my nascent career, and my higher income, caused rifts in our marriage. Following our break-up, I—always ambitious, highly responsible, hard-driving, hard-working, who helped support my mother since I turned twenty-one—decided I was ready to have some fun. Eager to taste more of life, I dove into dating.

One of the men to whom I'd been introduced invited me to go to Caneel Bay for the weekend. Well, I had been hearing about Caneel Bay from Olga and Pips for years! I happily accepted the invitation and speculated that my relatives might be there. Indeed, they were, and I couldn't wait to surprise them! But when I turned up with Evan, I didn't get the welcome I expected.

"Georgette suddenly popped up in Caneel Bay at night with a man. We thought it was Warren, but it wasn't. I practically told her that she was a hooker. She only stayed three days, and we eventually made up. Every night after dinner, we sat on the big terrace right outside our room, with beautiful tropical flowers all around. One evening before Georgette left, I had sandals on, and she kissed my feet. I think she wanted to show me she'd forgiven me for calling her all kinds of names. That's still one of the highlights for me."

Since I was far more comfortable hanging out with Olga and Pips than with Evan, I spent almost the entire Caneel weekend with them. Evan and I flew home together, but we never saw each other again.

Olga and Pips had been my confidants through the seven years I remained single after Warren and I separated.

"One of Georgette's many friends was F. Lee Bailey, the lawyer. He was at her Thanksgiving dinner one year. He hadn't said a word during the meal, but he drank a lot of scotch, which apparently was his shtick. Afterward, we all went to the living room. I said, 'Lee, you seem like an awfully nice guy. But there's one thing I don't like about you; you talk too much.' He laughed and started talking."

Bailey was a legendary criminal defense lawyer whose clients included O. J. Simpson, Sam Sheppard, and Albert DeSalvo, the "Boston Strangler." I had met him through my then-agent, Wayne Smith, who also represented Bailey. In the 1970s, I had been Personal Consultant to the NYPD Police Commissioner and worked with the US Department of Justice and police departments around the country. As an award-winning criminologist, I was tapped to do expert witness work and Bailey prepped me for my first trial, which became a landmark case in prosecuting police violence. But on this occasion, "FLee," as he was affectionately called, spent most of the holiday passed out cold in another room while my other guests celebrated Thanksgiving.

Through a young couple they met at Caneel Bay, Olga and Pips were introduced to Charles Schmaltz and his Puerto Rican lover, Geraldo Orlando ("Jerry") Perez, a seventeen-year-old, deeply troubled, gay hairdresser. Schmaltz eventually relocated to San Francisco for a job and dropped Jerry. But Olga and Pips quickly picked him up and came to think of him as an adopted son. "We immediately fell in love with Jerry. We tried to get him accustomed to middle class life, middle class values." They took him to their friends, to concerts, and on car trips. He came to their apartment for dinner at least once a week. But he was impulsive, and they frequently had to bail him out of trouble. Jerry, who felt badly mistreated by nuns, divulged to Pips that he wanted to be "baptized Jewish." Pips explained that Jews don't get baptized. Besides, he added, "Jews have enough troubles without you!"

Pips and Jack Podell were having lunch at La Toque Blanche one day. Across the street, they saw the finishing touches being put on a modern development, 860 UN Plaza. Pips had just read an article in the *New York Times* Real Estate Section about this being the finest new residence in New York City. Robert Kennedy had already bought an apartment there. Jack said, "That would be a nice place for you to live."

Despite Pips's misgivings, Jack insisted that they go after lunch to look at apartments. The on-site broker showed them a duplex. "It was a lot of money and just to needle my friend, I said, 'It's a little too big for my wife to clean.' You're supposed to have servants, and I wanted to embarrass Jack." Pips instructed the agent to show them the smallest available apartment. It was Apartment 21D, which overlooked the East River with dramatic cityscapes looking north.

With the sole exception of the $200 loan from Charlie Wyle to buy a ratty sofa for their basement apartment in Brooklyn, Pips had never taken a loan. His habit was to buy only when he had the cash to pay in full. That applied when, in 1967, he purchased, for $30,000 cash, that one-bedroom apartment in the brand new, ultra-luxurious 860 UN Plaza.

"When I told Olga about it, her reaction was exactly like mine: UN Plaza! It was like saying we're moving into the Waldorf Astoria."

Except for their beds, they brought very little of the Danish modern furniture with which their Kew Gardens Hills attic had been outfitted. Their new living room was kitted out with the great mid-century furniture sold by Knoll—some pieces completely custom-made. The low ledge below the tall, panoramic windows was overlaid with wall-to-wall plants, some imported from Caneel, in artistic pots. The weekly ritual of watering those plants and cultivating his private jungle was one of Pips's great pleasures.

Turtle Bay was the Phillips's home in Caneel, and 860 UN Plaza was located in a Manhattan neighborhood called Turtle Bay. The luxury cooperative was completed in 1966 and designed by the same architects as the adjacent United Nations Secretariat and General Assembly. At the time it was built, 860 UN Plaza was the largest mixed-use office and apartment complex in the country. With red carpets in a spacious lobby atrium and uniformed elevator men, the co-op was luxe all the way. In addition to Robert Kennedy, its residents included many bold-face names of the time: Truman Capote, Johnny Carson, Walter Cronkite, Yul Brynner, Angela Lansbury, Bonnie Cashin, David Susskind, Cliff Robertson, Secretary of State William Rogers. National Democratic Committee Chair Larry O'Brien.

O'Brien, who later died of an aggressive prostate cancer, had a Rolls-Royce. Pips occasionally went down to the garage to visit the Rolls, where he luxuriated in its cushy seats and took childish pleasure in opening and closing the doors. By the next year, he had his own cream-colored 1968 Cadillac Coupe DeVille convertible parked in the same garage. He would keep that car for the rest of his life.

"Because I once lost everything, I want to surround myself, not with riches, but with necessities. That gives me a feeling that I'm a little bit safer. I should know from experience that it ain't true, because when the chips were down, I learned that riches didn't mean anything, connections didn't mean anything. Exchanging something, getting rid of a pair of pants that have a big hole in the ass and buying a new pair is a change; to paint the walls is a change. A new carpet is a change. I hate change. I'm afraid of change. Any kind of change makes me insecure. I just try to keep the world that I have, my world, since the Shoah, since I came to this country."

Despite what looked like a luxurious life, Pips was proudly cheap—and financially conservative. He never invested in the stock market and bought only Treasury bonds—which paid handsomely during the Carter administration when dividends rose to more than 12 percent.

By every measure, the two unlikely Holocaust survivors had arrived.

CHAPTER 12

THE GLAMOUR YEARS

The years at Globe were ticking by and Pips had become a star salesman. "I knew practically all the major movie stars in Hollywood, and I socialized with the editors. I was the middleman between the consumers and the producers. That meant figuring out the ideal reader for each magazine. That's who we aimed at. I understood what the editors wanted and that was my biggest plus."

The editor of *Mechanics Illustrated* once said to Pips, "Gary, the stuff you're showing me is too scientific, too technical. Remember, our reader is Archie Bunker." Pips never forgot that, and every time he dealt with *Mechanics Illustrated*, he asked himself, "Would Archie Bunker be interested in that?"

"I always got from editors their idea of who their typical reader was. Once you understood that and were capable of interpreting that into material, you did all right. I was quite good at that and that was something I enjoyed. I didn't like selling, being a peddler. I demanded to be treated as an equal, and I was. Over time I gained respect and that's the way I was treated."

Although focused on celebrities, Globe was arguably a forerunner in photojournalism—the practice of telling a story through photos rather than looking at photos purely as art. It also pioneered the "special photographer" concept that was adopted by many of the major movie studios.

In publicizing a film, studios needed stills of both the film and the production. Their staff photographers tended to focus on scenes in the film to create content for ads. But Globe had the innovative idea of selling picture stories of what went on behind the scenes, making the production the story instead of the film. If an actor playing a cowboy had never sat on a horse, his blunders, as he learned to mount and dismount, would make an amusing or unusual story. That's the kind of picture story that Globe could sell to *Life* and other major outlets. After getting an assignment, a Globe editor read the movie script to determine how long a photographer would need to work at a particular location.

Globe had at least twenty-four photographers under exclusive contract. Many of them covered film productions in Spain and Mexico, where it was less costly to shoot a movie than in Los Angeles. "In LA, they had a union problem. In Mexico, nobody cared." Every week New York headquarters spoke to Globe's West Coast office, which curated photos and sent them to New York. Globe also sent sets of photos to their agencies in Japan and Germany. However, they never sold the photos themselves—only the limited rights to use the photos. Nor did Globe own the photos; they were agents for the photographers.

According to *Popular Photography*, Globe "contributed to the mythic creations of our time . . . Jayne Mansfield, Jane Russell, Anita Ekberg, and Raquel Welch."

Globe didn't just deal in film stories and movie stars. A letter to prospective contributors described Globe's subject matter as ranging from "general human interest to famous personalities, cheesecake, outdoor action, unusual inventions, oddities, interesting people, background stories relating to important news events, and many others."

Globe benefited from the demise of censorship and the growing permissiveness in displaying the body. "In the beginning, you could only show an actress's legs. Later, you could show her breasts. Eventually, you could show everything. There were a lot of magazines trying to compete with *Playboy* and they all made a living. It became easier and easier to get girls naked. I would say to an editor, 'We've seen everything on the outside of a girl. Now we have to go inside. The next thing is X-rays.' I was kidding, of course!"

Jack Podell had gotten Pips his job with Globe and Pips now returned the favor. Fred Klein, one of Pips's clients, was the publisher of *Gent* and other "adult" magazines. During their lunches, Pips kept bragging about Jack Podell as the best editor he had met because of his imagination, sensitivity, and risk-taking. One day, Klein bit: he called Pips and told him that he'd like to talk to Jack. Pips replied that he didn't think Jack would want to get involved with "girlie" magazines. Klein said he had something else in mind. Klein had been appointed publisher of MacFadden Publications, which published more than a dozen long-established pulp and trade magazines. When Jack heard the news, he urged Pips to immediately send Klein a congratulatory telegram.

"You think a telegram is necessary?"

"Don't be a fool! If he hires me, there's a good chance for you to become a partner."

"You're a real shit! Do you think I wouldn't help you advance your career even if there wasn't something in it for me?"

Well, he did and there was. Jack was hired as editorial director of MacFadden Publications and became one of Globe's biggest clients.

Jack was living in Westchester, an affluent county just north of New York City. He and his wife, Charlotte, were members of a Reconstructionist synagogue. A holiday was coming up and Jack nudged Olga and Pips to join the choir for that occasion. The "pipsy" voice that earned Pips his nickname in the youth *Bund* had long since become sonorous and deep. "I had problems with following the conductor because I always tended to sing one octave too low. He kept saying, 'Gary, up!' And I said, 'No, I'm comfortable down here.' At one point, he became flustered and impatient with the choir because the music wasn't coming together. In his frustration, he shouted, 'Yidn!'—the Yiddish word for Jews. I'm proud that I was one of the ones he addressed using that term." In this odd way, Pips could finally feel affirmed as a Jew.

A similar affirmation occurred when he was walking home from work one Friday, just as it was getting dark. Passing a synagogue, a man stopped him and asked Pips whether he was Jewish. Pips responded that he was, and the man asked whether he could spare twenty minutes to complete a minyan. In Judaism, a quorum of ten adults (men, for orthodox minyans) is required for certain prayer services to begin. "I didn't want to say no and I sat next to him in the synagogue. He took out his prayer book and showed me where they were, which meant nothing to me because it was all in Hebrew. Afterward, I asked the rabbi if I could call Olga to tell her I'd be home late for dinner. But he wouldn't let me because of Shabbat. After the service, the rabbi thanked me for attending and I, being a big jerk with a big mouth said: 'You know, according to your rules, I'm not even one of you.' Why did I say this? There was no reason. It just hurt me that, in some quarters, I wasn't recognized as a Jew, and I wanted to get back at them."

As in his Camera Clix days, there were many editors in Pips's orbit who became celebrities in other fields. Stanley Greenberg, whom he met through Jerry Podell, wanted to be a screenwriter and came up with an idea for a show. The odds were one in a million that anything would come of it. That show became *The Defenders*, which ran on TV from 1961 to 1964. He went on to write hit movies like *The Missiles of October*, *Pueblo*, and *Soylent Green*.

Mary Fiori, editor of *Photoplay* magazine, became one of the top editors at *Ladies' Home Journal*.

Bruce Jay Friedman, editor of outdoor men's magazines, became a best-selling fiction writer, with some of his books, like *The Heartbreak Kid*, becoming hit films.

To a limited extent, Pips also worked with book publishers, such as Random House. There he met Nan Talese, a leading editor in the 1960s, who was also the wife of Gay Talese, best-selling author of *Your Neighbor's Wife*. Pips pitched her a book idea, which she quickly shut down, but he was dazzled by her beauty.

Globe's best photographer in LA was Don Ornitz. His father, screenwriter Sam Ornitz, was one of the "Hollywood Ten" blacklisted after being accused of Communist affiliations by Senator Joe McCarthy's House Un-American Activities Committee. "Don Ornitz was our glamour photographer—not cheesecake, glamour. Many female stars asked Don to shoot them because they knew he would make them look better than ever. We sold these pictures to fan magazines and women's magazines as single glamour shots. Doris Day was one of his subjects. Another was Yvette Mimieux. She was young and pretty—never a top star, but he shot some beautiful stuff. We sent samples to *Life* magazine, which loved them, and they assigned Don to shoot a cover."

The worst crime in Pips's business was double planting. If you sold photos to one publication, it was anathema to sell it to another—particularly a competitor—until they were out on the stands and the issue in which they appeared was gone. Then you could sell the same photos to any outlet, so long as they were informed that the material had already appeared in another publication.

"We did that with lots of stuff, with cheesecake and adventure stories. It was okay as long as we kept our nose clean. But Mimieux turned into a classic case. *Life* assigned Ornitz to shoot Yvette Mimieux, and we asked them to return the samples we had sent. *Life* wanted to hold on to them for a while. Meanwhile we had similar photos in the office, and I sold one of these shots to *Modern Romances*, which was published by Dell."

Pips had previously encountered Dell's owner indirectly when one of his fellow refugees had become a driver for George Delacorte Jr. Delacorte, born George Tonkonogy, was the son of Hungarian Jewish immigrants. He founded Dell in 1921 and was known for his philanthropy—especially to Central Park in New York City. But Pips didn't think much of him.

"He paid for the theater in Central Park, all for self-glorification. He was a thoroughly unpleasant man, but he was rich. I sold a shot of Yvette for the cover of *Modern Romances*. Ornitz shot the assignment for *Life*, and we sent them those photos—of course, different from the samples we had sent. One day my partner's telephone rings and Delacorte is on the line: 'What the hell are you sons of bitches up to? What are you trying to do to me? Haven't you seen the newsstands this morning? You'd better go down and get *Life* magazine and *Modern Romances*. You'll see the same pictures on both covers. I'm going to sue the pants off Globe.' The guy was huffing and puffing like crazy and carried on like a jackass. I promised to look into it and get back to him. Elliott sent someone down to pick up copies of *Life* and *Modern Romances* and they were almost identical. A professional photographer doesn't shoot just one picture, he shoots at least one roll of film for any assignment, so this was from the same roll, only a couple of frames removed. For all practical purposes, the same picture. Elliott called *Life* and asked what the hell happened. *Life* had received the photos and mixed them up with the samples Elliott had originally shown them. *Life* realized it was their fault. They had taken one of the samples and put that on the cover instead of the stuff Ornitz had shot for them. Elliott called Delacorte and told him what happened. Delacorte stopped him: 'You don't have to explain. I've had second thoughts. If you can ever pull this off again, there will be a fat bonus for you.' For him, it couldn't have been better. His lousy romance magazine had the same cover as the big *Life* magazine. And *Life* couldn't complain because it was their fault.

The *New York Times* called us and did a story on it. Throughout that afternoon and evening, we got phone calls from all the newspapers in New York. In 1960, that was a journalistic coup!"

Globe had a photographer, Jerry Yulsman, who was known for his iconic photographs of the novelist Jack Kerouac. A writer himself, he also taught photography. Globe had sold *Playboy* on the idea of parodying popular TV shows with layouts of nude girls on their sets. One of the shows was *This Is Your Life with Ralph Edwards.* Ralph Edwards was to play himself as the host, and a male model would play the subject of that episode of the show. Jerry called Pips from the studio in a panic. "Gary, the male model didn't show up. I'm sitting here with seven nude girls and one guy, and they all get paid by the hour. I can't let them sit here forever and I can't, in a hurry, find another model. *Playboy* will have my head if I don't come up with anything. You've got to do it!"

"I said, 'You must be nuts! I'm not a model.' Well, I did it. I looked so damned stupid with a grin. But *Playboy* published it, together with six other pictures. I was never paid for it, but what the hell?"

As a salesman, it wasn't Pips's job to be in direct contact with movie stars. His job was to hawk photo stories *about* the stars to editors. But there was spillover, and he came to know many of them anyway.

Globe's President, Bill Eisnetz, died suddenly of a heart attack on a tennis court in 1963. His life insurance took care of his widow, but his Globe stock reverted to the two surviving partners, Elliot Stern and Charles Bloch. Pips, who had now been a Globe salesman for eight years, was offered a full partnership. "I thought they were going to hand it to me on a silver platter, but I had to pay for the stock, even though it was very reasonable: twenty-five thousand dollars. They made it easy by letting me pay over three years."

Pips moved into the executive suite of the Globe offices on 44th Street and Sixth Avenue in Manhattan. One of the first things that hit him as a partner was a lawsuit of which he had been only vaguely aware as a salesman. It was brought by two LA photographers, Larry Schiller and Billy Woodfield. Woodfield, a Globe photographer, "was a good guy. But Larry Schiller was a real hot shot, no conscience, and he would step over dead bodies to get where he wants to go, a real pusher." Both had been assigned to shoot a scene in a Marilyn Monroe film, *Something's Got to Give*, in which she is cocooned in a blue bathrobe. She slips out of the robe and slides nude into a swimming pool.

"The scene had been postponed for days because Marilyn didn't show up. She had always been a pain in the ass, but she was much worse now. So, they shot this scene, and the two photographers shot stills. Three months later, in August 1962, she killed herself. The film was never released and now Schiller and Woodfield were sitting on the last pictures taken of Marilyn Monroe: hot stuff. The two of them did the smart thing: rather than competing with each other, they decided to pool their pictures and offer an exclusive. Since Globe was Woodfield's agent, they gave all the pictures to Globe. Globe would split the fee with them, and they would split 50-50 with each other. In short order, Globe sold the cover and an inside layout to *Life* for a premium. We copied the transparencies and sent them all over the world and, after a decent one-year interval, *Playboy* ran a layout. Meanwhile, Larry Schiller declared that he had given Globe permission to sell only to *Life*. In those days, we weren't very tight with photographer agreements, and we learned from our mistakes. Later, we wouldn't touch anybody's photographs without an ironclad agreement about our terms and our relationship. Schiller wanted to get his pictures back immediately, but even if we wanted to, we couldn't give them back because they were all over the world by now. So, he sued Globe and got Billy Woodfield to go along with him. They used Melvin Belli, one of the top trial lawyers in the country, as their attorney. It finally came to court, and their claim was declared invalid. Meanwhile Globe had spent ten thousand dollars on legal fees, which was quite a bit of money back then. We returned Schiller's pictures anyway and washed our hands of the whole thing."

Larry Schiller went on to become a very big name.

Schiller collaborated for thirty-five years on books with Norman Mailer, including *The Executioner's Song,* and also authored his own books, such as *Marilyn and Me.* He later made many successful films. In the 1990s, he co-authored two books on the O. J. Simpson trial and its aftermath.

Charles Bloch was Globe's West Coast partner. "Charles was by far the best brain in the family, including my own. He's the guy who was in with all the movie people. He had a little publishing business on the side, but we didn't really mind because he did more than his share for Globe. He had a little office in Hollywood, an assistant, a couple of secretaries, and a darkroom setup. He also had staff photographers who covered candid photography for all the parties that go on. Of course, in Hollywood, they have a party every night. We had contracts with various magazines to supply them, for a monthly fee, with candid pictures every week."

Through the small publishing company he ran on the side, Bloch was in touch with an as-yet unknown woman, Helen Gurley Brown. Brown had written a book, *Sex and the Single Girl,* which she wanted to sell as a film. Charles, brainstorming new ideas in a meeting with film executives, said: "How about a movie called 'Sex and the Single Girl'? There's really no story but, what the hell, with a title like that you're going to make money." The film was released in 1964 with Natalie Wood as the lead. Although he had asked for nothing, she was so pleased with the role that she sent Charles a $10,000 check. Brown later became editor-in-chief of *Cosmopolitan* magazine.

The same year that *Sex and the Single Girl* was being filmed, Globe sent Pips to Los Angeles to talk to photographers about their needs. He spent the first night in Charles's house, sleeping in his daughter's empty bedroom. He then moved to Russ Meyer's home on Mulholland Drive and Meyer's wife, Eve, cooked for him. Pips's friendship with Meyer dated back to the 1950s, when Russ was a cheesecake photographer. In one of their early chats, he and Pips came up with the idea of adding a story line to the erotic photos. Out of that came "Nude Dude Ranch," in which Meyer went to a dude ranch outside LA with a few models to pose them naked on horses. The idea of adding a story kept percolating, resulting in a soft porn film, *The Immoral Mr. Teas*. Mr. Teas was played by Globe's LA darkroom man.

"The brilliant gimmick for the story was that Teas had an affliction, X-ray eyes: whenever he saw a pretty woman, he would see through her clothes. The pretty woman was always played by Eve Meyer. At one point, she played a doctor. While the doctor was examining him, he saw her in the nude. When she played a dentist drilling his teeth, he saw her tits looming overhead. There were half a dozen incarnations. He came to New York to show it to us first. He wanted us all together with our wives in the office. It was photographed very well because he was a good photographer, but that was all you could say for it. The rest was dumb, plain dumb. He told me that the movie cost him twenty-five thousand to make and he found a distributor. It didn't take him long to find out that the distributor was stealing him blind. Russ had only five prints of the film, which he took around himself from city to city and theater to theater. He controlled the showing. Within a short period of time, he made a hundred thousand dollars. He figured, 'I'm onto something.' Eve became his business partner and would oversee distribution, while he would make the movies."

Meyer was eventually put under a three-film contract with Daryl Zanuck. The first was *Valley of the Dolls*, released in 1967 to panning by critics. But it was one of Twentieth Century Fox's highest grossing films at that time and it put Meyer on the map as a filmmaker. Over time, his legend grew, and his *oeuvre* was seriously studied. But on March 27, 1977, Meyer lost his wife and business partner when Pan Am Flight 1736 from New York, taxiing on Tenerife airport in dense fog, collided with KLM Flight 4805 during its takeoff.

The year that *Valley of the Dolls* came out, another film inspired by Russ Meyer hit the theaters. "Russ and Charles were shooting the breeze, having a couple of beers, and Russ told Charles about some of his experiences during World War II. He was in a special unit, mostly guys who had a court martial hanging over their heads. But they were given a chance to redeem themselves by blowing up stuff behind the German lines. Russ told Charles the story and Charles said, 'That sounds like a movie. Do you mind if I get a writer to work on a script?' Charles got one of his writer pals and the script became a very successful film, *The Dirty Dozen*, starring Lee Marvin. That was Charles's brainstorm. He could smell things."

Frank Bez was another one of Globe's star photographers. His long career was catalyzed as a child when he was given the birthday gift of a 616 Kodak camera. From that innocuous beginning, he ended up shooting some of the biggest stars of the 1950s and 1960s. Among these were Natalie Wood and Raquel Welch.

"There was a lot of demand for color covers for confession magazines—*True Love, True Romance*. One of our main models was a gal who, at that time, was nowhere. Her name was Raquel Welch. She wasn't worth a picture story because nobody had yet heard of her, but she was a beautiful woman. Frank practically had an exclusive on her and shot a lot of stuff indoors, outdoors, and in the studio. He was a very good photographer, and she looked great. We tried to talk her into a layout for *Playboy* but she wouldn't do it. She felt the nudie stuff wouldn't be good for her career. But we sold a lot of covers of her to romance magazines. There were some pretty ghastly cover lines to go with the covers: 'I Loved My Father and Slept with

My Brother,' all kinds of incest or 'She was raped on the toilet.' The stories inside had nothing to do with Raquel Welch on the cover, but people associated her with the cover lines. We sold a lot of those, but we also sold Raquel Welch all over the world. She was one of the most beautiful women around at the time. We had sold about 150 covers, which was tremendous. I decorated the walls of my office at Globe with covers that I had sold. And that gave us an idea. My partner, Elliott Stern, mentioned the covers to *Life*, and they did a whole big thing on Raquel against the background of a hundred covers, of which Bez had shot ninety. That was a big feather in her cap, a tremendous push. Suddenly, she was a household name." It was 1966, and Welch had just made a box office hit, *One Million Years BC*. "I think she was a flop. She couldn't act her way out of a paper bag, never could."

One day, Welch came to Globe's New York office and forbade Globe from selling her pictures to any of the "confession" magazines—or to any magazine without her prior approval. Globe photographers had made thousands of color shots of Raquel before she achieved stardom, and the company was sitting on all those pictures. Pointing out that he had Raquel's valid release, which covered all the photos taken up until then and in the future, Pips claimed she had no legal leg on which to stand. She threatened to sue anyway. Pips and his partner decided it wasn't worth defending her suit, even if they won, because "you always lose on legal fees." Globe had already milked the Raquel Welch market as much as possible so there was little upside. After selling all those covers of Welch, "She turned out to be a ten-karat bitch. A beautiful woman but very unpleasant!"

Globe's star photographer was still Don Ornitz. But Ornitz didn't only work on assignment. In 1967, he shot a nubile woman with flowing blond hair, running nude through tall golden grass, leading a brown horse with a blond mane. It was a lyrical, intimate photo, which moved Pips deeply. He tried to sell it for a year.

"Nobody wanted to touch it. Finally, in sheer desperation I took it to the editor of *Popular Photography* and he said, 'It's gorgeous! I'm just doing an Annual. May I put this in the Annual?' I said, 'Sure' and it ran in the 1968 Annual. They paid lousy fees, a hundred and fifty to two hundred or something like that. But two days after the Annual came out, we got a call from Revlon's ad agency. They wanted to know if the picture was available because they wanted to use it as a Revlon ad. We got three thousand dollars from Revlon for this picture. From that moment on, we couldn't sell it fast enough—here and abroad. It was also used in a book. At first, I couldn't give the damn thing away. That's how crazy our business was!"

Pips's remit didn't usually include dealing with models because they generally worked directly with photographers. But, one day, he got a phone call from a model who wanted to meet with him. She was eager to get into *Playboy* as a Playmate of the Month. Pips told her there wasn't much he could do for her. But she persisted and he agreed to see her. When she arrived in his office, he was interrupted by a phone call. When he looked up, she was standing nude in front of him. He was speechless and worried that someone might walk in. "I just wanted to show you that I have a good body and could make a good Playmate," she explained. He passed her on to Globe's East Coast photographer for *Playboy.*

Entranced by all these stories over the years, I would occasionally plead with Pips, "What do I have to do to get into a magazine?" To which he invariably replied: "Grow a second head." It wasn't until I became an adult that I finally understood what he meant. If I grew a second head, I would be enough of a freak that magazines would want to write about me.

Among Pips's long list of contacts was Marika Aba, a Hungarian dancer and actress. After a brief performing career, she became an arts journalist for the *Los Angeles Times.* Having been a prima ballerina in Rome, she eventually returned to Italy to write about that country's film industry. Normally, Globe didn't sell articles. The only written content they provided was for photo captions. But Pips made a deal with Aba to combine her interviews with their photos. Out of that came a warm friendship.

Aba was close to Franco Zeffirelli, the Italian film director and producer. At that time, he was making *Romeo and Juliet*, which came out in 1968. The two lead actors, Leonard Whiting and Olivia Hussey, were teenagers and Zeffirelli asked Aba to serve as their chaperone while the actors were housed in a two-bedroom suite in New York's Plaza Hotel. Aba and Pips had business to discuss, and she invited him to the suite. As they were sitting in the living room, one of the bedroom doors opened. Not realizing that Pips was there, Hussey and Whiting emerged half naked. Embarrassed, they covered themselves up a bit, chatted with Pips for a while, and disappeared again into the bedroom. Turning to Aba, Pips quipped, "Is this how you chaperone? Young people, fooling around, what are you going to do? Let them do it."

Once, Aba was babysitting for Jean-Pierre Aumont, who was married to Italian actress, Marisa Pavan. They had an apartment on Fifth Avenue and Aba called Olga and Pips to say she was stuck in the apartment with the kids. Would they like to come over? "We spent the evening at Jean-Pierre Aumont's apartment and met the kids, who were charming. By coincidence, we later got acquainted with his stepmother, who was from Berlin. Jean-Pierre was a Jew whose real name was Salomon, so he called himself Aumont."

In 1969, Hollywood and the country were rocked by the brutal Tate–LaBianca murders. Sharon Tate, wife of the renowned film director Roman Polanski, was more than eight months pregnant when their home was invaded by the cultish Manson family. Globe photographers rushed into action. Directed by Charles Bloch, one photographer caught the bodies as they were carried from the house while another took photos of the scene from a helicopter hovering above. *Popular Photography* wrote a long story touting Globe's coverage: "In 48 hours, sales totaling $4000 were made to six magazines in both Europe and the United States." These included *Paris Match* and *Quick*. *Popular Photography* quoted Pips as saying: "Globe is a bridge between the picture markets and the photographer, and it tries to interpret each to the other."

Long before he got to Globe, Pips had done many shoots with Natalie Wood (née Natasha), starting with baby pictures of her naked on a bear rug. Now that she was a movie star, Globe did a lot of pictorial coverage of her films. She and Pips became phone chums and exchanged notes. Wood died under mysterious circumstances on a boat in 1981. She had married Robert Wagner for a second time nine years earlier. When they went to Paris for their honeymoon, Pips phoned Wood to tell her he wanted to send a photographer to Paris to cover her. Wood readily agreed but wanted to check with her husband. Wagner also agreed, but not so readily. In exchange for an exclusive, he demanded that Globe pay all their expenses, including their stay at Hotel Georges Cinq. Pips was taken aback. He calculated that Globe would never recoup the thousands of dollars they would put out. "Wagner was just that kind of guy. He was always a yuck guy, for me, anyway, and that really put the cap on it." Pips checked with his partners and phoned Wood back. "Natalie, forget it, it's not worth it, but nothing personal."

One day in the mid-1970s, a call came to Globe from *The Enquirer*, which wanted to do a layout on Henry Winkler. He had reached superstardom playing the Fonz on the TV comedy series, *Happy Days*. "In those days *The Enquirer* wasn't quite as objectionable as they became later." They wanted to add interest to the layout by including childhood pictures. The editor knew that Winkler's parents lived in New York and hoped that Globe could find them. Pips and his partner found a Winkler in the telephone book and dialed on the chance that they had the right person. Sure enough, it was Winkler's father. He had a very thick German accent. "I got on the phone and he invited us to come to his office, where he would bring pictures for us to select for the layout."

Harry Irving Winkler, Henry's father, had owned a lumber business in Berlin, which he restarted in the United States. While chatting in Winkler's office, Pips discovered that Harry had been married in the same synagogue—and by the same rabbi—where Pips had become a bar mitzvah. Harry had known Pips's father through Ernst's interior design business. He knew Pips's Uncle Martin even better because he, too, had been in the lumber business in Berlin. Martin committed suicide with his son when the deportations started. But Harry and his wife escaped before the worst of the Holocaust.

"Winkler was so proud; he couldn't talk enough about his son, whom he had sent to Yale. We tried to get the hell out of there, but he wouldn't stop. He gave us a slew of baby and childhood pictures of Henry. A few years later, he called and told us that Henry was going to be the Bacchus King of the Mardi Gras in New Orleans and asked whether Globe would want to cover it. It was funny, we were practically cousins!"

Pips also had a lot of dealings with Zsa Zsa Gabor. "She never amounted to anything in showbiz, but she was a personality. 'Oh, Gary, would you send me some lovely eleven-by-fourteen prints of these pictures that they took of me last month?' I said, 'They'll cost you six dollars apiece.' 'Oh, Gary, I posed for you people, I cooperated.' That wasn't how it happened; we weren't used to paying people or giving away photos unless they were outrageously accommodating. But she was an ass who always wanted everything for nothing. This bitch had money coming out of her ears. Every time she married, she walked away with a couple of million and jewelry."

On January 14, 1972, Charles called from Los Angeles with sad news. Don Hornitz had killed himself. "Don was a manic depressive.

He had manic periods where he would work twenty-four hours a day and everything would fall into place, and then he'd descend into depression in which he decided he was no good and didn't deserve anything. On this day, he had done a big advertising job. The art director called the LA office and said they weren't happy with the take Don had done and wanted some takes done over. I spoke to Charles and Charles relayed the information to Don. Don was in one of his down moods and said, 'That just goes to show you, I can't do anything right.' Charles noticed he was in bad shape. He called the art director back and told him, 'Don is really in the dumps, why don't you talk to him?' So, the art director talked to Don and said, 'Don, don't misunderstand me, you did a beautiful job. You're a genius! It's just a couple of little things that we want to do differently. It's probably my mistake more than yours.' He really lathered him. Don stalked out and Charles ran after him, but it was too late. Don had already taken off in his car and shot himself in the Hollywood Hills, where he was found dead a few hours later." He was fifty-two years old.

Don was more than a money-making photographer to Charles. Charles genuinely loved him, and Don's death hit him hard. In 1975, three years after Don's death, he gave notice to Globe and offered Pips and Elliot his shares. He had lost interest in the business and didn't want to do it anymore. Without Hornitz, it was no longer fun.

"Charles always had a peculiar notion that everything you do should be fun, that your job should give you some satisfaction. We didn't want anyone else to get in, so he made us essentially the same deal they made twelve years earlier with me. He charged twenty-five thousand—it was worth a lot more—and allowed us to pay it off over four years. If business is bad, he told us we could skip a year. He just wanted to get out and didn't want any hard feelings on our part. We really couldn't say no."

Charles offered up a colleague, who had been working with him for ten years, to run the west coast office. His designated successor was smart and Charles assured his partners that he was fully up to speed. But he and Pips didn't get along very well, and Charles's departure seriously damaged Globe's West Coast business. But the business went on, at least for a while.

Soon after Charles's departure, Pips's mother died in Germany at age eighty-seven. He did not attend the funeral. To the extent that he grieved, it was for the loss of his West Coast partner, not for Marie Philipsohn Ranke.

Actor and filmmaker John Derek married Bo Derek of *10* fame in 1976. He had photographed a nude set of his wife, which he turned over to Globe to sell to *Playboy*. "One evening I got a phone call from John Derek. I could tell from his voice he was very irritated and nasty. He started complaining loudly about the copy that ran with the pictures of Bo. I tried to explain that we have nothing to do with the text, we only sell the pictures. He kept calling me 'Gary.' In our business, people right away call you by your first name. But when he called me 'Gary,' it was not the friendly 'Gary.' It was contemptuous, like I was the cleaning woman or something, so I made a point of referring to him as 'Mr. Derek.' He threatened lawsuits and I just told him to go fuck himself."

One day, Elliot raced over to Pips: "You're not going to believe this. I just got a call from the CIA. They want to talk to us." Three days later, an agent came to the office and flashed his credentials. He had a proposition: The CIA had an operative in deep cover inside Africa and needed a vehicle through which to send him monthly payments that couldn't be traced to the US government. The operative had a camera and the agent proposed that he could pose as a contributing photographer for Globe. Globe could then send him payments for the pictures they allegedly sold. The CIA would provide the funds. "It occurred to me; how do they give us money? How do they record that? Why would the CIA pay Globe Photos? We figured it's going to screw up our bookkeeping. And what about taxes? We're going to have to report that. The agent promised to make a special accountant available to us. We said it's going to cost us more for our bookkeeper's time. But he said we would be compensated for that."

Elliot and Pips spent quite a bit of time with the agent. While chatting, the agent mentioned the failed attempt to rescue American hostages held by Iran in the late 1970s during the Carter administration. "I said, 'If they had used the Israelis they would have had better success. The IDF didn't screw up Entebbe in 1976 and it was much more difficult.' Tact was never my forte and I couldn't resist rubbing it in. I also asked him whether, before contacting us, he had checked our FBI file to make sure we aren't security risks. I then asked whether he knew that I was once in a union that was thrown out of the CIO for being Communist dominated. He said, 'No!' A week later we called him and told him that we'd thought it over: In principle, we would help our government, but he had to come again to straighten out the details. We never heard from him again."

In Berlin, Pips had never been much of a black-market operator and, courtesy of the Nazis, his formal education ended when he was fifteen years old. Like with all the jobs he'd been assigned as a prisoner, he had no training in the photo business either. Nevertheless, he was a big success at Globe. But technology was rapidly changing that industry.

"My two partners and I never got rich, but we made a living. We had some good times and some not so good times. We had to employ a lot of people, and our overhead was high. But we worked it out. Many jobs could now be done electronically, and my partners and I didn't understand the new technology. We decided it was time to sell the company."

Pips and his remaining partner, Elliot, put Globe on the market in 1979.

CHAPTER 13

THE GLAMOUR YEARS END

Elliot had a sleazy son-in-law, Joe, who couldn't find a job and tried his hand at various businesses—all unsuccessful. At one point, he started a movie business in Maine, where he wanted to make cheap films. He and his partner were covered with ample life insurance policies, and one day, the partner turned up dead. Although Joe was under suspicion, the police were unable to make a case against him. He cashed in on the insurance and lived on that for a while. When Pips and Elliot started making noises about selling Globe, Joe sent some leads, none of whom turned into viable clients.

One day, a detective came to see Elliot at the Globe offices. He advised Elliot that Joe had hired a triggerman to kill him, his wife, and younger daughter, everyone except Leslie, the daughter to whom Joe was married. "Joe imagined that his wife would inherit the business along with the payout from the key man insurance, and that he would be sitting pretty by being one of the Globe partners." Of course, for that scheme to work, the murders had to happen before Globe was sold. Fortunately, the killer-for-hire Joe tried to enlist was an undercover police officer. Joe was arrested and the impending murders foiled.

Selling Globe proved to be difficult, partly because of two contingent liabilities brought by unsettled lawsuits from photographers. There were no takers until Elliot's lawyer found a prospect who bought the company in 1982.

The prospect had a business that produced catalog photography for Sears & Roebuck. "He had a staff of photographers and people who hired the models and got the background and producer. It was like a movie production. He had about sixty people working for him on Seventh Avenue and he wanted to expand. He thought a photo agency might fit into his expansion ideas. I thought if we find a buyer, we would rather take less payout and have him invest at least a hundred thousand dollars in modernized equipment—like computers and other improvements—that would bring us up to date."

The buyer seemed amenable, and the deal was struck to sell Globe for sixteen notes to be payable for a few thousand dollars each over a four-year period. But he didn't buy the company; he bought only its assets, leaving Elliot and Pips stuck with the liabilities. One of the lawsuits was settled for $3,000 the day Globe was taken over. In the end, the company sold for less than it was worth.

The new owner transferred Globe to his space on Seventh Avenue and showed Pips and Elliot the premises. It didn't matter to Elliot, because he announced that he would retire in one month. But the new owner insisted that Pips sign an employment contract as manager of Globe Photos for a minimum of one year. He would be given a salary plus an expense account and, after one year, Pips could decide whether he wanted to stay. If so, he would get a 10 percent raise.

"It sounded good to me. I figured the new guy is going to invest. But it didn't start well. Instead of giving Globe the quarters that he had shown me, he gave us other quarters, which were really lousy. My office was a tiny hole in the wall with a broken windowpane. Then I found out this guy didn't have a pot to pee in. He was totally in debt to the bank, and he was getting into more and more financial trouble."

Globe's West Coast manager informed Pips that the photographers weren't getting their checks and monthly reports. Nor was Pips getting his expense money. Finally, the payments were made but it took a fight to make it happen. "Things went from bad to worse. I was very unhappy. I could have stayed and made more money, but I couldn't stand it anymore. It was yuck, icky, disgusting; we never worked that way."

Pips quit when his contract was up. Two months later, the bank called their loans. The new owner went bankrupt and sold Globe to Image Bank, which was owned by Kodak and later acquired by Getty Images. Image Bank paid nothing for Globe; they simply took over the liability of payments due to Elliot and Pips. "They said, we'll pay you off, but you have to wait three more years. A year later they sold Globe again to the guy who replaced me as manager. He paid off the rest of the notes, but it was always a cliffhanger."

Pips was sixty-one now and without a job. Nor was he eager to get one. He had a couple of offers, but they didn't suit him, and he was looking forward to a new life in retirement. "I've never been a typical American success story. I've always been much more interested in preserving than acquiring. It has to do with my German heritage and with the war. I just want my little cushion of security, whether it be money in the bank or food in the house. That's why I wear pants that are thirty-five years old. Even when I was in business, I never had an instinct for expansion. I was content with just making a living. Keeping things on an even keel was fine with me."

Pips's income was secure with the dividends from the Treasuries, which were his sole investment, along with the restitution that he and Olga received from the German government.

He walked out of Globe with a good reputation and was invited to lecture at photography clubs on the profession and how to market it. Word of mouth led to referrals for expert witness engagements. "The attorneys were very pleased to work with me because I knew what I was talking about."

Disputes between agencies and photographers usually revolve around lost transparencies, breach of contract or copyright, or the worth of a photo sale. In one instance, Pips was hired by the plaintiffs against Penthouse International.

Penthouse was launched by Bob Guccione in 1965, simultaneously in the United Kingdom and United States. But in 1969, he brought out an American version, specifically to compete head-to-head with *Playboy*. Guccione was a former Globe client whom Pips had met when *Penthouse* was interested in doing a story on Pips's friend, Russ Meyer.

"The plaintiffs were a couple of guys I'd never heard of who claimed to be photo agents. They had made a deal to represent their photographer. This photographer had, years before, taken pictures of now–Miss America, Vanessa Williams, in a lesbian layout. He had her release. She was nobody at that time, and he sold the pictures to *Penthouse*. Penthouse paid him fifty thousand dollars for all rights and the plaintiffs claimed that *Penthouse* should have gone through them as the agents and that my old friend, Bob Guccione, had underpaid the photographer. Bob was always jealous of Hefner and *Playboy* and he bragged in a long article how he snapped up those pictures right under Hefner's nose."

All this enhanced the value of the photos. In a four-hour deposition, Pips was asked to appraise the pictures and all the contact sheets. He determined that they were worth a million and a half dollars, arguing that full rights should never have been sold to *Penthouse*. "Anybody who knew what they were doing would have sold US rights first, and if *Penthouse* wanted more, they would have to pay extra for North American rights or distribution in England."

The case was settled for an unknown amount while Pips sat in the witness waiting room of the Washington, DC, courthouse where the case was being tried.

"I did a number of these things. It didn't involve regular working hours, and I could do it pretty much the way I wanted. I never liked the rat race, and I hated money. I lacked the killer instinct, the blood lust. I hated to consider myself a salesman. I was an editor's editor. It was my job to see that we produced stuff that they can use. I probably undercharged as an expert witness, but I enjoyed testifying."

During his Globe years, Pips was one of the founders of the Picture Agency Council of America (PACA), a trade organization of photo agencies that established industry standards and clarified rights. "Rights are complicated. Often magazines would want to buy North American rights, which meant that they had a Canadian edition. You want US rights? Fine. You want Canadian rights? Fine, but you pay extra for that. Canada is a different country, it's not the same."

The organization grew over the years, and by the time Pips withdrew, there were one hundred member agencies in the US alone and PACA was associated with similar trade associations in other countries. Pips was elected vice president for a three-year term and was reelected for another three-year term. But he and Elliot sold Globe before the second term was over. Pips resigned and was made an emeritus member. "For a few years after I quit, they sent me courtesy notices of their meetings and the newsletter. I came to a couple of meetings and realized they're talking about stuff I'm not really interested in anymore. Things became much more complicated with new technology, like transmitting photographs over fax machines. You can get a facsimile of a picture from here to Shanghai within thirty seconds. These things were beyond my comprehension, and I didn't want to be bothered anymore."

The things with which Pips *did* want to be bothered were his Jewish identity and his "adopted" son, Jerry Perez.

The year of Globe's sale was a milestone for Pips in more ways than one.

From here on, the telling of Pips's life and my own biography become more tightly intertwined. I had known Pips since I was five and a half years old, and although I am his authorized biographer, I also played a role in the American portion of his story.

In 1982, the year that Pips sold Globe, I married Rabbi Marc Tanenbaum, a towering figure in the rabbinate, a pioneer in interreligious relations, and a world-renowned human rights activist. Based at the American Jewish Committee, Marc had been ranked by newspaper editors as one of the four most respected and influential religious leaders in the US. Fittingly for Pips, as a *Mischling*, Marc was also known as "the father of Jewish-Christian relations," "the Secretary of State for the Jews," and "Judaism's foremost apostle to the Gentiles."

There was a twenty-one-year age difference between Marc and me. When he proposed to me, I agonized about that. The loss of my father had been devastating for me, and it took me years to come to terms with his death. Now I was facing the likelihood that I would suffer the loss of a husband. But, in thinking about it, I realized that ten good years with this man were worth forty years with any other man.

Olga and Pips were immediately enamored of Marc when they met him at a reception to which I brought him in 1981. Marc was a brilliant orator, with the style of a highbrow tent revival preacher. But on this occasion, he was there only as a guest. Nevertheless, when he walked in, he sucked the air out of the room. The other guests gravitated toward him as if pulled by a magnetic field. Pips had been with me for my graduations, school plays, dance recitals, piano concerts, Sophomore Father's Weekend at Vassar College, and every other milestone in my life. So, it was quite natural that, when the wedding date was set for June 6, 1982, Pips would be the one to escort me down the aisle and give me away.

Bedecked in a three-piece morning suit, silk tie, boutonnière, and yarmulka, Pips stood with me outside the sanctuary doors, awaiting our turn in the processional. The bride's appearance on the aisle is the climax of any wedding march. But at that moment, I turned to Pips and whispered, "I need to pee." Despite that urgency, he and I made it to the altar without mishap. In the recessional, a beaming Pips escorted Joan Walker, my maid of honor and Vassar classmate, out of the sanctuary and to the reception hall of Park Avenue Synagogue.

Pips was overjoyed that I had married a man with whom he connected so well: "They lived happily with each other, and Georgette really loved him. He certainly was crazy about her."

Marc's work revolved around diplomacy more than the pulpit. However, on the High Holy Days, he conducted overflow services at Sutton Place Synagogue, which was down the street from UN. Plaza. Olga and Pips were regulars on those days. Like most of the congregation, they were there to hear Marc speak, but they stayed throughout and were always there for lunches hosted by Marc and me between services on Rosh Hashanah. Right after one of these lunches, Pips fainted in the arms of State Senator Roy Goodman, just as Pips was recounting his Holocaust experiences to the man whose grandfather, Israel Matz, built the family fortune on the invention of Ex-Lax. It was the latest of three fainting episodes that foreshadowed future health problems.

Olga and Pips were always there for the Yom Kippur pre-fast and break fast meals as well as yearly seders that included an eclectic guest list. One of these was US Attorney for the Southern District, Rudy Giuliani, and his then-wife, WPIX anchorwoman Donna Hanover, who, in 1989, were attending their first seder. Donna, who was pregnant, was mugged on her way to the seder. Calls from the New York media, demanding to know whether the wife of the soon-to-be mayoral candidate was safe, punctuated the readings from the

Haggadah. In fact, she bruised her finger but managed to hold on to her handbag and the mugger ran away empty-handed. Devout Catholics, Rudy and Donna venerated the kiddush cup almost as if it were a Communion chalice and the matzoh as if it were the Communion wafer. In a sense, they were right. After all, Jesus's Last Supper was a Passover seder.

Marc was like a brother to Pips. Marc had been ordained in the Conservative movement, which, like the Orthodox, defines who is a Jew by matrilineal descent. Pips's mother was not a Jew. Nevertheless, with Marc, Pips felt fully accepted as a Jew. At long last, he was experiencing a semblance of Jewish life. And he was getting the Jewish education he missed in his childhood. For years, Marc and I marked Pips's birthdays with a gift of Jewish-themed courses at 92Y, a long-established institution on the Upper East Side of Manhattan.

To Pips, it was "a very cultural place, in addition to gymnastics and physical workouts. And being Jews, there's perhaps more emphasis on the mental activities than on lifting weights. I attended a series of lectures there for several seasons given by a rabbi who was a colleague of Marc's at the American Jewish Committee. We went through Jewish history in various countries at various times. He was a very good teacher, and we had a lively exchange. I was the star pupil in the sense that I spoke more than the others. At one point he said, 'Enough of Zionist propaganda, already,' which made me immensely proud. I asked him once, 'Do you consider me a Jew?' And his answer was noticeably noncommittal, but I learned a lot in these lectures."

Another rabbi, who gave a different course, asked the class to come up with a definition of God. For Pips, the answer was easy: man needed God, so he invented Him. Pips had hoped to spark a conversation. But the young rabbi just glared at Pips disapprovingly and never looked or spoke another word to him.

The "Y" offered formal day-long seminars on Sundays. It was these that caused Pips to turn his back on 92Y for good. "On one occasion they had a guy who originally came from Germany, a professor of Jewish history at Brandeis. He talked about the rise of antisemitism and the Holocaust. He remarked that no one could explain how this could happen in a civilized country in the middle of Europe in the twentieth century. I understood it only too well and thought he was full of shit. I was furious, so I raised my hand. The moderator was the head of the educational department of the Y, also a rabbi. He had already observed me on other occasions and noticed that I was an irritant, an *agent provocateur*. He wouldn't recognize me. I was so fucking frustrated that, when the lunch break came, I went home. I wanted to tell this old cocker he can't teach me anything; he doesn't know anything."

On another occasion, the guest lecturer was a non-Jewish professor at Hunter College. "He started talking about the Jews in general and the Holocaust in particular, but his remarks were offensive, outrageous, insulting, mean-spirited, and antisemitic. Among other gems, he said that the Holocaust wasn't altogether a disaster for the Jews; it got them a museum in Washington, which is quite a positive thing. To say that the Holocaust and Auschwitz gave the Jews prestige, so it wasn't all bad? And look how much attention Jesus got for the crucifixion. That, too, was a good thing. Really? He said that Jews feel morally and intellectually superior and that prevents assimilation. He cited Lebanon, indiscriminate shelling of Beirut, and the massacre in two refugee camps as proof that we are not superior morally. But what did that have to do with Jewish survival? He further unburdened himself by saying, 'Antisemitism is a meaningless phrase, a quasi-political statement like class struggle or communism, made out of mere conflict of interest.' Yeah, they want to kill us, and me, I want to live!"

Pips was stunned by the polite applause the speaker got from what he assumed was a Jewish audience. "Are they nuts? Didn't they hear what he said? Then the moderator came on and said he wanted to add a few things to it. I figured, now he's going to let him have it. Not at all! He nitpicked here and there but nothing to push back. No criticism. I was flabbergasted. Am I the only one who digested what this guy was saying? Up went my arm, and, of course, the rabbi wouldn't respond, so I just got up and walked out. A day or two later, I called him and said, 'How could you let this bastard stand there and tell us that Auschwitz was a blessing in disguise and antisemitism was really a political phrase that means nothing but a conflict of interest?' And he said, 'It got us fifty museums around the world, and the speaker compared the victims to Jesus.' Then he said we mustn't act as if the whole world wants to destroy us. Consider the French who lost many people from Napoleon on down and they don't feel that way. I mean, the comparison was so ridiculous, so odious. I was ready to spit. I was more insulted by the Jew and by the Jewish audience than I was by this lousy antisemite who stood there and spouted this crap. It just goes to show you that we Jews are as fucked up as anyone else, only more so."

Two years before I married Marc, Olga and Pips had learned that Jerry, their "adopted" son, was HIV positive. Jerry had been in their lives for nine years by then and they had already experienced many ups and downs with him. But this latest calamity devastated them. Jerry had taken to them as if they were his parents: "We could easily have been his parents, age-wise. He particularly loved Olga and Olga loved him passionately, like a son, the son she never had."

Pips had known that Jerry was gay from the moment that Charles Schmaltz had brought him to a dinner. "He was so sweet and beautiful; Olga and I couldn't help falling in love with him." Contrary to Pips's revulsion toward the homosexuals he had encountered in Berlin, Jerry's sexual orientation wasn't something that bothered him. In fact, he savored it. One of their early outings together was on July 4, 1976—the American Bicentennial. Pips met up with Jerry at Riverside Park to watch the flotilla of big ships sail up the

Hudson River. When time came to leave, Pips took Jerry's hand, and they walked out holding hands. "Here I was, a man in his fifties, with a young chicken hawk. People gave us funny looks, not hostile, but double takes. With my warped sense of humor, that amused me. I said to Jerry: 'I bet they think we have a thing going.' Jerry said to me: 'You know Gary, you are the only man I met in my life who neither wanted to sleep with me nor despised me because I'm homosexual.' I was very pleased when he said that."

One night, in 1981, Olga and Pips returned from a movie and found Jerry waiting in their lobby. The building staff knew him by then, so they let him stay. Jerry's head was bleeding, and the doormen called the police. At 11:00 that night, Jerry had decided to go to the small playground adjacent to the building and sit on one of the swings. Pips recounted: "There were some rowdies there and they hit him over the head with a pipe, stole his watch, and beat him up. Then they ran away. Because he didn't know what to do, he came into our building." Olga and Pips wanted to take Jerry to the emergency room, but the police arrived a few minutes later. They asked some questions and then pressed Jerry into the back of their patrol car so they could drive him around to look for his assailants.

Olga and Pips started climbing into the patrol car with him but were stopped by the officer. Pips was furious. "'We are going along and there's nothing you can do about it.' The officer was impressed by the fact that we lived in the UN Plaza and weren't exactly shmucks from nowhere. They drove around a bit and said, 'We want to look at some of the hangouts where the paid fags are.' Olga said, 'Don't use that word in our presence.' Of course they didn't find the guys."

Olga and Pips were finally able to get Jerry to the Bellevue Emergency Room. As the doctors started bandaging him, they asked for basic information. But Pips was so flustered that he forgot his last name and just referred to him as "Jerry." The medics became suspicious. "Aren't you a relative?" Pips replied that they were very close friends, almost like family. While they took Jerry for treatment, Pips called Charles Schmaltz, who was beside himself with worry because Jerry was still living with him at the time. Within a few minutes, he appeared in a taxi.

But this living arrangement didn't last long beyond that night's emergency. Pips recalled: "Finally, after years, Charles Schmaltz broke it off with Jerry. Jerry was tough to live with. He was always footloose and fancy free. Time had no meaning for him. He would say, 'I'll be home for dinner.' Then he would show up at midnight. He was like an irresponsible child, and Charles finally had enough. He also realized that Jerry wanted a father more than a lover."

Sometime after Jerry's relationship with Schmaltz ended, he met Robert Lang, who became his next father figure–lover. Olga and Pips embraced Robert, and he became one of Pips's avid hiking partners. On one of their hikes, a handsome young couple were trekking ahead of them on the trail. Robert quipped, "I wonder if they know that their respective asses are being watched by a dirty old man and a faggot.'

"Robert called me a dirty old man. I don't mind. I *am* a dirty old man!"

At one point, while Robert and Jerry were living together, Robert decided to get checked for HIV, and he tested positive. He urged Jerry to get himself tested and, he too, was positive. Robert, a trainer at the New York Health and Racquet Club, took a pill cocktail that kept him in terrific shape. Jerry, too, held up reasonably well for some years. But, tired of Jerry's shenanigans, Robert amicably ended the relationship in 1985, and Jerry was again on his own.

Earlier, Jerry had gotten a job at Lord & Taylor in White Plains as a hairdresser. But Pips was dismayed with the way Jerry managed his money. "As soon as he had a dollar in his pocket, he spent it. Now that he worked at Lord & Taylor, he bought me a cashmere sweater. He bought us other things and we gave him hell. 'We don't need your presents. You need to hold on to your money. You have your rent to pay, you have bills.' Then again, he would come up with a present, like a very fancy, expensive watch. It was a bargain—only a hundred and fifty dollars for this watch that was worth five hundred. I said, Jerry, twenty-five years ago, I paid fifteen for this watch and it's still running and I'm perfectly content with it.' There was one instance where he had five dollars in his pocket and ran across a beggar and gave him the entire five dollars. Then he had to walk because he had no money for carfare."

Jerry was fired from his hairdressing job at Lord & Taylor because he told a client, who always came late, that he didn't want to serve her anymore. Having been fired for cause, it seemed that he was ineligible for unemployment insurance. Pips sprang into action by making an appointment for Jerry at the court that handles employment disputes. When the day came, Pips accompanied Jerry and admonished him to keep his mouth shut.

"I went down there, and we waited almost the whole day to see the judge. I pled Jerry's case, arguing that he was a wonderful kid, but just barely out of the slum, and he doesn't know how to deal with frustration. He shouldn't be fired, and if he was, he should certainly get unemployment. I thought I was being very persuasive, but the judge didn't get it."

Jerry next found work in a salon that had an African American clientele. With two black grandmothers, Jerry understood their hair, was well-liked and acquired enough customers so that he could buy himself a car. "A piece of shit," observed Pips, "but he was proud as the dickens. I had given him some driving lessons. He was the only person I had allowed to drive my car, but only in an empty parking lot where there was no way to crash into anything. He got a license and could now come down from White Plains to visit us with his car." But Olga was worried every time he drove and insisted that he phone as soon as he got home to assure her that he had arrived safely.

Pips later noticed that the tires were bald. "Jerry, you cannot drive with these tires. You're taking your life in your hands. You must get new tires and if you don't have the money, I'll lend you the money.' But he never bought the tires."

The car didn't last long. One night in 1987, when Robert was visiting Olga and Pips, the phone rang at 11:30. It was Jerry. "I need your help. I've been arrested, and I'm in a police station in Westchester." His junker of a car had caught fire due to a leak in the oil pan. All the oil had drained out while the engine was running. The car was destroyed in no time, but Jerry jumped out safely. He was standing by the wreckage of his car when the police arrived. But instead of giving him a helping hand, one of the officers bent down and picked up a syringe from the gutter and accused Jerry of using drugs. Pips bridled at the injustice of the charge. "Whatever was wrong with Jerry, he never used drugs. He would smoke a joint occasionally but never used hard drugs. These sons of bitches either planted the syringe or there was one lying in the gutter. But Jerry certainly had nothing to do with it."

Pips asked to speak to the sergeant and pleaded that he not be kept overnight at the station. The sergeant replied that the only way Jerry could be released was if Pips came to pick him up in person. "I said, 'I live in midtown Manhattan; it's midnight; and the weather is lousy. But I'll vouch for him.' 'Sorry, Mr. Phillips, it's the only way.' Olga and I piled into the car with Robert. Even though he had broken up with Jerry two years before, he insisted on coming. We got to the police station and there was Jerry. Jerry had used the phone to call somebody else and when he put down the receiver, one of the officers came over with a rag to wipe it down because he had touched it. Olga was outraged that they could treat him like a leper. They issued a summons and let us take him away."

There was going to be a trial and Jerry needed a lawyer, for which he didn't have the money. Pips forked over $500 and the lawyer advised him not to fight the charges because he wouldn't win. The lawyer paid a $50 fine, and the case was closed. As always, Jerry reimbursed Pips, probably from the inheritance he got from his mother, who had died in 1986.

Jerry had two sisters in Puerto Rico, one of whom was a doctor. When his mother died, the only thing she had of any value was a house near Mayaguez. The house was left to her three children, but after a year, Jerry still hadn't received his share. Pips wrote a letter to the estate lawyer and found Jerry a Puerto Rican lawyer in New York. That did the trick, and Jerry finally was sent $3,200 in settlement of the estate. Pips told Jerry to let him open a bank account for him from which to pay his bills. But Jerry never followed up.

Pips explained, "He was an urchin, a kid. His education was practically nil. He was not illiterate; he could read and write, and he could speak Spanish as well as English. But he had no idea what the world was all about. I once told him something about the Russian revolution started by Lenin and Stalin taking over, and he asked, 'Was Stalin Lenin's son?'"

Jerry was generous, with himself and with others, particularly with Olga and Pips, who were uncomfortable with his magnanimity. When time came to pay his rent, he couldn't do it and got evicted from four apartments. With each eviction, Jerry called Pips in a panic and told him that the landlord was throwing him out and sending a truck to take his furniture. Each time, Pips would negotiate with the landlord and persuade him not to dump Jerry's belongings. Pips would then pay the overdue rent and put Jerry's things in his basement storage bin. Jerry always reimbursed Pips, but space ran out, and Jerry had to rent a storage locker.

"What a way to live! For a while he stayed at the 'Y' in White Plains in a tiny little cubbyhole. Then he rented a cheap hotel room near us. We couldn't have him stay with us because we had only a living room and a bedroom. But on some occasions, he slept on a makeshift bed we made for him on the floor. But this was not a permanent solution and there shouldn't have been any need for it. He made a living." But he never paid taxes.

At one point, Jerry took a trip to Puerto Rico with his little dog, Chulita. Olga gave Jerry a couple of tranquilizers for the dog to take on the plane so she wouldn't kick up a fuss. She instructed Jerry to give Chulita just half a pill. "So, what did he do? He gave her two whole tranquilizers and the dog was knocked out for twenty-four hours. But that was Jerry; he always screwed things up this way—not out of stupidity. His mind just worked differently; he couldn't focus on the practical things."

In mid-1988, Olga and Pips were again on the phone with Jerry, giving him advice. They could feel it wasn't registering. Finally, Jerry signed off and said he would call in a few days. Olga turned to Pips and cried that she could no longer take the stress of constantly worrying about Jerry. Swayed by Olga's outburst, Pips suggested that they cool it with him. "I can do without Jerry for a while. He's in his thirties and he can be on his own a bit, without having us to pull the strings all the time." They decided not to phone him. But he didn't call them either. And that had never happened in the seventeen years they'd known him. Pips speculated that he may just have become tired of constantly being harangued for doing the wrong thing.

Six months went by and in the first days of January 1989, Pips answered a phone call from a woman he couldn't place. The woman had been one of Jerry's clients in the salon in White Plains. Because he frequently talked about Olga and Pips, she knew that they were his surrogate parents.

"I just want to tell you that Jerry died."

"That really hit home. That, we didn't expect. I managed to suppress my terrible hurt and guilt by becoming very busy. Who's going to take care of the funeral? What arrangements are going to be made? Of course, we were the closest to him, so I was the one who had to do it all. I felt that I had to notify his sisters in Puerto Rico, if for no other reason than to get their Power of Attorney so I could act on their behalf. I recalled our contretemps over the inheritance when their mother died. But I left a message with their lawyer and one of the sisters called the next day."

Jerry's sisters would not come to New York for the funeral but did execute a Power of Attorney for Pips. Through the woman who had notified Olga and Pips of Jerry's death, Pips found other people who had been with Jerry in the salon. One who had been a particular friend to Jerry helped Pips find a funeral home. But where was Jerry's body? Pips contacted the medical examiner and got the full story.

Jerry was living in a small garden apartment with his little dog. A neighbor noticed a foul smell emanating from his unit and summoned the police. When they broke in, they found Jerry sitting upright in bed with a noose around his neck. By then, he had been dead for several days. It was around New Year's, the heat was turned on full blast, and the body was partially decomposed.

Pips recalled that Jerry had made a new friend—a young black woman. He learned that Jerry had spent Christmas with her while he was already in bad shape. He wanted to remain with her, but she had to go to work and gently pushed him out the door. "Apparently, that was the last straw for him. Why he didn't call us, I'll never know."

Jerry had been giving away his belongings to his clients. When they asked why, he said he didn't need them anymore. "He knew what he was going to do. All the evidence is that he committed suicide. I didn't tell Olga that and let her believe that he died of AIDS." Jerry was thirty-four years old when he died in January 1989.

The memorial service was held at a funeral parlor in White Plains, with a hundred people in attendance. Many more would have come had they seen the announcement, but it came out on a weekend and people missed it. The only white people at the service were Olga, Pips, Robert, and me. Pips delivered a eulogy in which he shared stories about their life with Jerry. He was touched and proud that so many people had come to Jerry's send-off—and racked with guilt for having neglected him in his final months.

Jerry Perez was now added to Pips's long list of losses. Marc Tanenbaum would be next.

Pips observed: "He was very busy all the time. He traveled a lot. He was a member of many committees, employed by the American Jewish Committee, and on the Executive Committee of the International Rescue Committee. He was the only rabbi at the Second Vatican Council. He was buddy-buddy with Cardinal Lustiger. When he went to Israel, he was received very warmly as a bigshot."

In 1988, the year of Olga and Pips's last phone call with Jerry, Marc collapsed in the bathroom while preparing to leave for the airport to deliver a lecture in Boston. I ran into the hallway yelling for help from neighbors and administered CPR while waiting for the ambulance. Marc was lifeless on the floor. After a short while, the EMTs managed to resuscitate him, with no brain damage. Marc had long suffered from a complicated arrythmia and had been given a drug by his cardiologist—who also happened to be Pips's heart doctor. The drug had triggered a near-fatal ventricular tachycardia—the same arrythmia which, a few years earlier, had killed Marc's brother while climbing subway steps in Philadelphia. But after many weeks in the hospital, Marc was able to resume his life.

Pips, as ever, focused on the nurses. "He had some pretty nurses and when I made cracks about the nurses which he didn't like, I said, 'Okay, rabbi, don't be such a bluenose.' Normally I didn't call him rabbi."

For the next four years, Marc was in and out of Lenox Hill Hospital, with various emergencies. I felt like I was living with an ax over my head. In 1992, Marc was to be honored by the New York Board of Rabbis. But he was in the hospital. Accompanied by Olga and Pips, I accepted the award on Marc's behalf.

At that time, I was pregnant with our first child. Marc and the fetus were on opposite trajectories. The more my pregnancy advanced, the more Marc's condition worsened. I began to feel like I was trading a life for a life. Finally, his doctors determined that he needed open heart surgery but had no confidence that he would survive. Nevertheless, he came through the surgery with surprising strength and seemed to be improving each day.

During this time, I was completing the equivalent of an Executive MBA in Banking. Up until the prior year, I had been Chief Marketing Officer and head of private banking for First New York Bank for Business, which had taken over the charter of the First Women's Bank. My final two-week residency on campus at the University of Delaware coincided with Marc's hospitalization. I knew that if I didn't finish now, I would never get back to it once I gave birth. Marc was stable and his recovery looked promising. So, I commuted to Wilmington every morning and returned every afternoon to be with Marc in the hospital. Pips often visited him during the day.

At the end of the residency, I was awarded my diploma with top honors, which meant that my thesis would be sent to the Harvard Business School. On the last day, I came to the hospital, proudly flaunting my degree to Marc, who immediately phoned his sister to boast of this latest achievement.

On July 2, I finally gave myself a break. I had a dental appointment in the early afternoon and allowed myself the luxury of a leisurely walk on a perfect summer day. I picked the wrong day to take time for myself.

Pips had been at Marc's bedside earlier in the day. "Marc just awakened from a half sleep as I walked in. He was obviously unhappy and, for the first time that I recall, fed up and complaining about being disturbed every few minutes and not being allowed to sleep. Then he felt nauseous and vomited all over his lap. I ran out to get help. The nurse came in shocked, told me to get out and wait. I sat in the solarium for about fifteen minutes and then tried to sneak in, but the nurse caught me and told me to wait until they called me. Marc was all cleaned up and feeling a bit better. 'I'm not going to eat that damned kosher chicken again,' he joked. He began to look sleepy, and I told him to rest, and I would see him tomorrow. 'Best to Olga.'"

Meanwhile, I headed to the hospital in the late afternoon to find Marc in crisis. Shortly after I arrived, he went into respiratory arrest.

At 8:30, I called Olga and Pips to ask them to come to the hospital because I thought Marc was dying. I could no longer turn to my mother, who was severely disabled with Parkinson's disease.

A team of four doctors and eight nurses valiantly tried for five hours to resuscitate Marc and they eventually allowed me to come into the OR where they were working. Marc had tubes running out of his mouth, arms, and chest. He had a plank over his chest where it had been opened to massage his heart. I leaned over him, whispering every word of love I could muster. I held his hand and put his hand on my belly where our son was preparing to be born in a few weeks.

That night was vividly imprinted on Pips's mind. "We were shattered. Georgette was more together than I was. Olga was in bad shape, but I was really in bad shape. I pleaded with the doctors to do something as they came in and out of the room and we sat outside on the bench. I was beside myself. Then they let us come in. Marc was there, unconscious but still alive. We stayed for a couple of minutes, and I started crying. I don't cry very often and one of the doctors helped me up and said, 'Better leave.' As we left, I started to shout, 'Marc, we love you, we love you, Marc.'"

Despite their heroic efforts, the medical team could not get Marc to sustain a pulse on his own. Marc had a medical directive which instructed that he not be kept alive artificially, so when the medical team said further efforts would do no good, I had to let them stop. I stood holding Marc's hand as I watched the monitor flatline. The team called his death a few minutes after midnight. Marc, age sixty-six, died one month after our tenth anniversary—almost as I had predicted when I agreed to marry him. I had been given ten good years with him and no more.

Afterward, we all sat in the solarium with Marc's lead doctor, who had saved his life after his 1988 ventricular tachycardia attack and been devoted to him over the past four years.

Pips recounted: "Georgette started telling anecdotes of her married life with Marc and she was so composed, I couldn't understand it. How could she? She was composed while he was there dying!"

Composed? I was numb! I was in shock! My worst fear had just been realized. The love of my life had just died. I was going to give birth alone and pass my own fatherless history to my son. Pips had lost Ilse, the love of his life. He had been in shock when they took her away, knowing he would never see her again. In that moment, he was numb, not hysterical with grief. He, of all people, should have understood what I was going through. But I now realize that, through the entirety of our relationship, we never connected on an emotional level. We were playmates, pals, confidantes. Our serious discussions were straightforward, candid, and practical. But displays of emotion had not been part of them. Affection, yes, but not emotion. Emotional support was not Pips's strong suit. In that sense, he felt he had failed Ilse, his father, and even his mother. And, as he would later realize, he had failed Olga in the same way. His only constant was his instinct for survival.

Pips confided to his therapist years later: "When we gathered Marc's belongings, I took one of his shavers home for myself." Was this an echo of the time, nearly fifty years ago, when Pips had taken a Gestapo officer's shaving brush as a memento? "Then we went with Georgette to her apartment, and we stayed until five in the morning. We were all very exhausted and she finally said she was going to sleep. We left."

On the day Marc died, July 3, TV broadcasts were interrupted with bulletins to announce his death. The next day people called from the *New York Times.* Some of these calls were transferred to Pips "because I was the last one to have seen Marc functional. Normally, Jews are supposed to be buried the next day, unless it's Shabbat. But this was Fourth of July weekend, and Georgette's rabbi gave permission to postpone the funeral by a couple of days." The *New York Times* obituary was one of many across the country. Numerous tributes followed, including the *Congressional Record* and a Mayoral Proclamation.

The funeral itself took place in the synagogue where Marc and I had been married ten years earlier. Pips recalled, "The place was packed with a thousand people, and various people spoke, including John Cardinal O'Connor, Giuliani, and several rabbis. It was a very good ceremony. And I was one of the pallbearers." Pips relished his role in the all-star cast.

The New York City Police Commissioner at the time of Marc's death was Lee Brown. I met Lee when he was Sheriff of Multnomah County, Oregon. We had been friends and colleagues since. I worked with him when he led the police departments in Atlanta, Georgia, and Houston, Texas, where he later became mayor. When he took on the post of Police Commissioner in New York City, he brought me in to work with him. When he learned of Marc's death, he couldn't attend the funeral because his own mother was dying. He instead provided a police escort from Park Avenue Synagogue, where the funeral service was held, to the Nassau County line, where NYPD's jurisdiction ended.

Pips was hugely impressed with the police presence. "When the service was over and we were walking out of the synagogue, the street was full of police. We got into the limousine right behind the hearse and we had motorcycle cops on both sides, as well as in front of us and behind. They stopped traffic along the entire route while we were in the city, and then when we got out on the Long Island Expressway. The motorcycle cops zoomed ahead and stopped the incoming traffic at the entrances to the highway. It was like a state funeral. When we hit the Nassau border they waved and took off. Then there was a ceremony at the cemetery. Shiva took place in their apartment. Georgette sat on a low stool, a sign of mourning. People came and brought food baskets and all kinds of stuff and there was a lot of coming and going. She later complained that I didn't spend enough time with her while she was sitting Shiva. I said, 'For heaven's sake, you know that I'm there any time you need me, but the place was full of people. You wouldn't have paid any attention to me if I had been there."

Marc and I had a three-bedroom apartment on the Upper East Side of Manhattan. One of the bedrooms served as my office and the other was Marc's. But with a baby due in a few weeks, I needed to clear Marc's office and turn it into a nursery. Marc had always had trouble parting with papers, and his office was piled high with them, leaving only a narrow center aisle leading to the archeological dig that was his desk. I turned to Pips to help. "Georgette asked me to see what I can do with all his papers. She didn't want to throw them away because this was an important man, and they were valuable. Marc's sister, niece, and nephew helped empty the room physically. A couple of days a week, I went to the apartment to sort papers. It was a mountain of stuff, and I'm not the fastest worker in the world. But I gave them some shape for an anthology of Marc's writings that Georgette had commissioned and their donation to the American Jewish Archives. I did it as a labor of love for Marc Tanenbaum and

Georgette's budding foundation. She called one day and said, 'I've received a grant for the anthology. You've certainly laid the groundwork and I'm sending you twenty-five hundred dollars.' I didn't expect any compensation and was kind of embarrassed, so I donated a thousand dollars to the Tanenbaum Center."

It was not the first book project with which Pips had helped me. In 1987, the first edition of my book, *Crimewarps: The Future of Crime in America*, had been published by Doubleday and was nominated for a Pulitzer Prize. Pips had got in the trenches to help with the book. "I made phone calls all day. I talked to the FBI a number of times. I talked to US attorneys to ask about specific statistics. I'd never done that kind of research, and I got quite good at it. When the book was in galleys, she gave them to me to proofread because she knew I'm a nitpicker. I found about four hundred mistakes, some just printing errors. But one sticks out in my mind: Georgette was quoting the Christian Right on homosexuality in relation to Satan. But they had misspelled 'Satan' as 'Satin.' I had a good chuckle and wrote in the margin: 'I'm a silk man myself.' Sometimes I didn't like the wording. She appreciated when I brought this to her attention, but finally she got annoyed. 'Listen, you want the perfect book, write your own!' I got paid about three thousand dollars. It was more a labor of love than anything else, but I did make a few thousand after my retirement."

Seven weeks after Marc's death, I felt some sharp twinges. I didn't pay attention to them because, with my due date still a week off, I assumed they were just Braxton Hicks false contractions. In my entire pregnancy, I had not taken a single nap. Nor had I stopped working. Nor did I have any morning sickness or strange food cravings. Although I was nearly forty-six years old, I'd had an extraordinarily easy pregnancy, physically. But Marc's decline and death—that part wasn't so easy.

On this day, I was preparing to go to a meeting at Police Headquarters. When I started hemorrhaging, I realized I'd better take my contractions seriously. Cancelling the day's meetings, I frantically tried to get hold of a friend who was to have been my birthing partner. He was nowhere to be found so I phoned another friend who arrived in a shot to rush me to the hospital. While waiting for him, I called Olga and Pips, who raced to meet me there.

Pips fondly recollected: "They let me into the room where she was surrounded by doctors and nurses, and she waved to me to come over. I sat by her side, and she held my hand and said, 'Pips, remember my papers are in this drawer.' I said, 'Georgie, don't be an idiot, you're not going to die now.' 'I know, I know, I just want to make sure,' she said. Then I saw the doctors whispering to each other and she was in a lot of pain. The baby's umbilical cord was wrapped around his neck, and they told me they're going to do an emergency Caesarian. I went out and they packed her onto a gurney, which they rolled past Olga and me in the hallway."

My son, Joshua-Marc Bennett Tanenbaum, was delivered at 6:05 p.m. on August 24, 1992—thirty-five minutes after I arrived at the hospital and seven weeks after his father's funeral. I was unconscious from the anesthesia, so the first ones to see and hold my newborn son were Olga and Pips. "Georgette was in great pain from her abdominal incision. I sat next to her and stroked her hand until one a.m., when her worthless birthing partner finally showed up. They put up a cot for him to sleep and we left. Of course, I was jealous but that's another story."

Pips later quipped that Joshua-Marc's conception, through invitro fertilization, and his delivery through C-section, was "like the Immaculate Conception and the immaculate birth; it never went through her vagina. I could talk to her like that."

Pansy Campbell, the nanny I had hired to help me care for Joshua, met Pips for the first time when I brought the baby home from the hospital for his *bris*—circumcision ceremony. At that time, Pips was just another face in the crowd. But he soon became a fixture.

Pips often met Pansy in Central Park when she took the newborn out in his carriage. Because the baby was usually sleeping, they fell into conversations about Pansy's West Indian background and Pips's Holocaust story. "But it was always about the baby. He loved the baby and always wanted to be with him," recalled Pansy.

Pips came a couple of times a week to sort through Marc's papers, bringing with him a ham sandwich for his lunch. Being that this was a rabbi's home, I wouldn't permit the sandwich to go into our refrigerator. But to Pips it was a joke.

In addition to our son, Marc left me with a large network of religious leaders and human rights activists. In 1992, there were at about fifty conflicts waged around the world that were based, at least in part, on religion. By then, I had had a diverse and gratifying career as an academic sociologist, criminologist, broadcast journalist, banker, consultant, and author. Olga and Pips had retained bragging rights on all of my achievements. But Marc's death gave me a chance to move beyond self-actualization and start giving back. I decided that nothing I had been doing professionally was as important as building on Marc's work. Accordingly, toward the end of 1992, I founded the Tanenbaum Center for Interreligious Understanding, which, with its subsequent leaders, would become the go-to organization for combatting religious prejudice.

Pips was cynical about my motives. "I told her, 'It's not doing you any harm becoming Marc's successor. Where Marc was a good networker and good at PR, you're even better!'" Nevertheless, Pips happily boasted about the bold-face names we attracted to the annual Tanenbaum fundraisers. He proudly cited just a couple of the programs: "Dan Rather of CBS; Felix Rohatyn, the big money man of the City of New York; Rudolf Giuliani, now mayor; His Eminence Archbishop Iakovos of the Greek Orthodox Archdiocese of North America; Governor Michael Dukakis; Ambassador Richard Holbrooke," and on and on. Then there was the ad that ran in the

New York Times with a photo of three innocent children: "If religious intolerance is a thing of the past how come 14,704 people died from it last year? It's going to take three of the world's great religions to get them to start hating each other."

Pips concluded: "Georgette found her real mission in life." And he was right.

Pips and I grew closer as I matured into adulthood, even though I had lost my childhood crush on him, and he felt I needed him less. To his mind, "We always had a friendly relationship, although not uncritical of each other. When she was a kid, she was in love with me. I kept telling her, 'Come see me when you're eighteen.' When she was eighteen, she wasn't interested anymore. But she and I are much closer than she is to my wife, especially in the last few years. Olga is on the fringe of things and disapproves of how she's bringing up her child. Georgette knows it, and Olga lets her know it."

After Joshua started preschool, Pips still occasionally immersed himself in Marc's papers. When Pansy picked Joshua up from school and brought him home, Pips's attention turned to Joshua. Joshua had a rotating globe in his room. And, just as he had done with me when I was a child, Pips drilled Joshua in geography. Joshua recalled that "For some reason, Novosibirsk in Siberia was his favorite fun fact city. Otherwise, he would just spin the globe and point to a country and demand that I tell him its capital. I didn't know the capital unless he had run through it with me multiple times."

"Pips was very proud of his command of English, and words were very important to him. He was a grammar purist. If you used the wrong words or pronunciation, it would be full stop, and he would show you how you were wrong."

The time spent with Pips wasn't limited to visits to Joshua's room. Joshua also visited Pips at 860 UN Plaza. Most of the time, Pips had photographs arrayed on the coffee table to show Joshua, telling him about his youth in Germany and his early life with Olga.

Occasionally, Joshua was Pips's hiking partner. Joshua remembered that "Driving with him in his car, I thought every two seconds that we were going to crash. It was a car that attracted lots of attention. Interestingly, it wasn't a chick magnet. It was mostly men who stared at his 1968 Cadillac," chuckled Joshua.

Pips became a substitute grandfather and wanted Joshua to call him "Pappy," and Pappy he remained for the rest of his life. Both Olga and Pips were selective in the gifts they gave Joshua. For birthdays, he received US Savings Bonds to help pay for his education. For random occasions, he received VHS tapes of operas: *The Magic Flute*, *Hansel and Gretel*, *A Daughter of the Regiment*. As a two-year-old, Joshua would stand in his crib, transfixed, and watch *The Magic Flute*, bawling if I turned it off so he could go to sleep.

Olga and Pips were always staples at any family or friend get-togethers. Pansy observed that "Pips was always kissing somebody. Olga didn't like it. She would reprimand him from time to time, but he wouldn't stop. It was always fun to be with him, but he loved the girls. When we were walking down the street, he always kissed someone. Sometimes I had to stop him—especially when a woman's husband was standing right there! But it made him happy."

Pips's early post-retirement years were a time of endings—his career, the passing of Jerry and Marc. And the year after Marc died, Olga and Pips made the last of their annual visits to Caneel Bay. But retirement also brought a seismic shift in their marriage.

CHAPTER 14

THE DECLINE OF A MARRIAGE

In retirement, Pips sensed that Olga had lost respect for him. He was home. He was no longer the breadwinner; and she became simultaneously more assertive *and* more depressed. They bickered constantly but neither could envision life without the other.

Pips had this pragmatic way of looking at it. "After fifty years of marriage the romance has worn off and there are many times when we don't like each other, but we love each other. If one can define love as need, we needed each other."

Pips had always dreamed of leaving New York once he retired. It would certainly be less expensive to live elsewhere. But more importantly, he loved nature. Santa Fe with its mountains, deserts, forests, and fresh air was one of the towns to which he aspired. He also fantasized about renting a Winnebago and bumming around the country for a couple of years, from Alaska to Baja California.

Olga nixed all these ideas. "I know you better than you know yourself, and you would be miserable," she observed. Pips didn't deny this. "But, when I came *kvetching* again, about getting out of this fucking city and going to Santa Fe or spending a few years in Israel, she finally said: 'You want to try it, go to Santa Fe, stay a month, two months, three months. See how you would react to it.' Well, that was like saying jump off the moon." In the fifty years that Olga and Pips had been married, they had been separated no more than fifteen nights.

Olga was no longer the stunning, pliant beauty she had been when Pips spotted her at Schulstrasse. But in their symbiosis, each lived in dread of losing the other.

Pips complained that, whenever he took a bath, Olga would come to the bathroom door every five minutes, to anxiously check whether he was all right. Conversely, when Olga went out shopping and was gone longer expected, Pips would begin to panic.

"I don't know what to do. Should I run out and look for her? And the same with her. I always must tell her when I expect to be back. I've learned to make it later, so she doesn't worry. That's how dependent we are. It may not be healthy, and it may be selfish. I need you; as long as I have you, I can relax. I can even be mad at you, but I've got you. There's never any danger that we would divorce or separate."

Early in 1995, Olga became ill. "That scared the pants off me. When, as a child, they took the piano out of the house, that trauma remained with me my whole life. You can imagine how I would feel if my wife of fifty years were in danger of leaving me. I wouldn't want to survive. As long as you have something and feel safe having it, you take it for granted. But when I begin, God forbid, to think that my wife might get seriously ill, I would die. All of a sudden, she becomes so much more valuable to me, something I might lose—and you know how I feel about losing anything or anybody. But my wife of fifty years, that beats losing a piano any day!"

There's an old Jewish joke about a telegram: "Start worrying, details to follow," which suited Pips perfectly. "Even without details, I really worry."

One day in winter, Pips wanted to go hiking in Harriman State Park. There was no snow and the roads were clear. But Olga was dead set against it. Pips could slip. He could sprain his ankle. He could break his foot or have some other mishap in the forest. And being that it was winter, he could freeze to death if no one else was around.

Pips was chafing against this limitation. "When I go hiking, she is beside herself with worry. Until a few years ago, I used to come back and tell her about my adventures, but that just reinforced her fear and anxiety. Now I don't tell her anymore. I just stress the positive and there's plenty of positive to stress. But Olga doesn't want me to go hiking. Yet, for me hiking is very important. So, I go hiking."

As an adolescent, Pips rejected limits being set on his behavior—even to the extent that he flouted the Nuremberg Laws. His determination to go on that day's hike to Harriman State Park was no exception.

"I put my foot down this time and said I'm a citizen. Since I have no companion to go with most of the time, I go alone. And I was ready to leave!"

At that moment, farcically, the anchor for Pips's bridge fell out of his mouth with a tooth in it. "That was a sign: Don't go hiking. Go to the dentist. Which I did." Pips had been having trouble with his teeth for years. I had urged him to get the work done properly with a prosthodontist. But he didn't want to spend the money. Instead, he kept on losing teeth and settled on bridges that never quite fit. Indeed, in later years, he preferred to leave his bridges on his night table, gum his food, and gleefully greet visitors toothlessly.

Continuing on the theme of his symbiosis with Olga, Pips recalled: "Just to give you an idea about how we are like Siamese twins, a friend of mine is leaving for the Galapagos Islands without his wife. I would love to go but Olga wouldn't go, and no way am I going away for two weeks. Our relationship is much closer, not necessarily happier or friendlier, but closer than anybody else that I know. The older I get and the older she gets, the worse it gets. So, I'm stuck in New York. I know I will never live anywhere else. But for her, this is the first home she's known since she was deported at the age of seventeen, and how can I take that away from her?"

Most of the time, Olga simply was not feeling well enough to travel. "She hasn't been feeling well for forty years," Pips said. It was breast cancer that they feared the most—and, for Olga, it was a near obsession. Each year, she approached her mammogram with dread, even though she had never been diagnosed with any malignancy. All this worrying compounded her chronic depression.

She tried to take the antidepressant Paxil for a couple of nights, but it made her nauseous. "It's hard to tell if she's exaggerating," Pips complained. "I mean, she's from Hungary, and they always exaggerate. She read the description of possible side effects, and I asked her whether she might have been influenced by what she read. 'No, no, no!' So, now I'm stuck with forty-eight Paxils. I paid a hundred and twenty dollars for fifty of them! When her nausea got better, she was worried it might come back. Why? If it comes back, that's the time to worry. This is typical for her. She's not happy if she doesn't have something to worry about."

Their sleep routines didn't help. Olga was usually up until four o'clock in the morning and Pips rarely went to sleep earlier than two or three in the morning. Up until then, he would sit in the living room reading and listening to tapes on the hi-fi system in which they took great pride. Meanwhile, Olga would be watching "some crap on television. She knows it's crap, but she wants to get tired. But when I come in and my lids drop, she leaves the room because everything wakes her up. And she won't take any sleeping pills."

Although his marriage to Olga was no longer gratifying, Pips realized that he'd never lacked for love. First the love of his parents, then the love of several girlfriends. Later, his great love, Ilse. He acknowledged that his mother loved him, even though they had little contact during the two years he was underground in Berlin. When the war ended, he met Olga, who'd been with him ever since. "I consider myself damned lucky that, with all the traumas that befell me, I've always been loved."

But, as with so many things in his life, Pips felt guilty. "I feel guilty that I have not made my wife's life better. And I'm not talking about money. I have not been as good a husband as Olga deserves." He had been less devoted to her than Olga had been to him and didn't fully live up to his end of the relationship.

For one thing, they didn't have much physical contact anymore. Although their beds were pushed together, Pips's side was a double bed and Olga's was a single bed, leaving a large space between them.

"Sometimes when we're both lying in bed, I stretch out my hand or she stretches out her hand and we just hold hands for a minute or two while we're watching television. It's a touch, but that's about it. I'd heard Barbra Streisand talking about her relationship with her boyfriend and she said, 'It's so good when we are spooning.' So I said to Olga, 'Let's try it.' She came over and we sort of spooned, but she wasn't comfortable, and I wasn't comfortable, and it didn't really click."

Nor did they kiss much anymore. But kissing had always held special meaning for Pips. In his youth, kissing was filled with romance and promise—as with Lucienne, Ilse, and the various women he encountered before his marriage. Once married to Olga, he boasted of never having cheated on her. He became a serial kisser instead.

"I was always a big kisser. I always like to ever so lightly fool around with girls, but nothing serious. I never even found out whether they were interested. Just sort of *en passant*, a kiss on the cheek and sometimes a little peck on the other cheek. I'm not sure whether they liked it; they may not have liked it; but they were nice enough not to complain to me. That would have embarrassed me."

It could be a stranger in the park. A fellow guest at a bar mitzvah. An Israeli visitor. A nurse. A police officer. For Pips, sneaking a peck on the cheek was akin to being a big game hunter bagging his prey. Each kiss was a notch on his gun, and he would brag about his "conquests."

"It's quite amazing to me that I get away with these things, kissing practical strangers, and young pretty women most of the time! My friends think what I'm doing is insane. They would never dream of doing such a thing. A few years ago, I went hiking with one of my pals at Lake Minnewaska. There's this trail that goes toward Castle Point. Halfway down the trail, there's a beautiful view and we sat down to eat a sandwich. Next to us sat another hiker, a young girl. Of course, I started talking to her and we ended up walking back together. My friend walked ahead of us. He was disgusted that I was paying attention to this total stranger. We walked behind him and had a lovely conversation about nothing in particular. As we parted in the parking area, I kissed her. It's a sport; it gives my ego a little boost. Of course, I couldn't tell Olga because I know she gets upset about these things even though you can hardly call it adultery." But Olga witnessed Pips's kissing adventures often enough and she was mortified—as was I when they happened in front of me!

But at age seventy-three, not even serial kissing could preserve Pips's zest for life. "I've withdrawn more and more from life, from getting excited about things I cannot change and things that don't affect me very directly. We don't like to leave our lair anymore and I've withdrawn more and more from social contacts. I guess I'm preparing myself for death. Olga is even more shut off than I am."

Even a visit from Olga's beloved cousin, Victor, from Israel was enough to throw them. "For us, this is a gut-wrenching event. How will I take my afternoon nap and entertain him? I get up late in the morning. He's used to getting up early so Olga will meet him for breakfast in the luncheonette until eleven or so, when I can see him."

Victor, who grew up in Olga's parents' home, was a precious reminder of the happy childhood from which she was so brutally torn, while Pips remained haunted by memories of his first great love. He had all of Ilse's letters but had been unable to open them for fifty years. "I really was afraid of again losing my equilibrium. I will do it. I will do it, but not for myself. I will do it because this is a transcendental way to keep Ilse alive. Her voice is speaking to me still, even though I can hardly bear it. All this is very much alive in me. I've never forgotten Ilse and never ceased to think of her. And now, she is with me almost all the time."

Pips was not in good shape and was experiencing frightening palpitations amid bouts of intense anxiety. "Once in a while my hands shake, particularly my right hand. I don't know what it is, and it never lasts very long. I get more palpitations than I did three months ago, particularly in the morning—but almost never when I'm walking or when I'm outdoors doing things. Even if I don't think of anything specific, palpitations come. Every morning, I look forward to taking my two Prozacs, as if they were instantly going to relieve me which, of course, they don't. But they help."

In 1996, something started stirring in Pips. "I'm hornier than I ever remember being, not in the physical sense, but rather in the psychological sense. I categorize women who interest me into two categories. First is the one who I just want to screw. Of course, I'm never going to do it, but I fantasize about going to bed with her. The other is one I would like to fall in love with, have a relationship with, not just the mechanics of sex. But I am almost incapable of looking at any woman who is younger than Mother Teresa without considering her as a possible one for either category. Then it fades away. I think it's a substitute for passion, the kind of love that is no longer active between Olga and me. It doesn't preoccupy me day and night and I don't masturbate physically. To a certain extent you might say I masturbate mentally. I take it with a bit of humor."

The following year, at age seventy-five, Pips turned his fantasies into reality and his fifty-two-year record of fidelity to Olga ended. He started going to a strip club—regularly. But he did it only on the days that he was scheduled to meet with the psychiatrist to whom he'd been referred for palpitations and anxiety. "Otherwise I can't get out without my wife asking me where I'm going."

Pips would leave home at 3:30 to get to his therapy appointment by 4:00. He then returned home by 7:30. That seemed like an awfully long time and Olga wondered, "How long do these sessions go?"

The other problem was that Pips returned home stinking of smoke. He had long ago given up smoking, so Olga wondered why he had this smell on his clothes. Pips thought that he should cool it a bit and wondered why he was even going to the club.

"First of all, it gets a little boring. You see the same pussy over and over again. Their prices are reasonable so it's not top quality and I should feel guilty about spending any dollar on something like this. I realize it's disgusting, it's filthy, it's lousy. It's like a whore house. And I'm not used to this kind of thing. All my life I've never gone to a whore house. The only time I ever spent a few days in a whore house was in Berlin in order to hide."

It certainly wasn't about sex. At this age, Pips was impotent. "I suspect it has to do with the Prozac, but also at seventy-five it's an organ that hasn't been exercised. So I go to this place and I'm aware of what a degrading thing this really is. And yet it gives me pleasure. I'm not used to seeing girls totally naked, parading their stuff right in front of my nose, literally. I know I'm not allowed to touch so it's a very peculiar and quite novel experience. But I know the names of most of the girls and they know my name, of course, only the first name. For just a few dollars they will do a lap dance. It's not a bad feeling but I don't get an erection. I tell them to turn around and I stroke their behinds. I'm not allowed to touch their breasts, only sort of put my face between the breasts. What throws me is, as soon as they're not being paid, they hardly look at you. A moment ago, they might let you stroke their asses, then finished! They don't turn around; they just walk away. For me this is hard to accept, hard to understand, hard to react to."

Pips got friendly with one girl in particular—Millie.[1] She was not a girl at all, but a woman in her forties. She exuded some warmth, so Pips decided to go a little further with her and booked her for the "VIP Lounge," where he could be alone with her for a "hand job."

"She fumbled my penis, which sort of managed to get half an erection. I wasn't trying terribly hard. I was more interested in her. I felt she wanted to make me feel better because I couldn't rise to the occasion. But I wasn't embarrassed. That's not what I went there for. I went there to touch her, to embrace her."

For the extra money, he could touch her anywhere, and he took full advantage of that. Pips was particularly enamored of her pubic hair, which most of the other performers had shaved "to give a clear and unobstructed view of the plumbing." She had not shaved and he told her he liked that. She guessed that he must be European, where unshaved pudenda are much in favor, and asked whether he was from Germany.

"For these few minutes in that VIP Lounge, I had a feeling that we were closer to each other than just meat. I said to her, 'I can't relate to you as meat.' She said, 'Most of my clients do and that's just as well.' If she were conscious of what she's doing, she couldn't look at herself in the mirror, it would be awful. By shutting things off, she's doing her job, she's making a living. I felt we understood each other. Then time was up, and she started putting on a black

---

1 Name changed to protect identity.

dress, which she had taken off. She pulled it over her breasts, and it reminded me of Gauguin and the Tahitian girls he painted. She knew right away what I was talking about. It pleased me that she's not a total idiot. She knew Gauguin, she knew Tahiti. It was a nice moment, and I said, 'I would like to talk to you, I would like to be a little closer to you.' She said, 'I never do that but with you I'm going to do it. I'll give you my home number, but I hope you're not going to hound me.'"

Pips called Millie the following week and invited her to a diner for a cup of coffee. He was stunned when she agreed to meet him. He sensed that this was to be a personal rendezvous, not a business transaction. It turned out that she was taking college courses, writing a critical essay about a novel, lived in the East Village, was a dog groomer, and had been a sex worker for many years. "I'm interested in what makes a woman do this and how she feels about it."

It's true that these encounters gave him some sexual stimulation. But more importantly, they were a form of relationship, something human and warm. The sudden intimacy started to feel to Pips like he was cheating on Olga.

"All of a sudden, I'm touching, I'm having sex with another woman without penetration, but I'm having sex. If my wife knew this she'd be devastated. All our married life, I've felt that's one thing that is taboo; one thing that can't be done; she cannot do it and I cannot do it. We may shout at each other, we may argue with each other, but we must be able to trust each other. Now I am breaking the trust. Partly it's resentment. I'm getting back at her for needling me, for bugging me. But strangely enough, I don't feel guilty."

When Pips "played" with Millie, it reawakened a desire akin to what was there when he was a young man. One day, he said to her, "I'm dreaming," and she asked, "What are you dreaming about?" Pips replied, "I'm dreaming that we're actually lovers." Of course, that was unreal. Millie could not be lover with ten men a week.

And why would she be interested in a septuagenarian if there was no money in it for her? In a way, Millie enabled Pips to relive the experiences he had with Ilse and the other girls of his youth—if only for a moment. Then the hour was over and he had to go home to Mama. Well, yes and no. If a child asks Mama if he can go out and play, she knows his plans. But, in this instance, Pips was not asking for permission. And if Mama weren't around, it would open the door for him to further explore his sexuality.

These encounters freed up Pips to mix and match his memories. Something that happened last week, five years ago, twenty years ago, or fifty years ago, could all be put on the table at the same time and connected in different ways.

The pseudo relationship with Millie had its ups and downs. During one of his calls, she gave him short shrift. "Maybe there was a good reason for it. Maybe she was sitting on the toilet." Pips decided to give it a rest for a couple of weeks. "I don't want her to feel that I'm pursuing her. Next time I call her, if she gives me any indication that she's not perfectly happy with my calls, I will ask her to tell me and I won't call her again. I'm not that crazy about her that I want to chase after her."

When he next called Millie, it was from his dentist's office and she was quite friendly. They agreed to meet for business as usual at the club. But she also said, one of these days, they should get together for a cup of coffee. Pips went so far as to tell her that he was eagerly awaiting her spring break so that he could introduce her to the glorious gardens at Wave Hill, Arturo Toscanini's lush estate overlooking the Hudson River. "I told her she would enjoy beautiful nature, flowers and blooming trees and that I would be driving my Cadillac. She didn't close the door, but it was probably a pipe dream. I might also take her to the Conservatory Garden on 105th Street in Central Park on Fifth Avenue, which is very pretty, but nothing compared to Wave Hill. That gave me a little bit of a lift."

Pips was a realist, and he knew that this pseudo affair with Millie couldn't last. "I will have to wean myself away from it and find something else, whatever that may be. If I had a real affair, that would be treason. This still is not that. It's show business more than anything else, but I would like to get a little more friendly with Millie."

Olga was getting more and more suspicious, and Pips promised himself he would return to the strip club only one or two more times. But when he was at the club, he wasn't thinking about anything else—not his teeth, not his losses, not Olga's depression, not his palpitations. The dark, seedy place lulled him into a kind of trance. The bad music and naked women had nothing to do with the outside world. They were their own universe, which was so gripping that, for the hour Pips was there, he didn't have a care. That was addictive. And nothing in his life did that for him, except for hiking. Hiking was intoxicating for Pips as a form of exercise, but more than that, it allowed him to escape his domestic life. And so did the strip club.

"After I've been in this club, it reverberates in my mind for several days, and I can hardly think of anything else. All my life, I've used some fantasy or another to fall asleep. Lately, I've used not fantasy, but the real memory of what transpired. I never have a sex dream, isn't that strange? I say to myself, if it wears off why push it up again? If I'm already off the drug, why light up another cigarette and start all over again?"

Each visit was another fix. A good feeling. A pleasurable escape. Something that helped Pips forget his problems and fall asleep at night. Pips was a sensual person, in a room full of sexy women who were friendly and giving with their favors. What's not to like?

As Pips got older, his sudden fainting spells, breathing difficulties, and assorted ills would make both driving and hiking dangerous. But not having an activity that gave him time to himself and took him out of his world, carried the risk of increasing his anxiety.

The strip club gave him the needed reprieve. But it came with a price. He had to lie to Olga and create a network of fake activities to explain his absences.

"I'm very concerned about running out of excuses. Olga is upset. She said to me today, why are you coming back home so late? I don't answer. It's getting to the point where she's smelling a rat. Whether she believes it or not, I'm stuck with this story. If I stop going, what am I going to do? I can't suddenly come back home an hour and a half earlier."

In 1998, Pips was diverted from his sexual preoccupations. His best friend, Jack Podell, had, years before, moved to Chicago to take a job as Director of the American Bar Association Press. In the late 1990s, he developed terminal cancer.

"My friend was on his last legs, not quite in a coma but getting there. I felt I ought to go to Chicago to be with him one last time and for the funeral. Olga was dead set against me going. She was afraid something might happen and didn't want to be without me. She was afraid she would worry twenty-four hours a day and thought it was ridiculous to go just for the funeral. But I felt I owed it to his wife, who's also a friend, even though she has a large family. I wasn't looking forward to the trip either, but Jack and I had been like brothers for forty-five years."

Pips didn't want to hurt Olga or cause her worry and decided not to go. It was another nail in the coffin of their marriage. But the two were still deeply entwined.

"Last week, I got up at six-thirty to pee and I noticed Olga totally covered by her blanket. One of her hands was hanging down off the bed. I said, 'My God, is she dead?' Finally, I realized she was breathing. But for a moment, it flipped through my mind, if that ever happens, would I still go to the strip joints? I said to myself, 'I can only go there as long as I know Mama is waiting at home, even if Mama gives me a hard time about smelling the smoke. But Mama is there. Once I'm alone, who knows? With Mama, I'm still playing. Doing something naughty behind Mama's back is fun and if Mama is not there, it's not fun."

Of course, Pips realized he wasn't alone. "I have a responsibility to my wife. I just feel that I'm on a different track. More and more, we are diverging. Not in our commitment to each other, not in our basic feelings for each other, our need for each other, but otherwise we are diverging. I hike without her. I would love to hike with her, but I can't. I see many neighbors of ours taking walks on a Sunday afternoon. We never do that. For one thing, for me to walk as slowly as she does is exhausting and frustrating. I'm not holding it against her, I know she cannot walk any faster. Every year we go to the Bronx Zoo. This year we couldn't because she says it's so terrible for her to walk. I said, 'Darling, you don't have to strain yourself; they have wheelchairs and you can sit in comfort while I push you.' A wheelchair? No! That's anathema! But it's no shame to sit in a wheelchair. It's not a sign that you are an old decrepit cripple. Young people break their legs skiing and they sit in a wheelchair."

The following year, 1999, it was Pips's health that took a downturn. He fainted in the bathroom. Olga heard the thump and came running in to find him on the marble floor. She took him to his cardiologist who insisted on sending Pips to the hospital in order to diagnose these episodes. "I wasn't very happy about that because for the fifty-two years we had been in America, neither of us had ever been an inpatient in a hospital. Each of us had to go to the emergency room a couple of times, but never more than a few hours."

On the way to the hospital, Pips stopped at his dentist to get yet another temporary bridge. At the hospital, he was assigned a room and got some sleep. The next morning, they served Pips breakfast. Feeling that he didn't need to stay prone, Pips sat up on the edge of the bed and started eating. But after a couple of minutes, he again blacked out—no warning, no dizziness, just out! A few minutes later, he came to and found himself surrounded by worried-looking nurses. Pips had cracked open his forehead and was bleeding profusely. "I stayed in the hospital for another week. They took every test known to man and found nothing particularly wrong." The culprit turned out to be Pips's prostate medication, one of whose side-effects is lowering blood pressure. And with his natural tendency to low blood pressure, the cardiologist ordered a pacemaker to be implanted. "Eventually, they took out the stitches on my forehead. I thought a big scar would be an interesting feature, but it was small and hardly noticeable."

Pips always assumed that he would predecease Olga and wanted to make sure that she would be looked after. As she had no experience managing finances, he turned to me because of my banking background. He was also preparing for his own death. In 2002, he wrote me a letter:

> *Georgette—my dear girl (I know that you want—and deserve—to be called a woman, but to me, you are my girl whom I love very much).*
>
> *This letter will become active when I've "gone to my reward," "kicked the bucket," and "bought the farm." As you know, our marriage is totally on the rocks. We no longer share anything but mutual hostility some of the time. Of course, Olga has a lot of pain and is in very poor shape mentally, physically, and emotionally. I'm pretty sure that some of her medications contribute to her condition (she takes four tranquilizers every day in addition to other drugs) but she refuses to get a really thorough physical and mental checkup, including psychiatric treatment. She is alienated from most people. We have not had a visitor in our apartment for years.*
>
> *Needless to say that I ain't no angel (at least not yet). Enough already of crying on your shoulder (the only one I've got).*

Nevertheless, I'm, of course, concerned about Olga's "innocence" in practical matters.

Please take care of my affairs (I mean the financial ones) when the time comes. I attach a list of where our papers are (at least the important ones).

Now, as "on dit," to something completely different. As you know, I'm leaving you the audio tapes of my sessions with my shrink. (We stopped taping in 1998.) There are about 80 of them, roughly between 1 and 1½ hours each. It's a long megillah, the story of my time on earth, and much of it is "off the cuff" talk, but at least half of it is rather unique. I'm talking about the years of 1925/6 till ca. 1947—particularly the Nazi years and the immediate post-war years.

As you may remember, I was not born a Jew nor was I ever in a concentration or extermination camp (as Olga, of course, was). However, what happened to me was in many ways exceptional and, I believe, very interesting.

Well, you'd just have to listen by yourself (or "deputize" an innocent soul). I know it's a pain in the ass but (as they say in England), "there it is." That's all for the present. Stay tuned for further developments.

Pips

On another occasion, Pips said, "Death is never far from my mind. Thank goodness I don't have to give my own eulogy. I can't think of a single thing of any importance that I've ever done in my life that was good, that was on the positive side. I can think of plenty of things that I feel guilty about. I can't think of a single thing of what they call in Hebrew a mitzvah."

By the time Pips wrote these reflections on death, I had been remarried for a year. My new husband, Leonard Polonsky, was an instant hit with Olga and Pips. They resonated with his cultural sophistication and his fluency in four languages. Leonard and I took Pips to the Four Seasons restaurant every year because he loved their *duck à l'orange*. In 2003, Pips sent me a letter to thank me for the eightieth birthday dinner that Leonard and I had hosted for him there, which also included notes for his eulogy:

> *Sweetheart, hope you can decipher this scribble. Use as much or as little of it as you want when the time comes or at my 100th birthday celebration. Just make sure to emphasize that I've been the salt of the earth and a boon to mankind (and womankind, too).*
>
> *Thanx much!*
> *Love,*
> *Pips*
> *P.S. Just selected my Jewish name—Yehudi—David. Remind me in case I forget.*

Somewhere along the way, Pips had made a list of all the things that were troubling him about Olga. Buried among other classical symptoms of clinical depression was "she wishes suicide." That should have been at the top of his list.

Pips dreaded the possibility of Olga finding out about his secret life. At the same time, he couldn't resist bragging about his escapades—at least to me. When the relationship with Millie fizzled, he found another strip club. This one happened to be across the street from the Tanenbaum Center offices in the Empire State Building. He would often come up to see me while waiting for the club to open. Perhaps a visit with me served the same purpose as a visit with his psychiatrist; it became an explanation for his absence from home.

On the evening of January 11, 2004, Olga and Pips were scheduled to dine with another couple at a restaurant across the street from UN Plaza. But first, Olga said she needed to stop at a nearby grocery store to pick up some item or other. Pips settled in to watch TV until she came back. With a start, he realized that a long time had gone by and still no Olga. He phoned around to find out if anyone knew where she was. Then he called Robert Lang. Robert told him to check on the roof of his building. Racing up to the roof, he saw Olga's shoes lined up neatly against the edge of the roof. When the building staff came, they found Olga splayed on the parapet, which had broken her fall as she jumped from the fortieth floor of the gleaming tower that had come to represent the pinnacle of their American dream. When the police came, they determined that she had lain there for some time, cold and broken, until she finally died.

It was a terrible death.

With all the tranquilizers and other pills she had, she could have ended her life painlessly. But maybe a terrible death is what she wanted. Perhaps, with her survivor's guilt, that's how she finally made her peace with the awfulness of the deaths of all those whom she had lost.

But what led her to take that final step off the roof? Had she somehow found out about Pips's adventures? Or was she just one more casualty of the Holocaust? Her doctor wrote:

> *I was the personal primary care physician for Olga Phillips, who is a survivor of the Holocaust. She had significant neuropsychiatric diagnoses related to her persecution and experiences during the Holocaust. She suffered severe intractable depression with hallucinations and nightmares, which dated back to experiences during the Holocaust, including the complete annihilation of her family at the hands of the Nazis. Mrs. Phillips' health continued to decline and her anxiety and depression worsened. Clearly this was directly related to her memories and experiences during the Holocaust. She was hospitalized in relation to this in December*

2003. Subsequently, while on anti-depressants she committed suicide on January 11, 2004. It is clear that her experiences under the hands of the Nazi murderers contributed to her demise.

CHAPTER 15

STILL THE SURVIVOR AND COMING FULL CIRCLE

The days following Olga's suicide were days racked with pain, guilt, and fury. Pips learned that Robert had known of Olga's plans and could not understand why he had withheld that information from him and failed to intervene. It may be that Robert had good reasons, but they were never revealed because Pips never spoke to him again.

Olga was buried in the gravesite that she and Pips had chosen at White Plains Rural Cemetery, a small, hilly burial place in Westchester County, just north of New York City. Just as they had never liked big resorts in life, they didn't want to be buried in a big cemetery in death. Founded in 1854, many of the tombstones at White Plains Rural Cemetery were so old that their inscriptions were faded and unreadable.

Olga and Pips became very fond of the woman who managed the cemetery, to the point where Olga, who, unlike her husband, was not a serial kisser, bussed her when they chose their gravesite. Never one to miss an opportunity, Pips kissed her, too. "We had a very positive feeling about her. It's not so important who she is, or who the other people are, once you are six feet under. But still, the surviving one of us will have an easier time and will feel more comfortable." Accordingly, Pips frequently drove to visit "my real estate up there" and to meet the congenial cemetery manager. "I want to see it while I still can, not when I'm horizontal." Coincidentally, Pips paid for the double gravesite on his seventy-fourth birthday, "an unintended symmetry."

Notably, it was not a Jewish cemetery. Olga felt strongly that she had spent enough time segregated among dead Jews in Auschwitz and had no desire to be segregated in her own death. Beyond that, it was the place where her "adopted" son was buried.

It was also less expensive than other cemeteries. Given that Pips believed, "We can't afford to die," this mattered.

After Olga was buried, the headstone that graced the grave was inscribed with both Olga's and Pips's names. When asked whether he thought this would confuse people, Pips argued that those who knew him would be aware that he was still alive, and the others didn't matter.

In those first days after Olga's death, Leonard, Joshua, or I were constantly with Pips. Twelve-year-old Joshua even stayed overnight to watch over him. Pips would not allow him to sleep in Olga's bed, so he slept on the floor at the foot of Pips's bed. Joshua recounted, "His leg wasn't working well, and it was hard for him to move around the house. I remember him ordering me around. He would yell 'Josh-oo!' and tell me to grab something from the kitchen, grab a particular record album, take something off the wall."

Gradually, a normal rhythm of life resumed.

In 2005, the year after Olga died, Pips, in a reflective mood, sent me a birthday note:

My dear girl,

In 1945, Olga became pregnant. (I was a pretty straight shooter in those days.) A very decent German woman gynecologist decided that she was too weak to risk a continuation of the pregnancy and recommended ending it. Abortion was illegal except in cases such as Olga's and it was performed in a hospital under proper medical procedures. We felt guilty about this and sometimes wondered whether you might have been that baby. That's why I always loved you as my virtual (though not always virtuous) daughter and continue loving you.

Have a good 59th—the timing is just about right.

Pips

Pips could now fully indulge all those activities that had been thwarted while Olga was alive. One of these was travel. Surprisingly, this took him not to Santa Fe, as he had dreamed. It took him repeatedly to Germany. And he could finally visit the country about which he was so passionate, and where Olga refused to go—Israel.

When Olga died, Victor's daughter, Tzila, immediately flew to New York to be with Pips and attend the funeral. It was during that visit that Pips seized the chance to arrange for his first trip to Israel.

His hunger for Israel was evident to Tzila. "When I came to see him, he pulled out maps and was keen to talk. He knew all the details about Israel—its history and geography, the wars, the people, the politics. He was so involved. He was very anxious to understand what was going on in Israel. It was almost as if he wanted to hold on to Israel through me."

That very year, in spring 2004, Pips made the first of four annual pilgrimages to Israel, where he was warmly embraced by Victor Hartmann and his family. The familial tie was Olga's, but it was Pips who held it close.

The first trip was tightly packed. The family took him all over Israel from the Negev to the Galilee; from Tel Aviv to Jerusalem; from the Ramon Crater to the Dead Sea. Tzila recalled, "He was thrilled. He just wanted to walk around the hotel in the little streets, to see the view. He stopped to talk to almost everyone—especially soldiers. I thought he should be tired. But absolutely not! He was full of energy all through the tour." Until he fell. Pips's visit coincided with Israel's Independence Day, and the Hartmanns had tickets for the highly symbolic ceremony on Mount Herzl. But Pips spent the evening in Hadassah Hospital instead.

It was in Israel that Pips felt his greatest fulfillment as a Jew—even though, under Israel's Law of Return, he would not be recognized as such. Yet, he told Tzila, "I'm more Jewish that many Jews in Israel because I chose to be a Jew." Tzila agreed.

His sojourn in Israel was a true "Return" for Pips. But it coincided with another return—this one to Berlin.

Since 1969, the mayor of Berlin had been offering free one-time, one-week visits to Holocaust survivors who had formerly been residents of that city. Olga would not have agreed to ever again return to Berlin, but she was now gone. Pips, again invoking his mother's admonition, "When one gives, you take," jumped at the chance. Although it was a one-time offer, he would manage to finagle a second free junket.

The first return followed his second trip to Israel in 2005, where he went to Natanya to visit a relative of Olga's. Then the entire family took him to the north, where he rode the cable car up the Manara Cliff to see the borders with Lebanon and Syria arrayed before him. And he got to see Masada, that ancient fortress where the Jews made a last stand against the Romans in 960 CE. Fortified by these experiences, Pips felt ready to face his first visit to Berlin since 1959—the year he had seen his mother for the last time. He flew directly from Tel Aviv to Berlin, with Tzila accompanying him.

No one was more surprised than Pips with how welcome he was made to feel.

Tzila observed, "He was received as such an important guest, especially by the interpreter." The interpreter, Vivi Bentin, was working with the mayor's office and accompanied the visitors to the meetings that had been scheduled for them.

Vivi later said, "I remember vividly how we went to the German parliament and met with one of the deputy speakers. It was around May 8, the anniversary of Germany's surrender in World War II. The political representative was telling how everybody was so pleased to be liberated. Then Pips raised his hand to say that not everyone was all that happy. In fact, they had been scared because nobody knew what was going to happen. The Russians were coming and not everyone welcomed them with open arms. I hadn't heard that perspective before and I found it really interesting. Later we went on a boat tour, and that's how we got to talking."

Tzila and Pips were booked into the five-star Kempinski Hotel, facing the Brandenburg Gate. Tzila remembered a sofa in the lobby. "Whenever we came into the hotel, he sat on the couch like a king. All the people in the tour came to talk to him—and he talked almost nonstop!"

But it was the off-tour sights that moved Tzila the most. "Pips took me to the synagogue where he had been married to Olga, and he found the book in which their marriage had been entered. He was in tears." He took Tzila to the Polizeipräsidium, where he had made his second escape under the noses of Eichmann's officers. He showed Tzila an underground bunker where he had been held, and Schulstrasse, the prison-turned-DP camp, where he first encountered Olga.

For Pips, the experience was bittersweet. Vivi recalled, "In a way it felt like he never left, and the culture was still there. He was happy to get to know people better and to talk about the war. Of course, he was very critical of many things. He didn't want people to get away with just apologizing for what happened. He wanted to make the point again and again that it won't be forgotten, no matter how well we get along today."

The conversations with Vivi weren't limited to the Holocaust. They frequently spoke on the phone and much of the focus was on music. "He loved the opera and the German and European composers. He would always tell me about the concerts and operas he attended and who took him. For the rest, it was just about normal things. He was like a grandfather."

Pips could still recite Goethe by heart and thrill to German "Marschmusik" (marching music). Vivi puzzled over how to reconcile Pips's love of German culture with the bitterness he felt toward his home country. "I imagine it must be very hard."

The encounter with Vivi became a friendship that endured for the rest of Pips's life. Vivi twice brought her family to New York. "He had given me a very generous birthday gift, and I was thinking I wanted to spend the money on something that he could also benefit from." Of course, Pips took them to the Bronx Botanical Garden in his huge old Cadillac and Vivi recalled how Pips would chat up everyone along the way. And, of course, kiss the women. "He kept telling me I was too old for him and he had younger and prettier girls. And that's just fine for me!"

Pips returned to Berlin a second time in 2006 with Tzila. "This time he returned not as a Jew; not as a German; just as a proud man. We went to the Reichstag, and he never stood in line; he was always the first to go in."

Pips went back to Berlin for the final time in 2007. For this visit, he traveled with Tzila's adopted daughter, Sharon, and Sharon's sister, Meital. Joshua was with them, too. They were back at the Kempinski, where Joshua shared a room with Pips. This time Pips was there to bear witness with the third generation. Although none of the young people were his own flesh and blood, they were all part of his virtual family—a family that had replaced the one he lost to the Holocaust. That year marked also the last time he returned to Israel.

Hector, our driver, started working for Leonard and me in 2007. Starting in 2008, we tasked Hector with taking Pips for drives. The first time they met, Hector described Pips as a "nice, elderly gentleman" with whom he had fascinating conversations about the war and the celebrities whom Pips had known. He particularly remembered Natalie Wood. "It was like a history book, talking to Pips about his experiences."

But once Pips was let loose at the Botanical Garden or Harriman State Park, Hector didn't know what to make of Pips's serial kissing. "His behavior definitely seemed odd to me, but I guess it made him feel good to get a kiss from one or another woman."

But it was his shocking humor that stood out to Hector above all else.

Ram Amit, a cousin from Olga's Israeli family, was visiting New York. Hector, who was unfailingly punctual, was picking up Ram to take him to Pips. Ram got into the car a few minutes late and Hector tried to make up the time in order to get to Pips on time. When the car pulled up, Pips was waiting in the lobby and impatiently checking his watch. "You're one minute late," he chided Hector. "But Ram was delayed," he explained—to which Pips countered, "Go ahead! Blame it on the Jews!"

Another time, Leonard and I took Pips for an outing to the Pepsico Gardens in Purchase, New York. Pips sat up front with Hector. When we returned home that evening, Hector dropped us off first. No sooner did we get out of our car than Pips turned to Hector and said, "Agh! I thought they'd never leave!"

In 2008, Pips developed a friendship with an unlikely young Texas woman—Kristin Smith. As a Christian, she had grown up believing in the importance of connecting the New Testament to the Hebrew scriptures that preceded it. In junior high school, she had read Eli Wiesel's *Night*, in which he records his experiences under the Nazis in Buchenwald. "I was so moved that I felt I had to do something to respond," explained Kristin. While at Baylor, she took a course, "Hitler and the Holocaust," that motivated her to enroll in a class on Jewish ethics and complete a minor in religion. Kristin then started graduate school studying musical theater at NYU. There, she signed up for a program at the local Hillel that matched students with Holocaust survivors. Apparently, Pips had also registered for that program, because he was paired with Kristin. Pips always loved sharing his stories of the Holocaust. Yet, neither he nor Olga were willing to be interviewed for the Survivors of the Shoah Visual History Foundation that was preserving survivor testimonies for future generations. Of course, Olga had been dead for three years by then, so it's possible that he felt freer to formalize his storytelling.

After Kristin graduated, she and Pips remained close. For the next seven years, she visited him at home, attended concerts or dined out with him. She brought her friends and parents to visit him. And when Kristin married and had children, Pips was embraced by them.

"I loved going to experience music and the arts," recalled Kristin. "I think that really connected us—not only in understanding each other, but as a faith journey. We did pray together. And that is one of my favorite memories." Pray together? This was a Pips I never knew.

Kristin also prayed when she was in Pips's car. "I loved seeing the car, but riding in it was quite another thing. Going to the Bronx Zoo, I really didn't know if we were going to make it!" she exclaimed.

Kristin had trouble dealing with Pips's salty language, but she looked past that to the hurt behind it.

In sharing his feelings about Olga's suicide, Kristin remembered Pips saying that he learned from that how serious depression is. "I do know he loved her very much. But he didn't know how to respond. He knew there was something going on but not the severity of it. He would also talk about missing the intimacy of having another person there with you. So, I was thankful to be able to spend time with him."

Pips also talked to Kristin about dying. "'I thought dying would be easy. But even that requires paperwork!' It was one of my favorite things he said."

In 2008, Pips fell while getting off a bus and broke his hip. Following a hip replacement, he was left with one leg slightly shorter than the other. He was chair bound and had intense back pain. Jonathan Schaefer became his personal trainer. "He stayed in that chair for the first few times, and I barely got him to move. As I matured as a trainer, I worked hard to never let anybody seduce me into conversation. But he talked and talked and talked. He was a captivating speaker and very funny."

Eventually, Jonathan got him out of the chair, moving around the apartment, and up to the gym. The conversations deepened. Jonathan, a Dartmouth graduate, actor, and writer in addition to being a trainer, observed that Pips was a voracious reader. "He was very erudite. He loved dramatic literature and could converse at length on it. Schiller wrote the words for the aria in Beethoven's Ninth. Pips taught me that in German while moving around the machines in the gym."

The two sometimes watched films together. *Ninotchka* was a favorite. "He was into it and he was very good a discussing it. His deep analysis of some of these films was impressive."

From time to time, Jonathan helped Pips to take a shower. Pips would finish by combing his thick hair and beholding himself in the mirror, "You handsome devil, you!"

By 2009, Pips's failing health precluded any more travel. Although he had stopped smoking decades before, it was too late to prevent full-blown emphysema from destroying his lungs. He used a nebulizer three times a day along with supplemental oxygen. He had long borne a curvature in his spine that left him stooped and a lower back problem that was unsuccessfully treated with injections of bone cement to stabilize his vertebrae and relieve pain.

Frequent blockages of his urethra repeatedly took him to the Mt. Sinai Emergency Room. He finally opted for a catheter and a bag rather than natural urination, relief that he regarded as a godsend.

When Pips got sick, Pansy sometimes went to the hospital with him. Pips wanted her to work for him. Of course, I still needed her for Joshua. But she went to Pips a couple of mornings a week to do Pips's laundry while Joshua was at school. Each time she went, she stopped at Au Bon Pain to pick up a carton of soup for Pips and for herself and spend a couple of hours with him. And while he was still able to travel, she watered his massive collection of plants while he was away.

In his current condition, visitors were Pips's balm. When Joshua started college in 2009, he was no longer able to keep up his visits to Pips. This angered Pips.

Joshua reflected, "He was always keen to remind me that he was the first one to see me when I was born and how he helped my mother and grandmother get settled. So, I felt very guilty about not spending enough time with him. But I was just growing up, trying to find my own way, and things fell through the cracks," said Joshua. "Just because I wasn't closer doesn't take away from his importance to our story. I always cared about him. He was always the personality in the family, and he was very present in my life."

But Pips, who always wielded his Will like a cudgel, disinherited the boy.

One of Pips's favorite pastimes was revising his Will, depending on who was in and who was out of favor at the time. That included Jonathan, his trainer! In this case, it was about a bequest of his 1968 Cadillac. Jonathan recalled, "I went with him a couple of times to the Botanical Gardens. He drove and he loved it, but I feared for my life. So, I made a deal with him. 'I'll go anywhere you want, but I'm driving.' He really fought me on this, but eventually he let me drive. Then he played this game with me. 'I'm going to leave you my Cadillac.' I would say, 'I don't want it.' Finally, I gave in and said, 'If you want to leave me your Cadillac, I'll drive it cross-country and write a book about you. That's my solemn promise.' Then he kept putting me in the Will and taking me out of the Will, which I never took seriously. It was a game. He'd tell me to bring him a CD or watch a movie 'or I'm taking you out of my Will.'"

On one occasion, Pips again dangled a bequest of the Cadillac before Jonathan. Jonathan, whose hair was thinning, shot back, "Just leave me your hair!"

Jonathan also went with Pips to the strip club a few times. "I met his little community there. He had a real feeling for the girls. What he liked best was massaging them. That was his big joke. He said, 'I'm the only massage therapist in town who pays the clients!'"

After a while, it became clear that Pips could no longer manage on his own, and that's when Diane O'Dwyer entered his life as a caregiver. "I was with him for seven years, seventy-two hours a week," she recalled. During overnights, Diane slept in Olga's bed, a comfort to Pips and a convenience for Diane, so that she could monitor his breathing and keep him safe. Exceptionally, he never tried any funny business with her.

"He had nothing but the utmost respect for me. Honestly. I never ever worried about anything like that. Plus, he knew I could take him!" Yes, she could. Diane was a former Master Sergeant in the US Air Force.

Pips eventually needed round-the-clock home care, which Leonard and I arranged. But Pips always wanted to fire his other caregivers. Not because they did anything wrong; just because, except for Diane, Pips felt they didn't sufficiently anticipate his needs.

"Because you're a needy bastard," Diane rejoined. "He goes, 'Fuck you.' I mean, we were like a married couple! Oh my God! We had good times. We had bad times, too."

Pips had always been frugal. "I hate waste, particularly waste of food but also other waste. This is due in part to my upbringing.

Germans, in that sense, are very different from Americans. Germans believe in preservation rather than acquisition."

This applied to toilet paper as well. Diane reported, "Whenever he took toilet paper—whether he was sitting on the toilet or blowing his nose—he took three sheets at a time. One time, he asked me to get him some tissues to blow his nose, but he was out of tissues. So, I got toilet paper. But it was more than three sheets. He goes, 'What are you giving me all this for?' I said, 'Have you seen the size of your nose?'"

His impulse to preserve could take bizarre turns. A few months after Olga's death, he went to one his much younger neighbors to offer her the shoes that his late wife had left on the roof before she jumped. His neighbor was horrified and Pips never understood why she had reacted in that way.

Then there was the 1968 Cadillac, which he finally had to stop driving. But he couldn't give it up. Pips explained, "To me the idea that something is old does not devalue it. In fact, it makes it even more valuable." The car, which in later years he kept just for hiking, was now stored in the garage of my assistant, Joelle Zito.

"He loved and missed his Cadillac so much," observed Diane, "and it was at Joelle's house. So, we did a road trip. I took him up there, just so he could drive it again. I'm blessing myself because I'm in the passenger side. I just wanted him to be able to drive again. And we just went very slowly around the cul-de-sac." That was the only time Diane ever let him drive her.

One day, Diane and Pips were walking down the street and ran into one of the mechanics who used to work on the old Cadillac. When he learned that Pips was no longer driving the car, the mechanic confided: "You do know you're the worst driver in New York City. Whenever we saw you coming down the road to turn into our garage, if any of our mechanics were outside smoking a cigarette, they ran back inside because they didn't feel safe when you were on the road."

When his driving days were over, after much resistance on Pips's part, it was either Diane or Hector who drove Pips to the nearby nature spots that he loved: Harriman State Park, Lake Mohonk, the High Line, and Lake Minnewaska. An excursion to Lake Minnewaska often concluded with Pips taking Hector to a favorite German restaurant, where they would feast on sauerbraten while Pips regaled Hector with his stories. By the time they finished, it was 10:00 p.m. and pitch-black outside. Pips deadpanned, "Can you drive at night?" to which Hector rejoined: "We'll find out!"

During another one of their many chats, there was talk of making a film about Pips's life. Hector asked, "Whom would you like to see playing you?" Pips answered, "Paul Newman, even though he's not handsome enough."

The Bronx Botanical Garden was the place to which Hector squired Pips the most often. Pips had a favorite koi in the Japanese garden, which he named Charlie. He fed Charlie pieces of bread at every visit. The Botanical Garden also held special events, for which it charged an extra fee. But Pips, the geriatric fare-beater, refused to pay and brazenly kept going through the gate so as to avoid the extra charge. He got away with it every time!

"He would tell me, 'Keep walking; keep walking.' I'd say, 'You're going to get me shot or killed here.' But he just didn't care. He was fearless. He was very confident, and I admired that about him. He was very good at sweet-talking and turning things around," remarked a red-faced Diane.

Interestingly, Diane was not embarrassed about Pips's shadow life. With Olga gone, he had found a substitute for Millie: Arina.[2] Arina was a dancer at the strip joint Pips frequented near my office. He found a real home there. The manager, Yola, took a genuine liking to him, and he became her pet client. Whenever Pips came, she

---

2 Name changed to protect her identity.

would give him a meal. She and her girls threw birthday parties for him and even put together a scrapbook for his ninetieth birthday. Yola looked in on him at home from time to time.

Diane took Pips to his club a few times and glimpsed the girls dancing. But Pips had eyes only for Arina. He fervently wished that she would come to his apartment, but she refused. He was so fond of her that he put her—as well as Yola—in his Will. Finally, a friend advised Pips to let Arina know about his Will and, instead of waiting for his death, offer her some money now. The advice worked! Pips called it the best advice he had ever received in his life. Arina came to Pips's apartment on Fridays—a day to which he always looked forward. While he did whatever it is he did with her in the bedroom, Diane would wait in the living room until the hour was over. But she eventually decided that this was a good time to get some fresh air and give Pips and Arina their privacy.

By now, Diane was paying his bills for him. That's how she discovered how much Arina was getting paid. "I called Joelle because I almost had a heart attack! Arina was getting paid four thousand dollars a month! I asked whether I should speak to Pips about this. I'll say something like the family is very worried about where he's spending his money because, down the road, he'll need it for healthcare expenses. So, I literally took it from four thousand to two thousand. And I said, 'Dammit! I'm in the wrong business!'"

Did any of this make Diane uncomfortable? "I didn't really think too much about it. I just laughed. I was happy that he found some happiness. Where I drew the line is when he asked me to wash his glass dildo!"

Meanwhile, the serial kissing continued. "No matter where we went," said Diane, "the mission was to break the previous record. The last record was fourteen kisses in one day. I was busy just keeping him in line, but he was entertaining. One time, we were in the park and he was being a brat. Joelle happened to call me, and I asked, 'Can I just leave him here?' But she said I have to bring him back home."

When he wasn't with Arina, Pips occupied himself with a huge collection of pornographic films that he had amassed. Because he was hard of hearing and refused to wear hearing aids—mostly because he choked on the $4,000 price tag—he played his VHS tapes at high volume. Diane was known in the building and was always seen going in and out of Pips's apartment. She didn't want people to think that she was the one making all the orgasmic noises. "I said to him, new rule: The acting sucks. You don't need to hear. You don't need audio. You need only video for this shit. So let's mute it and you can just watch. But I introduced him to *Hogan's Heroes* and he loved it. Every night we went to bed watching either Carol Burnett or *Hogan's Heroes*."

To be fair, Pips also had a vast cache of operas, classic films, nature tapes, and ballets on VHS tapes—all of which he watched repeatedly with deep appreciation.

All the pseudo sex was substitute behavior, which Jonathan theorized was a carryover from Pips's coping behavior in prison. Pips was still obsessed with Ilse and her name came up often. He confided to Diane, "I don't know what I'm going to do when I die, because there's going to be Ilse and Olga there." "Yeah," replied Diane. "Well, you made your grave, buddy, you sleep in it!"

In 2011, Pips was in Room 1622 at New York University Medical Center, hospitalized with emphysema. Jonathan visited him there several nights in a row and observed that Pips's usual wry humor had left him. "He was very soulful. Most of the time, I could feel the community around him. But this time, it seemed like he felt lonely. It was the first time, in my presence, he fully embodied that sense."

Pips had said to Jonathan, "When people asked me about my career, I said, 'My career was survival.'" "He really did see himself as a survivor and was kind of surprised that he might not survive this time," mused Jonathan.

But Pips did survive. And he resumed his usual outrageous behavior.

Pips adored Leonard and Leonard adored Pips. Leonard was surely the most generous man whom Pips had ever met. One day, he dropped off a gift envelope in Pips's lobby. It contained a check for $50,000. When Pips came home and opened the envelope, he called Leonard. "You cheap bastard! You couldn't even put a stamp on the envelope?"

Diane was flabbergasted. "But that was Pips."

CHAPTER 16

DEATH OF A SALESMAN

Pips went into Mt. Sinai Hospital for the last time on November 25, 2015. He was ninety-three years old. His oxygen saturation had dropped precipitously, and breathing was an enormous effort. When he was admitted, Diane was standing behind me. She recalled, "I had to turn away because I was so pained by Pips's condition. With all these doctors around his bed, I felt he must be petrified. I was heartbroken while they were telling us his status."

Pips wanted more than anything to live. His goal was to make it to a hundred. His lifelong will to survive was still with him, despite chronic pain and short windedness. "It beats the alternative!" he repeatedly quipped. After a few days, the doctors gave Pips the choice to transfer to palliative care, where he would be made comfortable.

Pips's mischievousness, his lack of respect for authority, his self-centeredness are the factors that had enabled him to survive his life's traumas. But above all, there was his need for close human contact. None of this changed during this hospital stay. His "thing for nurses" remained with him, even in the Palliative Care Unit.

Ethelee, Herb Hahn's widow, and one of their daughters, Alexandra, visited Pips in the first days of December. Pips gazed at them with the deep affection that develops in a fifty-year friendship and jibed, "I never thought I would see you on my deathbed." Ethelee was wearing a necklace that had belonged to Olga. That day, I also came in, carrying a beige alligator bag that Pips had bought Olga in 1968. Two of his caregivers dreamed that they saw Olga and Pips, and when Joelle came to visit, he told her that Olga was there.

Hector also visited. During his first visit, Pips confessed to Hector that he was ready to die. Then Arina came to visit. When Hector returned shortly after she left, Hector asked Pips: "How are you doing today?" Pips, impassive, declared, "I've changed my mind."

Hector and Pips speculated about whether there would be any way that Pips could communicate after death. "We'll have a code word," Pips declared. "Ahoy."

"Pips was a survivor," reflected Hector. "With everything he'd gone through, he was still able to have a sense of humor. I think that's part of the reason he was able to survive."

Not everyone uses humor as a defense against horror, pain, and fear. But for Pips, it was reflexive. "My mother always said to me, it's better that you should laugh than you cry about it. I apparently took it to heart."

During my last visit, I leaned over his bed as Pips reminisced about the five-and-a-half-year-old girl I had been when he met me for the first time on the pier where the *Ile de France* had docked after bringing me from France. Then he opened his eyes wide—as if he was about to embark on a new adventure—and asked with both trepidation and anticipation: "Am I going to die today?" I patted his hand and assured him, "No, today is not the day you're going to die."

And he didn't. Pips had a party that day and indulged in copious amounts of ice cream. Pansy, who always treated Pips with utmost care, was one of his visitors. Pips confessed to her, "I have a deal with the guy upstairs. I don't bother him, and he doesn't bother me."

Through his morphine haze, he must have sensed that death was imminent. As Diane's shift ended and she was leaving his room, he said, "Hurry back!" At 2:00 a.m., the hospital phoned her to say that Pips had died peacefully in his sleep—just as he had hoped. She jumped into a taxi and raced to the hospital so he wouldn't be alone while they prepared his body for the funeral home. This devoted Irish Catholic caregiver probably didn't realize that she was performing a *mitzvah* that is part of Jewish practice following death. She was serving as Pips's *chevra kedisha.* It was a fitting close for a man who wanted nothing more than to be accepted as a full Jew.

Pips was buried next to Olga at White Plains Rural Cemetery. His grave was not cold or unfamiliar because he had visited it so often while he was alive. He had put his name on the headstone eleven years earlier, but the names of Olga and Pips are written so large that there is no room for the date of his death: December 5, 2015. Nor is their space for Olga's.

Perhaps Ilse was waiting for him, too.

But Pips had no illusions about an afterlife and believed that he had nothing meaningful to leave behind. "I have not created anything that is going to survive me. I have not lived an exemplary life. I don't even have children. There's no more family; I am the last of my family. So, when I'm dead, I'm dead, finished. My family will have become extinct, so my only hope for survival beyond me is the knowledge that my tribe, the Jewish people, will survive.

"The disappearance of the Jews would mean my death, too. Not that I consider myself a perfect Jew. I'm a Jew boy courtesy of Adolf Hitler. But it's my identity, and I feel every human being needs an identity beyond just being a human being. That identity is the one thing that makes me feel as if I'm leaving a legacy."

What remains of Pips are dozens of tape recordings with his life story—"a record of a life nobody will give a damn about." I give a damn and hope I have done his story justice in this book. This is Pips's legacy.

I'm waiting for him to shout, "Ahoy!"

ACKNOWLEDGMENTS

The first person I need to acknowledge is Pips himself for entrusting me with his story—warts and all. He was correct when he wrote to me that "it is rather unique." But the person who helped me give the story shape is my editor, Bernard Schweizer. He was a gentle and responsive partner, who totally "got" the concept for this book and enthusiastically shepherded it along.

I must also thank my agent, Karen Gantz—who has become a good friend—for putting my proposal in the right hands and always intuiting the right editors for me. My last three books could not have been made without her unwavering belief in me and her steadfast support.

The tapes of Pips's sessions with his psychiatrist, Dr. Alexander Sasha Bardey, on which this book is based, were enhanced by people in his ambit who shared their stories with me. These included Dr. Bardey, who gave me valuable perspective on parts of the story that made me uncomfortable. Among the others were Hector Amoedo, Pansy Campbell, Tzila Hartmann, Diane O'Dwyer, Jonathan Schaefer, Kristin Smith—all of whom were part of Pips's late-life support system. Then there was my son, Joshua-Marc Tanenbaum, who was Pips's virtual grandson. Last, but certainly not least was my husband, Leonard Polonsky, who died just as I was writing the final chapters of this book. His warm friendship with Pips was deeply imprinted in his memory. Leonard frequently invoked Pips's name and witticisms long after Pips died—and that helped keep Pips alive for me.

INDEX